Memory
What Every Language Teacher Should Know

STEVE SMITH

and

GIANFRANCO CONTI

Edited and formatted by Elspeth Jones

With illustrations by Jean Liew

By the same authors

Steve Smith and Gianfranco Conti (2016)
The Language Teacher Toolkit

Gianfranco Conti and Steve Smith (2019)
*Breaking the Sound Barrier:
Teaching Language Learners How to Listen*

Dedicated to Elspeth, Joel and Amy.
Steve

Dedico questo libro alla mia bellissima e dolcissima bimba,
Catrina Jade, alla sua mamma, Golnaz (per averla messa alla luce)
e ai suoi affettuosissimi nonni paterni, Mario e Ketty.
Gianfranco

ABOUT THE AUTHORS

Steve Smith taught French for over 30 years in UK secondary schools, including 24 years as Head of Department at Ripon Grammar School. After graduating in French and Linguistics, his Masters degree focused on second language learning and acquisition. He now produces resources for his widely used website www.frenchteacher.net, writes a blog about language teaching, and is a professional development provider. Steve's popular YouTube channel has videos relating research to practical pedagogy youtube.com/channel/UCO7TVqgdbfovyu6skiF6Gag and he curates the website www.informedlanguageteacher.com. He is Visiting Lecturer and Lead Subject Tutor for the Modern Foreign Languages PGCE course at the University of Buckingham. Steve is author of *Becoming an Outstanding Languages Teacher* (Routledge, 2017) and *50 Lesson Plans for French Teachers* (2020, Amazon). He tweets as @spsmith45 and can be reached at spsmith45@aol.com.

Gianfranco Conti taught English, French, Spanish, Italian and German for over 25 years. He has been a university lecturer, holds a Masters degree in TEFL and a PhD in Applied Linguistics. He is now an author, independent educational consultant and active professional development provider. In 2015 he was awarded the prestigious TES Best Resources Contributor award for the 1,600 resources he has shared on TES. He has recently co-authored with Dylan Vinales and Ronan Jezequel a popular series of vocabulary-building books, based on his lexicogrammar approach, including the best-selling *Spanish Sentence builders* and GCSE French revision workouts. Gianfranco writes an influential blog on second language acquisition called The Language Gym, co-founded the interactive website language-gym.com and the Facebook professional group Global Innovative Language Teachers (GILT). He tweets as @gianfrancocont9.

CONTENTS

ACKNOWLEDGEMENTS

We are grateful to the many language teaching colleagues and researchers who have informed and inspired us over the years.

If you have read our previous books or blogs you will know that we attempt to draw on research to help guide language teachers in their choice of pedagogy and classroom procedures. In the end it is how teachers apply their knowledge to their own particular settings and classrooms which counts the most. Below are three quotations to get you thinking.

The purpose of school – indeed, the purpose of all learning – is to change long-term memory. The problem is that much of what we do in school takes little account of what we know about how memory works (Dylan Wiliam, educationalist).

...we must learn how to adjust the materials to facilitate learning and education with the working memory abilities that the learner has (Norman Cowan, cognitive psychologist).

When we access things from our memory, we do more than reveal it's there. It's not like a playback. What we retrieve becomes more retrievable in the future. Provided the retrieval succeeds, the more difficult and involved the retrieval, the more beneficial it is (Robert Bjork, cognitive psychologist).

Introduction – why this book?

To learn is to remember and language learning places such huge demands on memory that it's no wonder many students find it hard-going. They need not only a large store of vocabulary in long-term memory, but also an underlying command of a repertoire of grammar. In addition, they need to retrieve all of this instantly in order to understand, speak or write.

As language teachers, therefore, one of our main jobs is to get students to remember sounds, words, chunks, structures and conventions of the language, not to mention all the cultural information associated with the target language community. To do this most effectively, you need a curriculum, a pedagogical approach and a repertoire of classroom activities. Underpinning all of these we believe you need an understanding of how memory actually works.

That's where this book comes in. Our aim is simple: to provide a readable introduction to memory, one key component of the science of learning, and to relate it to language teaching. We believe that insights from the research on cognitive science can contribute to an informed understanding of classroom language learning and should be an essential part of language teacher education.

Firstly, however, what areas are covered by the science of learning, or **cognitive science**? Let's get some definitions out of the way. **Cognitive psychology** refers to the scientific study of mental processes such as attention, language use, memory, perception, problem solving, creativity and thinking. **Neuroscience** is a branch of science concerned with the anatomy, physiology, biochemistry, or molecular biology of nerves and nervous tissue and especially with their relation to behaviour and learning. The general term **educational psychology** refers to how we learn and remember things. **Psycholinguistics** is the study of the relationships between linguistic behaviour and psychological processes, including language acquisition.

Our book dips into all these areas, but particularly the findings of cognitive psychology which, since the 1980s, has become increasingly influential in second language learning research. We'd like to convince you that to understand language learning and teaching more clearly, it's useful to understand the mind, the source of all behaviour and experience. How do we perceive, process and retrieve information we receive? How do we gain expertise in our specific area of learning? What factors boost or inhibit language learning? In sum, how do we get students to remember what they learn?

We need to issue some words of warning, however.

First, we have to be wary of taking findings from cognitive psychology and applying them in a simplistic fashion to language learning. Research is a theoretical affair, whereas teaching is very much practical. It's unwise to take the findings of research and apply them uncritically to the classroom. In addition, many psychological research studies about memory focus on recalling facts, sequences of digits, nonsense words, images, artificial mini-languages, to name a few. Laboratory experiments necessarily have to focus on isolated elements in the learning process, so they bear little resemblance to classrooms where all sorts of factors come into play: personal, social and mental. In the jargon of cognitive psychology it is said that laboratory experiments lack **ecological validity**, namely they don't replicate classroom experience.

Second, language learning is not of the same type as found in some other subject areas. In the popular book called *Why Don't Students Like School?* psychologist Daniel Willingham writes that "memory is the residue of thought". This may not apply as well to language learning as other subjects. Why? Because language is not 'subject matter' of the type you might encounter in science, history or geography. In these disciplines, the challenge is often to learn concepts or solve problems, whereas as language teachers we know that the aim is to help students combine knowledge and skills to become proficient *users* of the new language. Knowing *about* the language is a small factor in the equation. Perhaps we could dare to suggest that, for language learning, memory is the residue not of thought, but of input and practice!

Third, there is a danger of simplification in a book like this. We've done a good deal of homework and have had to grapple with understanding the subject matter, in order to be clear and concise about findings without sacrificing accuracy (a bit like explaining an area of grammar to a class!). We decided from the outset not to shy away from using academic references, but let's be clear: this is not what could be called an academic, scholarly work. Some readers may wish to take their study further, so we've provided a bibliography, along with links to further reading and videos at the end of each chapter.

The more you read about memory, and learning in general, the more complex it seems and the more provisional the research appears. When reading about different models of working memory, for example, you quickly discover how many of the competing claims are speculative. A lot has been learned through careful experimentation, but explanations of such a complex process as learning often remain uncertain.

Before we get into the main body of the book, let's begin by dealing with an issue which has preoccupied writers and teachers for centuries. It's one which we believe every language teacher should consider from the outset when thinking about memory.

Two ways of learning

Learning has been an area of inquiry for centuries and many theories have been put forward. In the psychology and second language acquisition literature one distinction that's been made is between two types of learning: *implicit* and *explicit*.

Implicit learning is 'learning without awareness'. It's how children pick up their first language(s), with no intention to learn. It's unconscious - natural, if you like. It's also the most powerful process in second language acquisition, and occurs when we're immersed in the language, for example living abroad, taking part in an exchange or through immigration. Indeed, some have argued that all we need to do to learn a new language is understand spoken and written messages and nature will take its course (Krashen, 1982).

In contrast, explicit learning happens consciously, with intention, and what you learn can often be explained. It's the type of learning you do when thinking through the solution to a problem or following a teacher's explanation on the board. It comes into its own in formal classroom settings and clearly has a role to play (see, for example, Leow, 2015). For various reasons, teachers often believe it's the most important type of classroom language learning.

The result of implicit learning is *implicit* or *procedural* knowledge – knowing how to do something without necessarily being able to explain it. This is the kind of knowledge you use when speaking your first language(s). In contrast, the result of explicit learning is *explicit* or *declarative* knowledge – being able to describe what you know, for example being able to say that we usually form the plural in English by adding an 's'.

If you're a native speaker of English your implicit, procedural knowledge is excellent, but your explicit knowledge may be poor. For example, could you explain why the following two sentences look similar but have a very different underlying structure?

    1. John is eager to please   2. John is easy to please [*]

---

[*] This pair of sentences is well known to those who have studied Noam Chomsky's work in the field of Linguistics. It appears in a book he wrote in 1965, *Aspects of the Theory of Syntax*.

Implicit knowledge of language develops through large amounts of interaction with **comprehensible input**, that is, spoken and written messages we understand. This is why language teachers are urged to use the target language in meaningful ways as much as possible. Explicit knowledge develops differently and, although it's a hotly debated issue, some researchers (for example DeKeyser, 1995), and most teachers, believe that with enough practice, explicit knowledge can become implicit. Just as when we learn to perform any complex activity, such as driving a car or learning to play tennis, a process of explicit instruction - learning how it's done - is needed until we can do it 'without thinking'.

Our focus in this book is partly on explicit (conscious) learning and we make the assumption, supported by a good deal of research, that this can help students become proficient second language users. We also believe that this conscious process may be relatively more important in the early stages of learning a language in a classroom. In addition, the book considers the important role of implicit learning – put simply, how we pick up a language unconsciously through exposure.

You may think this distinction is a bit theoretical, but it actually underpins everything you do in the classroom.

What's happening in a student's head?

For many years psychology wasn't very interested in this question. When behaviourism ruled the roost in the first half of the twentieth century, research was all about observable behaviour, stimuli and responses, and it was thought impossible to peer inside the 'black box' of the brain. Newer theories have subsequently been developed, and technology is allowing us to observe what actually happens in the brain when people learn.

If a language teacher shows a sentence and asks students to read it aloud, what's going on inside the student's head? To start with, they might read the sentence well, or they might make some mistakes. This is helpful to know, but doesn't tell us what's going on beneath the surface. And what's going on is immensely complex and increasingly well understood.

To read a sentence aloud successfully the student needs to direct attention to it. They need to know about the sound system (**phonology**) of the language and be able to match this sound system to the marks they see on a page (**phonics**). To understand the sentence they need to have knowledge about **vocabulary**, **grammar** (**syntax** and **morphology**) and even **background knowledge,** both of the topic and of the world in general.

For example, imagine giving an 11 year-old this sentence:

The growth rate of GDP in 2019 was below average

They would usually be able read it aloud, but would not be able to explain what it means without some knowledge of economics.

The highly complex set of processes just described is carried out astonishingly quickly in the brain, when you think about it. If we can understand these processes better, perhaps as teachers we can use this knowledge to our advantage.

Metaphors are often used to talk about how the mind works, and one of them is this: we can observe a car – how fast it goes, the noise it makes, whether it works or not – but to really understand it you need to look carefully under the bonnet to see what makes the car go. Only when the interaction of the engine or battery, motor, electrics, fuel system and so on is understood, can you really grasp how a car works and know how to fix it when it goes wrong.

Over many years, cognitive psychologists have used observable behaviours to produce theories about how people think and learn. But in the last decade or so, imaging techniques from neuroscience have enabled researchers to look under the bonnet of the car, so to speak, to understand much more clearly what's happening in the brain when people learn and use language. Although there is still a huge amount to learn, we're getting closer to a better understanding of how we learn and remember.

Did you know?

Modern brain scanning (neuroimaging) procedures allow researchers to observe brain activity, including when language learning tasks are being carried out, such as learning words or thinking about grammar. The main types of scan are summarised below.

- Electroencephalography (EEG) is used to show brain activity under certain psychological states, such as alertness or drowsiness.
- Positron emission tomography (PET) shows brain processes by using the sugar glucose in the brain to illustrate where neurons are firing.
- Magnetic resonance imaging (MRI) scans use echo waves to discriminate among grey matter, white matter, and cerebrospinal fluid.
- Functional magnetic resonance imaging (FMRI) scans are a series of MRIs measuring brain function via a computer's combination of multiple images taken less than a second apart.

The scope of this book

"I've gone over the imperfect tense loads of times, but they still don't use it correctly."

Many of our students make fantastic progress in a short time, but every language teacher has recounted at some point how frustrated they are that students have forgotten what they've been taught. To understand how students remember and why they forget, we not only need to have an understanding of the general principles of second language acquisition, but also how learning and memory work in general.

In each chapter of this book, aspects of cognitive science or applied linguistics are explained, along with the implications for language teaching. Questions for reflection are offered at the end of each chapter, along with further reading or viewing references. Scholarly references are also included in the text, in case you want to go into the subject more deeply.

Please be aware that space doesn't allow us to describe many specific classroom activities in this book. For much more practical detail, see our previous publications *The Language Teacher Toolkit* (2016) and *Breaking the Sound Barrier: Teaching Language Learners How to Listen* (2019).

In this book we consider the following themes in sixteen chapters:

1. What is memory?
2. The multi-component model of memory
3. Working memory
4. Phonological memory
5. Visuospatial memory
6. Cognitive Load Theory
7. Managing cognitive load in the classroom
8. Long-term memory
9. Declarative and procedural memory
10. Prospective memory and metamemory
11. Making it stick
12. Remembering vocabulary
13. Learnability
14. Emotional factors which affect memory
15. Learning from mistakes
16. A memory-friendly curriculum

Each chapter contains explanations, references to research and what we see as implications for the classroom. Along the way we've provided information boxes, descriptions of important experiments, teacher tips and specific classroom activities.

This is the first of two books we're writing about cognitive science for language teachers. While this book focuses on memory, the second will look closely at the acquisition of language skills and fluency building.

This is definitely not a 'how to teach' manual. In any case, we don't believe there is one best way to teach a language since, among other things, every classroom context, every syllabus and every teacher is different. As researchers Rod Ellis and Natsuko Shintani put it: "… there is no simple second language acquisition recipe that can be applied to language pedagogy" (Ellis and Shintani, 2013, p.27). But we would urge teachers to take any ideas they find useful here and evaluate them to inform their current practice. What is known about memory does make some practices more effective than others. Our aim is to provide an introduction to memory which can help you better understand, plan or refine your practice to enhance students' learning by creating more durable retention.

What is memory?

1

Key concepts

In this chapter we consider:

- **The importance of memory**
- **Types of memory**
- **The information processing model – the brain as a sort of computer**
- **The multi-component model of memory**
- **The social aspect of learning**

The importance of memory

Have you ever wondered why you remember some things and forget others?

Why is it you can remember how to conjugate a Spanish verb, but can't remember how to do a quadratic equation? How come you remember the capital of one country, but not another? Why do you remember how to ride a bicycle, even after twenty years of not having done so? Why is it you remember one funny moment on holiday, but not another? How do you remember the name of that person you met last week, but not the one you were introduced to two minutes ago? How is it that you remember how to speak your first language(s) without having to think about it very much?

Memory is complex, isn't it? But we know just how important it is to us all and how it defines our very existence. It has been said that we are the sum of our memories. Without a memory of the past, we cannot operate in the present or think about the future. Without memory, we could not learn anything.

For us as teachers, memory is an exceedingly important thing to understand since we spend much of our working time trying to help students remember what they've learned. Will they remember next week the words and phrases we covered today? Will they be able to apply that grammar rule in the exam at the end of the year? Will they remember to check their written work for mistakes, as I told them to? Fundamentally, what can I do to help students remember language and be confident, happy linguists?

What is memory? To start with, the Oxford Dictionary of English says that memory is "the faculty by which the mind stores and remembers information". More technically speaking, cognitive psychology tells us that memory is the term given to the structures and processes involved in three stages: *encoding*, *storage* and *retrieval* of information.

- **Encoding**: the process by which sensory information is converted into a form that can be used by memory.
- **Storage**: the process of maintaining information in memory.
- **Retrieval**: the process of recovering and using stored information.

So we receive input, encode it in memory and store it there to be available for retrieval. Language learners need to have a huge amount of stored information for retrieval: phonological, lexical and grammatical. In addition, students need to be able to recall other aspects such as cultural information and rules of appropriacy. But in cognitive psychology memory is not conceived as a single, unitary faculty or process. Let's look next at how memory is broken down into different components.

Types of memory

Just think of the vast amounts of information our memory has to cope with every day. No wonder we don't pay attention to all of it and that we are selective in what we do pay attention to and recall. The latter depends a lot on our goals and priorities at the time. These may well be different for a teacher than the student, so a challenge for teachers is to get those goals in sync.

The information we receive can take the form of images, sounds, smells, tastes and physical sensations. Each of these has a role to play, but psychologists believe that what we *see* is crucial. As linguists, however, we know that what we *hear* plays an even greater role. Combining the visual and aural is powerful when it comes to learning a language.

As noted above, we can remember facts and concepts, like capital cities or knowing what a phone is used for (known as *semantic memory*) and things that happened (known as *episodic memory*). *Autobiographical memory* (remembering what happened to you) is one type of episodic memory. Interestingly, women consistently perform better than men on verbal tests of episodic long-term memory and autobiographical memory, whereas men consistently outperform women on tests of spatial memory (Loprinzi and Frith, 2018).

A memory can be consciously recalled and brought into consciousness, like a verb conjugation (**declarative memory**), or we can just do things from memory without thinking, like riding a bike (**procedural memory**). When students use language in the classroom they might be using a combination of all these types of memory – using a sentence automatically, without thinking much about it, consciously trying to remember that word they heard last lesson, remembering the teacher hobbling around the classroom to demonstrate *I have a bad leg* or struggling to remember what the teacher just told them to do in the pair work task.

What complicates matters is that the mind is not like a recording device which simply receives, registers and stores information. Each person shapes the information they receive based on a whole range of factors: their existing knowledge, the context in which they receive the information, how they feel at the time and their level of attention, to name a few. What's more, every time a memory is reactivated, it is altered by the new context in which this retrieval takes place.

Did you know...?

If you are one of the 15% of people who are left-handed, you may have a better memory of past events.

Aparna Sahu and colleagues found in a study (confirming previous ones) that people better remembered whether they had seen a word before if they were 'mixed-handed' (or were even relatives of left-handers) or were shown the word twice on different sides of the visual field. The advantage only occurred when participants were intentionally trying to remember, that is, not picking up the information unconsciously (Sahu, Christman and Propper, 2016).

The fact that left-handers and their relatives seem to have larger *corpus callosums* (the bridges of neurons linking the brain's hemispheres) suggests that the interaction between the two halves of the brain strengthens memory for events.

Is the brain like a computer?

There are a number of schools of thought concerning how people learn and remember. These days, a very influential one is the ***information-processing*** model. In this view of things the brain is compared to a computer. Now, computers can do some things that the human brain can do, like store information and perform rapid calculations, though much better. So it's tempting to see the computer as a kind of brain and the brain as a kind of computer, but ultimately the analogy is misleading. While the brain has its own network of brain cells (neurons) - think of semi-conductors in a computer - computers perform the same operation repeatedly exactly the same way, whether the end result is the calculation of the average speed of your run, or the landing trajectory of an aircraft.

In contrast, the repeated use of a brain circuit changes the performance of the circuit, so the same input on two separate occasions can produce a different outcome. This is because the circuit in the brain is biological. What's more, whereas a computer has identifiable components and circuits, things get much more complex with the human brain. Although it has areas which are mainly responsible for certain tasks (listening, seeing, paying attention, etc), the brain can often bring in different areas to help out. This is referred to as ***brain plasticity***, and explains why some people can still perform activities with parts of their brain missing. In other words, the neural networks of the brain grow and adapt to new learning.

So what makes the brain special is that, unlike a computer, It has many different neural pathways that can replicate the function of another. This means that errors of development or temporary loss of function through damage can easily be corrected by rerouting signals along a different pathway. This is why stroke victims can often gradually recover the power of comprehension and speech even though those areas mainly responsible for those abilities have been damaged.

In sum, the brain doesn't just record, make calculations and retrieve that same information, it changes those memories every time they are reinforced or called upon again.

Did you know...?

The brain can hold at least a petabyte of information (some claim much more). That's about as much as the World Wide Web currently holds. (A petabyte is one thousand million million computer bits of information – quite a lot!)

The brain has roughly 100 billion neurons (brain cells). A study by Bartol et al. (2015) into synapses (the interconnectors between brain cells) indicated far more possible types of connection between those neurons than had been imagined.

The researchers calculated that in every 2 to 20 minutes, your synapses grow or shrink in size in response to the signals they're receiving. The variation in neuron size was far greater than previously thought.

The multi-component model of memory

Although there are competing models about how memory works, most cognitive psychologists believe in what's called the **multi-component model of memory** (also known as the **multi-store model**). In this view of things, the brain is indeed likened to a computer which processes, stores and reproduces information in different ways and, broadly, in different areas of the brain.

But a word of warning here about what we mean by storage. Memories aren't 'stored' in the usual sense of the term. They don't *exist* in the mind, kept in a file. How could they be? The idea is a little absurd. A memory is really a reactivation of electro-chemical connections between different parts of your brain that were triggered at some time in the past, perhaps very often. Think of the same circuit lighting up again. To get a bit more technical, it's to do with strengthening the **synapses**, the junctions between neurons. We often perceive these connections as conscious thoughts, but not always. For example, every time we switch on a light we are unconsciously reactivating a memory. For our purposes in this book, like many writers in education, we'll continue to use the term storage.

The social brain?

Books and articles about memory usually focus on the brain as if it exists in isolation and functions like a computer. A growing number of researchers believe that this undervalues the ***social aspect of learning***. In a famous experiment, Patricia Kuhl wanted to find out whether social interaction improved babies' ability to pick up an unfamiliar language. American babies exposed to Mandarin Chinese through watching DVDs did not pick up new phonemes (sounds of the language) as well as those who were exposed to the same language 'live'. It seemed that the social aspect enhanced perception and memory (Kuhl et al., 2003).

Perhaps it's the very interaction between people when learning a language which is key to positive outcomes and better memory.

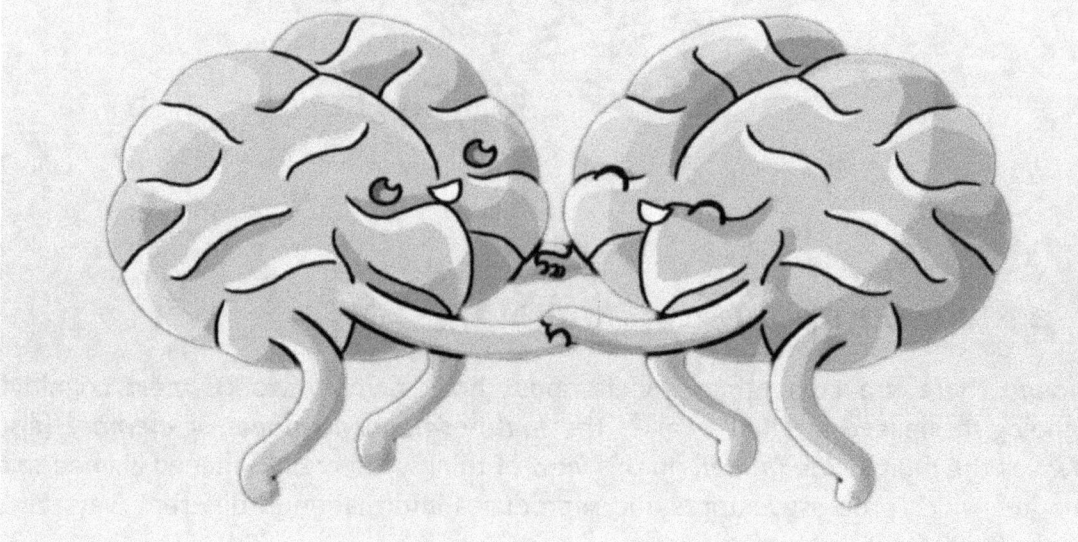

Summary

✓ Memory is complex; we remember some things more easily than others.
✓ Memory is about the structures and processes involved in the encoding, storage and retrieval of information.
✓ Psychologists talk about different types of memory, such as semantic, episodic, autobiographical, declarative and procedural.
✓ The neural networks of the brain grow and change every time they are reactivated by events or new learning.
✓ The mind can be compared to a computer – up to a point.
✓ Many psychologists think of brain activity as a multi-component system.

For reflection

- What do you think is the relative importance of declarative and procedural memory? How important is it to know the *facts* of a language?
- What do you think students remember more easily: vocabulary or grammar?
- Which is the more powerful language learning route, in your opinion, explicit or implicit?

Further reading and viewing

- Fiona McPherson's website *About Memory* is a rich source of information, with a large number of summaries based on research studies. Available at: https://www.memory-key.com
- Neuroscientist Catharine Young explains how memories form and why we lose them in this short video. Available at: https://www.youtube.com/watch?v=yOgAbKJGrTA
- Tulving, E. (1972). "Episodic and semantic memory," in *Organization of Memory*, eds E. Tulving and W. Donaldson (New York, NY: Academic Press), 381–403. Available at: http://alumni.media.mit.edu/~jorkin/generals/papers/Tulving_memory.pdf

The multi-component model of memory

2

Key concepts

In this chapter we consider:

- **Two types of memory, often known as working memory and long-term memory**
- **Controlled and automatic processing**
- **Metaphors for memory**
- **The areas of the brain most important for language learning**

Two types of memory

The distinction made between two types of memory, originally called primary and secondary memory, goes back to William James in 1890. He defined the two memory systems in this way:

- *primary memory*, which lasts for a few seconds and holds information in our consciousness, and

- *secondary memory*, which has unlimited duration and can be brought to consciousness if desired.

This is remarkably similar to the modern multi-store models of memory, the first of which was introduced in 1968 by Richard Atkinson and Richard Shiffrin. Their multi-store model consisted of **long-term memory** and **working** or **short-term memory** and was later improved by an additional component, the **sensory memory** (Atkinson and Shiffrin, 1968).

How does this two store model work? At a simple level we can imagine the mind working as in Figure 2.1.

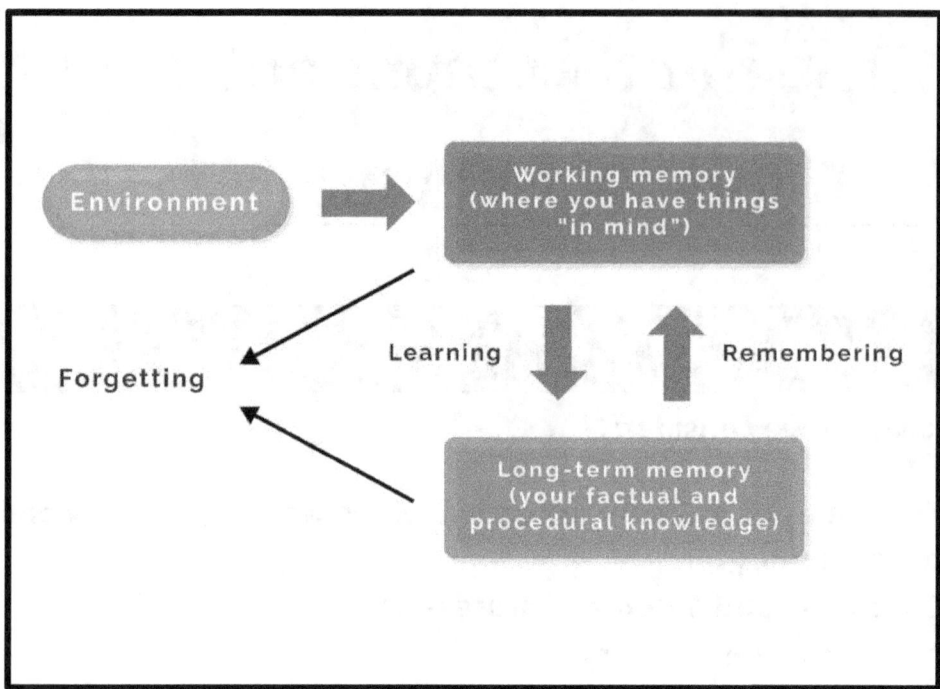

Figure 2.1 A simple model of the mind

If we look at this in a bit more detail, the brain records, very quickly, all the information it is bombarded with in a **sensory register**. This is a sort of ultra-short term memory for each of the five senses: sight, sound, touch, smell and taste. Each rapidly encoded memory lasts for under two seconds, although different senses have different durations. This initially encoded information is sub-conscious – we aren't aware of it. But when we pay conscious attention to something, it is transferred from the sensory register into **memory**. The act of paying attention filters out unwanted information to focus on what is worth processing – what you are interested in. This allows us to process information more efficiently.

These days most cognitive psychologists refer to our two types of memory as working memory (short-term memory - the 'mental workspace') and long-term memory. When we consciously receive sensory information we handle it initially using working memory, which decides what to focus on and processes it (takes it in, organises and stores it).

Types of processing

A distinction is sometimes made between two types of processing: **controlled processing** and **automatic processing**. Language psychologist Norman Segalowitz compares the two types of processing to the difference between an automatic and manual ('stick shift') car.

An automatic car changes gear without any conscious intervention by the driver whereas, in a manual car, a deliberate operation is needed (Segalowitz, 2003). In linguistic terms, automatic processing is involved when you are using a language spontaneously and fluently, while controlled processing is in use when you are beginning to practise a new grammatical structure or item of vocabulary. Automatic processing requires far less mental effort than controlled processing. Producing sentences is hard work for novices.

You might be asking what the evidence for this model of memory is. Well, it partly stems from what are called **dual task** laboratory experiments. If one task selectively interferes with one type of processing but not another, then those two types of processing must rely on different aspects of the brain's systems. For example, studies show that if a person is asked to speak out loud, this interferes with their ability to take in visual information. Secondly, **neuropsychological evidence** from patients with brain impairments is further evidence for compartmentalised brain processes. If one part of the brain is damaged, this limits what a person is able to do.

Metaphors for memory

Many metaphors have been suggested for human memory, but you might like to think of working memory as a work desk, where you're thinking about things now, or you hold things consciously 'in mind' in order to solve a problem, make a decision or carry out a task.

Long-term memory, on the other hand, is like a huge warehouse where you can access all the things you know about the world, whether it be the capital of Spain, the price of a litre of milk or the meaning of the fact that French adjectives agree with nouns. This warehouse is never full, but things are often hard to locate.

Another way to think of memory is as a large, leaky bottle with a very narrow neck and huge body. Working memory is the neck which only a small amount of liquid (information) can enter at a time (Baddeley, 2000). If you pour liquid into it too fast much will be lost; only a proportion will enter the main body of the bottle and some of that may evaporate over time.

The implications of this are clear enough. We need to be really careful to limit the amount of new language presented and practised, especially with beginners, in order for it to pass through the neck of the bottle. We go into more detail on this in Chapter 5.

Main areas of the brain involved in language learning

In the nineteenth century French anatomist Pierre Paul Broca and German physician Karl Wernicke carried out studies on aphasia (the inability to comprehend or formulate language) that indicated which areas of the brain play a key role in language use. In these early days of brain research, before scans were possible, much was learned from autopsies of patients who had suffered damage to parts of their brain. ***Broca's area*** (above the left ear) and ***Wernicke's area*** (behind the left ear) were found to be fundamental to the ability to understand and speak. Damage to Broca's area leads to poor fluency and a lack of correct grammar, while damage to Wernicke's area produces fluent, but vague and hard to follow speech.

With modern neuroimaging scans neuroscientists are able to localise the parts of the brain which are activated when we perform different learning tasks. But we shouldn't imagine that the components of memory models correspond perfectly neatly with regions of the brain. We can't simply say that working memory is in one precise place, and long-term memory in another. As we saw in Chapter 1, when the brain suffers trauma, it is often able to adapt by engaging different areas to compensate for the damage, and many parts of the brain play a role when we learn.

To give an idea of where the main areas of the brain involved in language are situated, Figure 2.2 gives a side-on view of a few main areas of the brain, while Figure 2.3 picks out four key areas, as far as language perception and production are concerned. The word ***cortex*** is used to describe an outer layer of the brain's grey matter (darker tissue consisting largely of nerve cells).

In the next four chapters we look at key components of this model of memory: working memory, phonological memory, visuospatial memory and long-term memory. We focus specifically on a well-known model associated with psychologist Alan Baddeley and consider the implications of the model for language teachers.

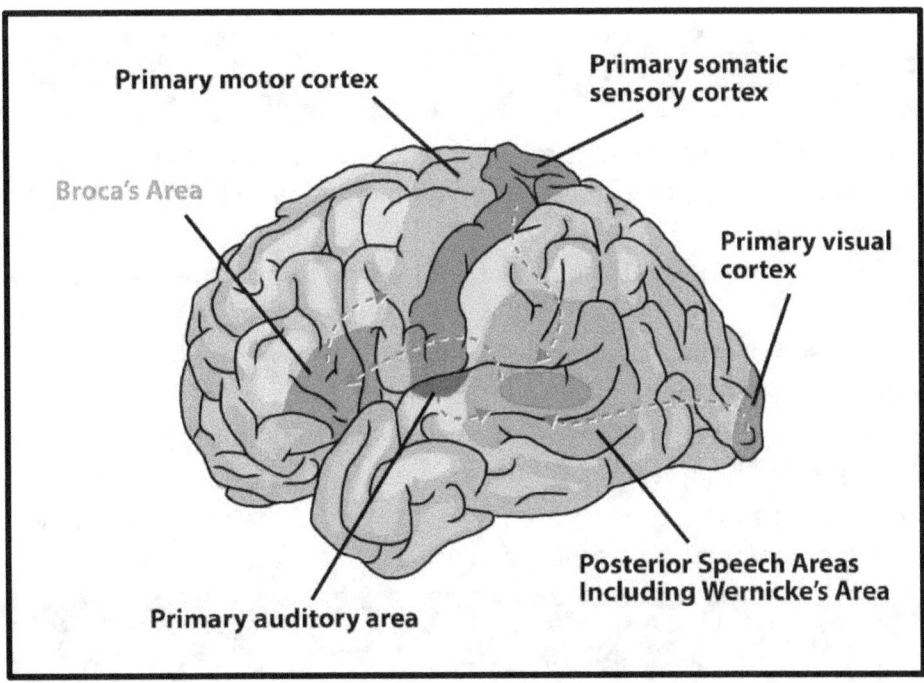

Figure 2.2 Basic anatomy of the brain (side view, with the rear of the brain on the right)

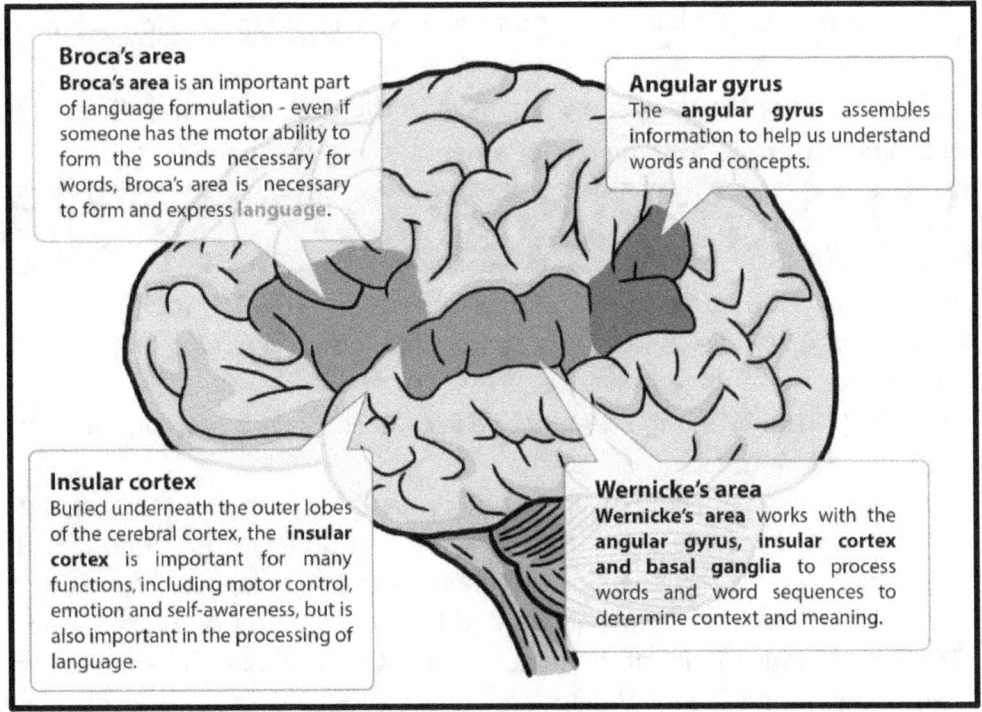

Broca's area
Broca's area is an important part of language formulation - even if someone has the motor ability to form the sounds necessary for words, Broca's area is necessary to form and express language.

Angular gyrus
The **angular gyrus** assembles information to help us understand words and concepts.

Insular cortex
Buried underneath the outer lobes of the cerebral cortex, the **insular cortex** is important for many functions, including motor control, emotion and self-awareness, but is also important in the processing of language.

Wernicke's area
Wernicke's area works with the **angular gyrus, insular cortex and basal ganglia** to process words and word sequences to determine context and meaning.

Figure 2.3 Key areas of the brain for language perception and production

Summary

✓ Most cognitive psychologists tell us that we possess two types of memory: a 'mental workspace' called short-term memory or working memory, and long-term memory.

✓ There is good evidence to support the idea of a compartmentalised view of the brain.

✓ The bottleneck of working memory is narrow, so only small amounts of new knowledge can enter at a time.

✓ Different parts of the brain are generally responsible for different thought processes, but it's not simple.

✓ Broca's Area and Wernicke's area are two parts of the brain long known to be important for language learning and use.

For reflection

- To what extent do you think language is picked up incidentally (sub-consciously) and to what extent does it need to be taught for it to stick?

- If the memory bottle has such a narrow neck, what might this imply for language teachers?

- When you have learned a new language in the past, what specific strategies or techniques were used to help you remember new language?

Further reading and viewing

- Baddeley, A. D. & Logie, R. H. (1999). Working memory: The multiple-component model. In A.Miyake & P. Shah (Eds.), *Models of working memory* (28-61). Cambridge: Cambridge University Press.

- Wen, Z. (2016). *Working Memory and Second Language Learning* Bristol: Multilingual Matters.

- This video by Carol Yue explains more about the information-processing model of memory. Available at: https://www.khanacademy.org/science/health-and-medicine/executive-systems-of-the-brain/memory-lesson/v/information-processing-model-sensory-working-and-long-term-memory

- This fascinating illustrated lecture by Karen Froud examines, from a neuroscientific view, what happens in the brain when we process language. https://www.youtube.com/watch?app=desktop&fbclid=IwAR1FwhIdASt6_Pdr4DzbdfQq5d01J58Y6LbKGyPPKnN-f2JBxMKY_25Pnhc&v=N4KuS08TRsE

Working memory 3

Key concepts

In this chapter we consider:

- A definition of working memory
- How working memory is thought to function, including its components known as the Phonological Loop, Visuospatial Sketchpad, Central Executive and Episodic Buffer
- One way that working memory capacity is measured
- The limited capacity of working memory
- The importance of chunking in building memory
- The importance of automaticity in skill acquisition
- Cognitive overload and divided attention
- Inattentional blindness
- The fragility of working memory
- Working memory in action
- The dynamic relationship between working memory and long-term memory
- The relationship between working memory and language learning aptitude
- How to identify students with working memory deficiencies

What is working memory?

Roughly equivalent to what for many years has been called short-term memory, working memory has become a great focus of research in the field of second language acquisition. Some researchers go as far as to say that it's the major part of second language learning aptitude (Wen, 2016).

What we can't say, however, is that having a larger working memory actually makes you smarter in general. It can have an impact on how well students perform on tests, but when it comes to what psychologists call **fluid intelligence**, "the ability to reason through and solve novel problems" (Shipstead et al., 2016), working memory is not crucial.

In any case, knowing how working memory functions helps us understand how our students learn a language and how we can refine our teaching. To be clear, there are many competing models of memory in the scholarly research, without even a clear consensus about what precisely the terms short-term memory, working memory and long-term memory mean. We decided to keep our description clear and (relatively!) simple by sticking to one particular model. Research in the field is rapidly evolving. For example, while some psychologists believe working memory is a temporary storage facility separate from long-term memory, others argue that working memory is the part of long-term memory which is activated as we perform a task.

We also need to emphasise once again that in the description which follows, working memory is not a separate 'box' or 'place' in the mind or brain. When we describe it, we are really talking about processes or functions rather than physical structures, even though functions can be very broadly associated with different brain areas, as we saw in Chapter 2. Remember how the brain is 'plastic'? Many parts of the brain can play a role in learning and forming memories.

Even the term *memory* itself may be a little misleading in this context. Working memory is not so much about *remembering* things, but using thinking processes to perform functions such as learning, processing language, planning ahead, rehearsing, manipulating ideas and reasoning. To give you a definition from the literature:

> *Working memory is those mechanisms or processes that are involved in the control, regulation and active maintenance of task-relevant information in the service of complex cognition, including novel as well as familiar, skilled tasks* (Miyake and Shah, 1999, p.450).

We only use working memory when we process new information or carry out tasks consciously. When we perform routine tasks or process familiar information, we use subconscious processes which by-pass working memory. So, to give a practical example, when a student stops in a middle of a spoken sentence to form a challenging structure (for example, the perfect tense of a reflexive verb in French), they are using working memory, consciously slowing down production to apply the grammar rule while monitoring the accuracy of what they say.

On the other hand, a student who has automatised saying a sentence (such as a high frequency sentence such as *J'ai joué au foot* – 'I played football') says it in one go, effortlessly, without engaging working memory much at all. In fact, fluent speech is said to consist of a process called **chaining**, where we produce a series of utterances with connectives to join them together. Fluent speakers seldom pause in the middle of a sentence unless they are under stress or are forming complex sentences.

By the way, working memory varies between individuals, and those with a larger working memory capacity generally do better at the type of tasks students do in school. Working memory capacity is also pretty much fixed for each person. However, it does vary with age, developing slowly through childhood, peaking during the mid-twenties, then declining in later adulthood. Some studies suggest that with training, working memory for specific tasks can be improved.

How does working memory function?

This is where it starts to get technical. Look at Figure 3.1 which shows a commonly used and highly influential model of how working memory operates. It is from the work of Alan Baddeley (2000), building on an earlier model from the seminal 1974 model by Baddeley and Hitch.

We get information from the environment through various means: visual, acoustic (language, noises and music), touch, taste and smell. Of course, it's what we see and, and especially what we hear, which are the most important for language learning. In this model, incoming speech is held and processed in an auditory storage area called the **Phonological Loop**, which plays a key role in language processing and acquisition (see Figure 3.1). The Phonological Loop temporarily stores and rehearses language we hear.

Visual information, for instance the images on your flashcards or the spelling of words on your classroom screen, is held in working memory in what is called a **Visuospatial Sketchpad.** Think of this as a place where images and space are consciously held in mind. It appears that we draw on it when we process any words which refer to location (such as right, left, above, below).

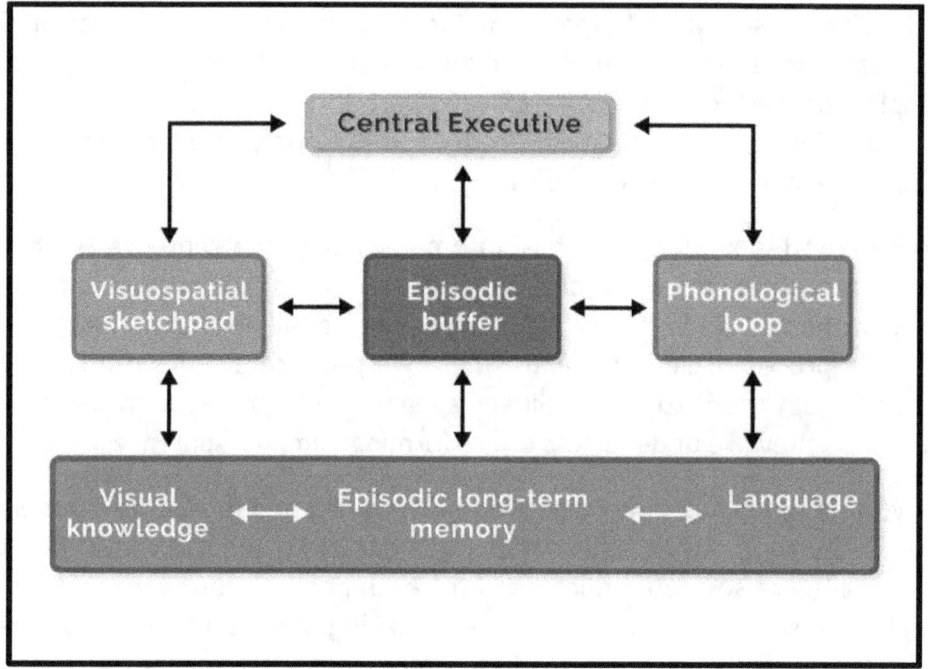

Figure 3.1 The Baddeley (2000) multi-store model of working memory

Both of these stores have very limited capacity, and each one is thought to be separate. However, they often operate in tandem to form links or associations, thanks to a **Central Executive** and **Episodic Buffer** which regulate the flow of information in and out of the Phonological Loop and the Visuospatial Sketchpad, using information from long-term memory to help. Remember that in this model, long-term memory plays an integral role in working memory. Think of a complex, dynamic two-way relationship between working and long-term memory.

By the way, apart from brain imaging when people carry out verbal and visuospatial tasks, the strongest arguments for separating out the phonological and visuospatial parts of working memory in this way come from the study of patients in the field of neuropsychology. For example, some patients with a deficit in the temporary storage of verbal information have no visuospatial impairment and vice versa.

The Central Executive in this model is like the conductor of an orchestra, managing all the processes occurring in working memory, for example it decides what to pay attention to, suppressing any distracting stimuli to ensure that the brain operates as efficiently as possible. The Episodic Buffer binds together information from the Phonological Loop, Visuospatial Sketchpad and long-term memory. It also calls on information from working memory needed to make sense of any information or perform any tasks which can't be carried out automatically in long-term memory. Tasks which can be done effortlessly, without conscious attention, are said to have been **automatised** (see section below on Automaticity).

In recent years, the idea of the Central Executive has come under critical scrutiny, with some psychologists suggesting, for example, that it's really long-term memory which manages the whole system.

Linking long-term memory knowledge of language to the Phonological Loop allows learners to understand much more quickly what they hear as they combine their existing knowledge with new, incoming material. Research suggests that the Central Executive reaches its peak performance during our twenties, and declines somewhat thereafter.

Measuring working memory: the digit span test

In 1887 a London school teacher called John Jacobs decided to test the abilities of his students. He dictated a series of numbers which the students had to read back from memory. The more numbers they could recall, the longer their digit span.

This type of short-term memory test is still widely used today, for example in the Wechsler Adult Intelligence Test. In itself, the digit span test is not a great measure of general intelligence, but more elaborate tests of working memory span are good at predicting a range of cognitive skills and, as mentioned earlier, some researchers relate working memory to language learning aptitude.

Digits Forward

I am going to say some numbers. Listen carefully, and when I'm through, say them right after me. For example, if I say, 4-3, then you say, 4-3. Ready?

Series	Time 1	Time 2
3	7-4-9	1-7-4
4	8-5-2-1	5-2-9-7
5	2-9-6-8-3	6-3-8-5-1
6	5-7-1-9-4-6	2-9-4-7-3-8
7	8-1-5-9-3-6-2	4-1-9-2-7-5-1
8	3-9-8-2-5-1-4-7	8-5-3-9-1-6-2-7
9	7-2-8-5-4-6-7-3-9	2-1-9-7-3-5-8-4-6

Did you know...?

Musicians and bilingual people have long been shown to have a better working memory. A study by Alain et al. (2018) found that musicians and bilinguals were better at identifying and locating sounds (human, natural and musical).

Participants were asked to identify whether the sound they heard was the same type as the previous one, and if the sound came from the same direction. Musicians remembered the type of sound faster than individuals in other groups, and bilinguals and musicians performed better than monolinguals on the location task. Although bilinguals remembered the sound about as well as monolingual non-musicians, their brains showed less activity when doing the task, suggesting less effort was needed.

Bilinguals showed increased activity in language-related brain areas, which may reflect a need to limit interference from their other language(s).

The limited capacity of working memory

When following a recipe, do you keep forgetting the instructions you just read? Do you have to keep returning to them before you do the next step? It's an everyday reminder about how limited our working memory is and how easy it is to forget stuff really quickly.

How restricted is working memory exactly? Well, it depends on what psychologists choose to measure and how they measure it. Originally, George Miller (1956) wrote about "seven plus or minus two", but he was talking about recalling lists of numbers. In general terms, more recent research suggests that a young adult can hold around three to five 'pieces of knowledge' in mind at one time and that these are quickly forgotten (for example, Cowan, 2010). Bits of knowledge could refer to verbal chunks, idioms, whole sentences.... or steps in a recipe. Think of it another way: we have about 3-5 slots available for pieces of information. Young children have about half as many (Riggs et al., 2006).

The limited capacity of working memory is one of the most fundamental things language teachers need to be aware of when planning and delivering lessons. We'll go into this in much more detail in Chapters 6 and 7.

Chunking

When you think about the sheer complexity of learning a language, you might wonder how we manage it at all. Researchers believe we use a range of processes when we learn the structures of a language, one of which is known as **chunking**.

Chunking means compressing large units of information into smaller more meaningful ones, so that they take up less cognitive space. So for instance, as we learn to read, instead of processing texts one letter at a time, we learn to chunk the letters into words and words into phrases or sentences. This allows us to read quickly and easily.

Furthermore, when it comes to bits of language, because we have grammatical knowledge which binds words together into meaningful units, a whole sentence of, say, eight words, can be held in memory much more easily than a random list of the same words. Look at these two sets of eight words, then try to remember them afterwards:

PONG BROTHER WITH THE PING HIS PLAYED BOY

THE BOY PLAYED PING PONG WITH HIS BROTHER

The second set of words is much easier to remember, of course, and might count as one chunk of language in working memory because the words are bound together by our knowledge of grammar, its relationship with meaning, and our usage. The more we use a string of words, the stronger the associations between those words become in long-term memory and the easier they are to retrieve. So, thinking back to those two sets of words above, whereas we have never come across the first one, we are familiar with the sentence pattern underlying the second (Subject + Verb + Object + Complement). This familiarity makes the sentence easy to chunk, even if it's the first time we've seen it.

By the way, this gives an advantage to learners whose first language is syntactically similar to the target language, for example a French speaker learning Spanish. Research (and experience) shows that, to some extent, we impose the grammatical patterns of the first language(s) on to the second. (Think for a moment of how often you use the patterns of your first language when speaking or writing your second.)

Chunking as a key to listening

At a normal rate of speech humans produce between 10 and 15 phonemes per second. But the ability to process discrete sounds is limited to about 10 items per second (Miller and Taylor, 1948). In addition, as we have seen, working memory holds fewer than 10 items in a random sequence. How do we manage to process this large amount of short-lived sensory information?

The answer is chunking. Incoming items are rapidly grouped and passed to higher levels of representation (syllables, morphemes, words and so on), before the next onslaught of incoming data.

A little context is useful here. For a long time language learning was seen to be a case of knowing how to retrieve words from memory, then combine them by an underlying knowledge of rules. You could call this a 'words and rules' view of things, where grammatical rules define a sentence skeleton which is fleshed out by words.

More recently, researchers have tended to move towards a different perspective, namely that vocabulary cannot be separated out from grammar in this way. The word *lexicogrammar* is used to describe this way of looking at vocabulary and grammar. In this view, we learn a language through hearing, seeing and using multi-word units (chunks). As Michael Lewis put it, language is "grammaticalised lexis, not lexicalised grammar" (Lewis, 1993, p.24).

We sub-consciously pick out statistical patterns (those we encounter most often, others which are not acceptable) and gradually learn to chain them together in utterances. Analysis of child language use shows that, rather than combining words with grammar to make novel sentences, very often children use ready-made chunks. A 15-month study by Kenji Hakuta of a Japanese child learning English found evidence of initial use of pre-fabricated chunks which were later sub-consciously analysed and used to make further language development easier (Hakuta, 1974).

Adult language users also use ready-made chunks much of the time (estimates range from 40% to 80% of the time, depending on context).

One conclusion for language teachers is that we could attempt to emulate this type of learning by constantly modelling multi-word chunks, centred around the most useful words. This is likely to be more productive than a 'words and rules' approach. Indeed, some writers have suggested that for many students, being able to manipulate and combine a repertoire of useful chunks, together with vocabulary knowledge and a narrow range of grammatical rules, is the best we can hope to achieve given the limited time we have with them (Lewis, 1993). In sum, working with chunks makes more efficient use of working memory and may well reflect to a good degree how we pick up our first language.

Automaticity

Alongside chunking, humans have learnt to make retrieving information and performing skills fast and automatic. The term *automaticity* comes from a skill acquisition model of learning proposed by John Anderson. The idea is that, with practice, knowledge can be become automatically retrievable without having to think about it (Anderson, 1982). This means that, when we perform a complex task, the brain can bypass working memory, calling on automatised knowledge from long-term memory. This avoids clogging up working memory, allowing more efficient focus where it's needed the most. In other words, automaticity frees up cognitive space in working memory.

Automaticity is vital for fluent production of language. A fluent speaker doesn't devote much working memory capacity to the pronunciation of sounds or to applying grammatical rules, for example. In this case, automatic processing is in use (Segalowitz, 2003). Most conscious attention is focused on higher order skills, such as ensuring language is meaningful, coherent, engaging or persuasive.

It's very common to come across students of French, Spanish or German who, after three or four years of language learning, still struggle with adjectival agreement, verb formation, word order and other basic grammatical structures. They find it hard to speak or write with any fluency. Apart from lacking knowledge in long-term memory, this could be for a couple of other reasons:

> (a) teaching doesn't include a component focused deliberately on building up fluency;
> (b) students haven't had enough practice with target structures across a sufficiently wide range of contexts.

So the main point is this: working memory capacity is very limited and language learners, especially beginners, don't have much long-term memory knowledge to help them deal with incoming language. Work focused on automaticity can speed up retrieval and lighten the load on working memory.

Cognitive overload and divided attention

Whenever a task requires cognitive space and resources which exceed working memory capacity, we experience **cognitive overload** which we'll consider more carefully in Chapters 6 and 7. Suffice it to say for now that cognitive overload is often caused by **divided attention**. This is when the brain has to cope with multiple demands on conscious attention. It happens, for example, when a student attempts to produce a long sentence containing several items of vocabulary and grammar structures they are not familiar with and which are beyond their current level of proficiency. Errors and forgetting are the consequence.

In addition, stress and anxiety significantly increase cognitive load and the pressure on working memory. This is discussed further in Chapter 14.

Inattentional blindness

Working memory can usually successfully cope with only one challenging task at a time. So, for instance, when students check through an essay, they pay attention to features such as content relevance, structure and organisation, often missing spelling or grammar mistakes. This phenomenon is sometimes referred to as **inattentional blindness**.

This has significant implications for language learning. Think for instance of a student listening to an aural text while doing a typical textbook comprehension task, for example, true/false or answering questions. Their attention is focused on the meaning of the text, so they are unlikely to notice and learn any useful linguistic features the text may contain. This is why it's helpful when working with texts to do a range of different tasks which focus the students' attention on different levels of processing (such as phonology, vocabulary, grammar, meaning and overall structure). In a nutshell, working with texts intensively, rather than superficially, leads to more efficient learning and better memory.

The fragility of working memory

Whether it's processing input from the outside world or retrieving material from long-term memory, working memory holds information for a limited time – the precise time is hard to measure, but a classic study by Peterson and Peterson (1959), where psychology students had to remember three letter nonsense words, suggested around 18 seconds. After that, the information fades away, unless you make a conscious effort to keep it there by focusing a good deal of attention on it through what cognitive psychologists call **rehearsal.** So if you wanted to remember the steps of your cooking recipe better, you'd need to keep thinking or saying them out loud. Do you ever repeat a phone number out loud to help remember it?

Rehearsal through Delayed Dictation and Delayed Copying

Try dictating short chunks of language or short sentences to a class, but instead of students writing down what they hear immediately, get them to wait 10 seconds before writing. This forces them to think through the language multiple times.

Or have students look at a sentence on the board, then hide the same sentence and ask them to write the sentence 10 seconds later.

This simple challenge makes students rehearse language, making it more likely to be remembered later.

Storage in working memory is not only temporary, but also extremely fragile. The slightest distraction can cause us to lose information we are processing. For instance, as we listen to something, any new incoming speech signal completely erases the previous one. Or, when we interrupt a student as they're speaking to correct a mistake they've just made, we may cause them to forget what they were about to say.

The distinctiveness of the language input (how much it stands out) or its relevance (how much it matters to a person) also affect how long something stays active in working memory. Furthermore, the more meaningful or **elaborate** the rehearsal is, the more likely it is that the information will pass into long-term memory. So-called **shallow rehearsal** is less effective than **elaborate rehearsal**. (We look into this whole issue in Chapter 11.) For example, simply repeating a series of unconnected words over and over is less effective than giving some added meaning to them – mental associations or images, say. As we have seen, words which are connected meaningfully or grammatically are much easier to recall later.

Working memory in action

Every operation the brain performs when decoding a message takes place in working memory. Take vocabulary learning: any rehearsal we do when trying to commit vocabulary to long-term memory (for example, repeating aloud) is performed in working memory, which temporarily holds that information for as long as we rehearse it. In speaking and writing, all the operations needed to put ideas into words, all the while monitoring for accuracy, happen in working memory too.

When we read, for example, our eyes jump from point to point along a line of text (looking ahead by a few words) as we decode the words individually or in groups. When reading silently an average adult reads between 200-250 words per minute. Speech is also sequential. In either case, it's essential to hang on to the first part of a sentence until the last words are encountered. It's our working memory that holds the necessary information to allow this to be done.

Whether our students are reading or listening to target language input, translating a passage into French, planning an essay or performing an oral task it is working memory that processes what it hears or sees in the moment, or draws on knowledge from long-term memory. Anything language teachers can do to help working memory operate efficiently will lead to better long term retention.

And don't forget that it's beginners who depend most on working memory, given how little long-term memory knowledge, conscious or sub-conscious, of a second language they have. They have to do more 'thinking' than students who have made a lot of progress. As Sweller, Ayres and Kalyuga (2011) put it: "Novices use thinking skills, experts use knowledge" (p.21).

Working and long-term memory: a dynamic relationship

We mentioned previously how we use background knowledge from our long-term memory to help us think. View this as a dynamic relationship between working memory and long-term memory. As new information is noticed, it interacts with all sorts of information held in long-term memory (phonological, lexical, grammatical and semantic). The new information is processed, combined with pre-known information and creates new memories. It's a highly complex, fast process, in constant flux.

To give a concrete example, when a student reads a target language word or phrase they know, they hold its graphic image and its sound (if it is pronounced or sounded out in the student's head), while matching it to the word in long-term memory. If a match is found, the process can stop there. However, if the word or phrase is new, the student can call upon a range of interpretive processes as well as other knowledge from long-term memory to attempt to decode it.

When reading a text sentence by sentence, the meaning of the preceding text is held actively in working memory so that, when a new sentence is processed, the interpretation of the new sentence and the previous text influence each other. One implication here is that reading and listening lessons need to include activities which promote these so-called *discourse building* skills, for example, reordering sentences or jigsaw reading, where paragraphs have to be placed in the correct order.

Is working memory linked to language learning ability?

Zhisheng Wen and Shaofeng Li summarise the research about the degree to which working memory capacity and span predict the ability to learn languages (Wen and Li, 2019). Many studies have been carried out, but there are still large gaps in knowledge, particularly with regard to listening and writing. The authors conclude that both working memory and a separate measure called *language aptitude* correlate more strongly with explicit (conscious) than implicit (unconscious) learning. Language aptitude shows a stronger correlation than working memory, even if working memory is thought of as part of language aptitude.

The authors also note that phonological short-term memory, explained in Chapter 4, is a factor for beginners learning new vocabulary and grammar, but not so much for experienced learners. In a summary of the literature, Lourdes Ortega tentatively suggests that "good memory helps vocabulary learning in the beginning and grammar learning later on" (Ortega, 2013, p.157).

Working memory has been shown to predict reading comprehension ability (Geva and Ryan, 1993), while Mitchell et al. (2013) point to growing evidence that learners with higher working memory capacity are more likely to attend to and remember vocabulary and morphology. Working memory capacity also predicts the ability to keep track of the ideas presented in a long or complex sentences (Zhou et al., 2017). In addition, research by Goo (2012) suggested that students with better *attentional control* (part of working memory) responded better to teacher reformulations during information-gap tasks, that is, they noticed and responded more accurately to the teachers' input. O'Brien et al. (2006) reported that phonological working memory predicted fluency and accuracy in speaking.

A takeaway here is that we need to be particularly aware of working memory limitations in general, but particularly if beginners have less efficient working memory. In addition, we can't assume that all students will notice improved versions of their answers unless we specifically point out mistakes. Suggestions for identifying students with poorer working memory are given on the next page.

In the next two chapters we describe how two components which many psychologists label the **Phonological Loop** and **Visuospatial Sketchpad** work together, processing sound and visual images respectively, to enable learners to process and remember incoming language.

Drill and skill

Various types of oral drill can combine the use of working memory and long-term memory, allowing students to hear, rehearse in memory, manipulate and retrieve comprehensible language.

- Read a sentence in one tense which students must put into another, e.g. *I play football* becomes *I play**ed** football*.

- Read a sentence one or more elements of which students have to change by retrieving a word or phrase of their own, e.g. *I went to the* supermarket becomes I *went to the baker's*.

- Read a sentence to which students add new elements, e.g. *I went for a walk with my brother* becomes *I went for a walk with my brother in the park*.

- Begin a sentence which students must finish, e.g. *I went into the kitchen and...* becomes *I went into the kitchen and made a coffee*.

- Read a sentence and tell students to change the subject pronoun (which often requires an associated change in the verb form and other parts of a sentence), e.g. *I played tennis with my friend could* become *We played tennis with our friends*.

- Read a sentence which students must put in a negative form, e.g. *I often go to the cinema* becomes *I never go to the cinema*.

How to identify students with poor working memory

Incomplete recall. Students may skip steps when carrying out a task, rather than working through them as asked.

Difficulty getting started on tasks. This is often because the student's working memory has been overloaded with all the instructions they've just received. Even if the task itself involves only one or two steps, the students may have also heard all sorts of other information, such as which book to use, how long they have to work on the task and how to start things off.

Slow to copy things down from the board. This is because the student may find it hard to remember more than one or two words at a time, so they frequently need to check and recheck the original sentence.

Not answering questions in class. Students are often reserved when participating in class. They may have forgotten part or all of the question, be unsure whether some of the information they are volunteering has already been discussed or have forgotten parts of the topic that everyone is discussing (such as vital parts of a book that has just been read out loud to the class).

Trouble following through on instructions. This happens especially when more than one instruction is being given at a time. With young children, this can relate to activities at home and at school, such as packing up and then sitting quietly on the carpet, or brushing your teeth and then choosing a story to read before bedtime. Teachers need to be careful about how they precisely give an instruction.

Struggling to take notes. Again, this is because students can only remember a short amount of information in the time taken to write it down.

Taking longer to write original pieces of work. Students with poor working memory have to go back and re-read what they've written because they can lose track of their train of thought in the middle of a sentence. Failure to go back and refocus on what they were trying to say can mean they tend to create incomplete or poorly written sentences. This is obviously a big factor when it comes to speed and coherence of writing in the later years of secondary school.

Summary

✓ There are competing theories and models of how working memory operates.

✓ Some psychologists believe working memory is a temporary storage facility separate from long-term memory, while others claim that working memory is the part of long -term memory which is activated as we perform a task.

✓ Whatever the model, working memory plays a key role in language processing and acquisition.

✓ In the most popular model of working memory, the latter consists of a control system, the **Central Executive** and three so-called slave systems: the **Visuospatial Sketchpad,** the **Phonological Loop** and the **Episodic Buffer**.

✓ The Phonological Loop is the language learning device. It processes sounds.

✓ The Visuospatial Sketchpad is where we process images and any spatial information. It would appear that we draw on it also when we process any words which refer to location (such as right, left, above, below).

✓ The Episodic Buffer is a system which binds information coming from the Phonological Loop and Visuospatial Sketchpad. It also calls on information from working memory needed to make sense of any information or perform any tasks which have not been automatised.

✓ The Central Executive is an attentional system which monitors the functioning of the other systems. Its main function is to suppress any distracting stimuli to ensure that the brain operates as efficiently as possible.

✓ Working memory has very limited capacity. It can only process three to five items simultaneously. Learners with a working memory capacity below average are like to be at a disadvantage as they are more easily affected by cognitive overload.

✓ Information lingers in working memory for a limited time before decaying, unless we keep rehearsing it.

✓ Elaborate (more meaningful) rehearsal, which involves creating associations between the item being learnt and other known information, is more effective than shallow rehearsal.

✓ We need to be aware of which students may have more working memory issues than others.

For reflection

- What different ways can you think of to get students to rehearse words, chunks and sentences?
- Why does using comprehensible language help students make the most of working memory?
- How might knowledge of working memory guide the amount of new language you introduce in a lesson?

Further reading and viewing

- Baddeley, A.D. and Hitch, G.J. (1974) Working memory. In *The Psychology of Learning and Motivation* (Bower, G.A., Ed.), pp. 47–89, Academic Press.
- Cowan, N. (2010). The Magical Mystery Four: How is Working Memory Capacity Limited, and Why? PMC US National Library of Medecine. Available at: ncbi.nlm.nih.gov/pmc/articles/PMC2864034/
- Craik, F.I.M. & Watkins, M.J (1973). The role of rehearsal in short-term memory. *Journal of Verbal Learning and Verbal Behavior, 12* (6): 599-607.
- Alan Baddeley talks about the origins of the Central Executive. Available at: https://www.youtube.com/watch?v=aseitqCZKQo#action=share

Phonological memory

4

Key concepts

In this chapter we consider:

- The Phonological Loop
- The role of the Phonological Loop during silent reading
- The role of phonotactics in language processing
- The Phonological Loop and vocabulary learning
- Phonological memory difficulties: the case of dyslexia

The Phonological Loop

In the multi-store model described in the previous chapter, the *Phonological Loop* is the most important part of working memory as far as language learning is concerned. How does it work? Consider how you hold a word or phrase in your head as you make sense of it or prepare to say it; or how you say words in your head as you read from a book; or how you try to make sense of some spoken language. These processes are carried out by the Phonological Loop, what psychologists sometimes call verbal or *phonological working memory*.

The Phonological Loop has been described as the mind's ear, processing and storing sounds. Think of it as our language learning device, activated in a particular part of the brain, the temporal lobe of the left hemisphere (above and around your left ear). In the model of working memory we have described, the Phonological Loop consists of two components (see Figure 4.1).

- The ***phonological store***, which has a limited capacity and holds acoustic information briefly.
- The ***articulatory loop***, which allows us to mentally rehearse language to prevent it from decaying, for example when you repeat a sentence in your head a few times.

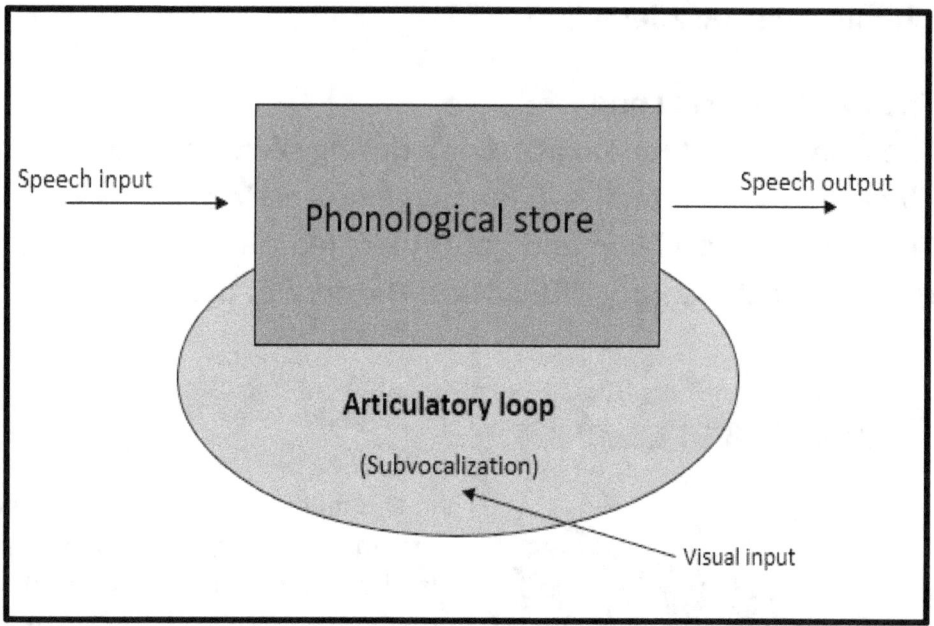

Figure 4.1 The structure of the Phonological Loop

The Phonological Loop interacts with long-term memory, playing a vital role in the long term retention of the phonological form of new words and phrases. As new phonological forms are held in the phonological store during rehearsal, so more permanent memory representations are constructed. This is one reason why it's so important to allow students to hear and repeat new language as often as possible. They need to have a phonological representation of words, not just know what they mean or look like. This makes it easier for them to recognise words and chunks in the continuous stream of speech.

We know some other significant things about the Phonological Loop. Its capacity or span, as we saw in the last chapter, is as few as three to five items of language at the same time: but recall that these can be sounds, words, phrases or even whole sentences.

Interestingly, the number of words working memory can hold at any given time depends on the native language of the speaker. For instance, Mandarin speakers can hold more words than English speakers in working memory for reasons that are not entirely clear. It may be to do with the fact that Mandarin-speaking children must do a good deal of rote learning when mastering the characters of their language (Mattys et al., 2018).

Faulty Echo

For phonological decoding and modelling the listening process.

1. Display a list of words or short phrases which produce sounds you want to focus on.
2. Read one of them aloud as clearly as possible.
3. Read the same item aloud a second time, pronouncing a sound wrongly. Make sure that the wrong pronunciation reproduces mistakes commonly made by students, for example, faulty 'r' sounds in French, Spanish and German, or common vowel sounds.
4. Students must spot which sound you mispronounced and give suggestions about what is wrong and why.

The limited capacity of the Phonological Loop means that a novice second language learner can hold fewer words in working memory than in their first language as they pronounce the words more slowly. The more rapidly a second language speaker can utter a word or phrase, the less space it takes in working memory. So the more you know, and the more fluently you can speak, the easier the job becomes for working memory. This means that teachers need to carefully control the amount and difficulty level of language that students hear and read.

As we saw above, the phonological store holds sounds very briefly (about two seconds, before one sound is erased by the next and is erased by the one after). This means, for instance, that any distracting sound, including a correction by a teacher or a giggle by a friend sitting next to you may result in forgetting.

Furthermore, research shows that learners can recall pairs of words which sound the same less well than those which sound different. For example, students might find it easier to remember the pair of French words *violon* and *trompette* than the pair *fraise* (strawberry) and *frais* (fresh). This is called the **phonological similarity effect**. Research suggests that the interference caused by this effect on memory is stronger than the one caused by the **orthographic similarity** effect (when two words have similar spellings). Usually the two effects combine to make it harder to learn words which sound similar. In essence, pairs of words which look and sound similar are harder to remember.

This phenomenon has important implications for learning and helps us understand why learning verb conjugations in highly inflected languages (such as French and Spanish) can be so challenging, especially for students with a less efficient working memory. In the case of French verbs, the phonological similarity effect is particularly strong, as many verb forms are pronounced exactly the same (for example, *je mange, tu manges, il mange, elles mangent*). Not surprisingly, many learners of French find it hard to map the phonological form of these verbs to the correct spelling.

To deal with this, you can do a range of phonics (sound to spelling) activities, focused on verb forms (for example, partial dictations in which the verb endings are omitted, crossing out silent letters, correcting faulty transcripts, and so on). **Input-enhancement** techniques can also be used, for instance where a problematic verb form and its associated pronoun are highlighted (for example, in French **je** mang**e**, **tu** mang**es**, **il/elle** mang**e**, **ils/elles** mang**ent**). These provide students with an extra **retrieval cue** to help them remember.

Did you know...?

The ability to hold things in your head and remember them starts quite young.

A study by Tam et al. (2010) of 117 6-year-olds and 104 8-year-olds found that the ability to keep information in working memory begins around the age of 7. The study revealed that, while any distraction between learning a set of words and having to recall them hindered recall, having to perform a verbal task was particularly damaging. It suggests their remembering was based on phonological rehearsal (verbally repeating the names of the items to themselves).

The Phonological Loop during silent reading

As you read silently to yourself you cannot resist saying the words in your head. Try it now! This shows that when we see written language, we simultaneously hear it. By combining what we see with its mental, phonological activation we engage both visual and phonological processes to reinforce memory. In Chapter 6 we refer to this as dual coding. More of that later, but for now, suffice it to say that quiet reading, reading while listening, or reading aloud, all help to build memory and therefore long term proficiency. But the quiet reading will be far more useful if students already have a firm grasp of phonics. To put it more snappily, our visual field says 'shapes!,' while our Phonological Loop says 'sounds!'

Phonetics, phonology, phonics and phonotactics

Phonetics concerns the physical aspect of sounds, their production and perception. Articulatory phonetics is the study of speech sound production by the articulatory and vocal tract. Acoustic phonetics concerns the auditory qualities of sounds.

Phonology is about the sounds (phonemes) of a particular language. Phonemes are sounds that can make a difference in meaning between two words, for example the sounds in *ship* and *sheep* are two of 44 phonemes in English. Phonology is also concerned with non-segmental features such as intonation.

Phonics is concerned with the relationship between phonemes and spelling.

Phonotactics concerns the acceptable combinations of phonemes in a language. For example, the fact that in English we can start a word with the first sound cluster in the word *throw*, but it cannot end a word.

The role of phonotactics in language processing

The Phonological Loop is also the area which 'knows' the acceptable sounds that can appear together, or at the starts and ends of words, when we decode incoming speech (known as **phonotactic** rules). For example, in Spanish the combination /str/ never occurs at the start of a word. This means that a common mistake made by many Spanish native speakers is to add an extra 'e' before words beginning with /str/.

When we acquire our first language(s) we learn the acceptable sounds and sound combinations within the first few months of life. Not surprising perhaps that when phonotactic rules for a first and second language are the same, words are more quickly detected by the Phonological Loop.

Basically, words which are easier to pronounce are learned more quickly. This means that **cognates** (words which mean, sound and look similar across two languages) are more easily remembered, when spoken, than other words, as the Phonological Loop recognises their similarity with the first language phonology.

Since words which are easier to pronounce are learned more quickly, internalising the phonotactics of a language is important. It therefore helps to explicitly teach the phonotactic rules of the target language and give plenty of opportunities to use connected speech right from the start.

This helps along the process of chunking words together, speeding up both acquisition and spoken fluency. Why is that? Fluent speech is about sequencing meaningful chunks (a process we called chaining in Chapter 3). With this in mind, the common practice of teaching words in isolation is not the best way to develop fluency. Better to do individual, choral and interactive reading aloud activities, structured question-answer sequences, structured drills or any task requiring the repeated use of common chunks of language. Providing large amounts of comprehensible listening input, flooded with the same chunks also contributes to building memory, speeding up language processing and developing oral fluency.

Phonological short-term memory and vocab learning

Giovanna Speciale and colleagues demonstrated the importance of phonological short-term store capacity when learning new words. They found that being able to learn phonological sequences is a predictor of new vocabulary learning ability, both in a lab experiment and during a 10-week university Spanish course. Students' skill in learning sequences of phonemes predicted their ability to recognise Spanish words and also their ability to repeat invented Spanish words (Speciale, Ellis and Bywater, 2004).

From this and other studies, it is believed that, in second language learning, the role of phonological short-term memory may be especially important for less proficient learners, as it is for young first language learners. This is further evidence that a focus on phonology and phonics pays dividends with beginners in particular.

Sentence Stealer

This popular reading aloud task is great for building phonics knowledge and phonological memory.

1. Display a list of 12 model sentences students are familiar with. Each sentence has a number from 1 to 12.

2. Give each student four blank cards or slips of paper. Tell them to secretly write on each card any one of those sentences, or simply its number.

3. Students must 'steal' as many cards as possible from other members of the class in five minutes, i.e. student X approaches student Y and reads out from the board any four sentences; if a sentence that X reads is on one of Y's cards, X can 'steal' that card. To make it more fun students can play rock, paper, scissors (repeating the three words aloud in the target language) to win the right to guess.

4. The student with the most cards at the end of the game wins.

The Phonological Loop and vocabulary learning

The Phonological Loop plays a key role in vocabulary acquisition. One source of evidence for this is research carried out with young children learning non-words (made up words). Those who are good at repeating non-words accurately learn new words in their native language more quickly. In addition, other research has shown that children who are good at repeating native language syllables are also good at learning second language words (Baddeley, Gathercole and Papagno, 1998; Service, 1992). What's more, children with greater phonological memory capacity can produce longer utterances and narratives of increased grammatical and semantic complexity (Adams and Gathercole, 1996).

Phonological memory difficulties: the case of dyslexia

In your teaching career you will often work with dyslexic students. Dyslexia, also known as **developmental dyslexia**, is a learning difficulty that primarily affects the skills involved in accurate and fluent word reading and spelling. It is partly genetic in origin. Figures vary, but according to the British Dyslexia Association, the number of people with dyslexia in the UK is around 10%, with 4% of the population at the severe end of the dyslexia continuum.

Levels of dyslexia vary depending on the particular language. For example, it is more of an issue in **orthographically deep** or **opaque** languages like English, French and Arabic, than in **orthographically transparent** languages such as German, Italian and Spanish, where the correspondence between letters and phonemes is much more predictable.

Researchers believe that a deficiency in phonological processing underpins the reading difficulties of people with developmental dyslexia and a variety of explanations have been proposed. These include issues with phonological awareness and verbal memory. Recent studies suggest that developmental difficulties in reading may also be related to visual processing problems, which are particularly relevant for visually complex stimuli such as alphabetic writing. Some researchers have suggested that students with poorer phonological working memory struggle most when classroom work focuses only on speaking and listening, both of which demand lots of attention. This means that, rather than avoiding writing with struggling students, it should be used as beneficial support.

Working memory (and the Phonological Loop in particular) is known to play an important role in dyslexia. Dyslexia causes difficulties in phonological awareness, verbal memory (recalling sounds and words in the spoken form) and verbal processing speed. In particular, dyslexics have problems in extracting phonemes from written text.

What about non-alphabetical languages such as Mandarin? As neuroscientist Stanislas Dehaene points out (Dehaene, 2009), all types of reading involve co-opting areas of the brain which evolved to handle visual and spatial information, not to read – after all, reading is a recent, 'biologically secondary' sort of activity (Geary, 2008). The brain can function inefficiently in any language and the most recent research tends to suggest that, whatever the language, the key processes are universal.

Reported figures vary wildly, partly because dyslexia operates across a spectrum from mild to severe, but according to research published in 2016 by the Chinese Academy of Sciences, an estimated 11 percent of China's primary school students have dyslexia. Some brain scan studies have shown that where it is images, not letters, which are being deciphered, then dyslexia still comes into play, but it is of a different type, and brain areas are activated differently. In a study by Siok et al. (2004) Chinese children with reading difficulties showed less brain activity than usual in a particular region, the left middle frontal gyrus, an area used for visual perception, spatial relations and cognitive skills. More recent studies have shown dyslexia to be associated with abnormal structure in the cerebellum. In essence, whereas for English speakers dyslexia is primarily a phonological issue, for Chinese it has an additional visuospatial aspect.

These findings could also explain the rare cases of people who read normally in one language, but are dyslexic in another.

Language teachers, in conjunction with special needs coordinators, would do well to be aware of any children with dyslexia and make a particular effort to ensure help is given with decoding issues. All students benefit from training in phonics, but especially those with particular reading difficulties. It can't be assumed that students will just pick up the relationship between letters and sounds without specific activities aimed at helping the process along. We devote a lot of attention to phonological awareness and decoding activities in **Breaking the Sound Barrier** (Conti and Smith, 2019).

Advice for teaching students with dyslexia

- ☒ A language with a transparent spelling system such as German, Italian or Spanish will be easier while other alphabetical languages may pose a greater challenge.
- ☒ Dyslexics may benefit the most from phonemic and phonics tasks and games.
- ☒ Make sure students get to pronounce all the words they see.
- ☒ Be more tolerant than usual about spelling and pronunciation errors.
- ☒ Encourage reading aloud syllable by syllable.
- ☒ Consider using suitable apps to support learning such as Quizlet.

The power of inner speech

Most people go around the world silently talking to themselves. People are often willing to tell psychologists about their private monologue. By asking them to write down internal speech as soon as possible, useful evidence has been accumulated.

Psycholinguist Gary Dell showed that inner tongue twisters produce errors that are similar to tongue twisters spoken out loud (Dell and Sullivan, 2004). In your own inner speech, try saying the French tongue twister *Un chasseur sachant chasser sans son chien* ('a hunter who can hunt without his dog') as quickly as you can. Do you notice any pronunciation errors? But you have no inner tongue to twist - or do you? This tells us that silent practice can be effective. This makes a lot of sense if we use similar brain regions for mental and spoken practice.

Summary

- ✓ The Phonological Loop, a storage and rehearsal system, is our main language learning device.
- ✓ Its capacity is as few as three to five items of language at the same time - sounds, words, phrases or whole sentences.
- ✓ For memory, students need to hear lots of comprehensible target language.
- ✓ The more you know and can say fluently, the less space is taken up in working memory.
- ✓ The phonological similarity effect means that words which sounds similar are harder to recall.
- ✓ Phonological and phonics activities help students remember new language and recognise it in the stream of sound.

✓ The Phonological Loop 'knows' the rules of phonotactics. Particular attention is needed to deal with discrepancies between the phonotactics of different languages and to ensure learners get regular practice hearing and using utterances beyond the single word level.

✓ Students with poor phonological working memory or dyslexia need particular attention when it comes to phonology and phonics teaching. They benefit from the support of the written word.

For reflection

☒ To what extent do you bear in mind the limited capacity of the Phonological Loop when designing and carrying out everyday activities such as repetition, drilling and listening comprehension?

☒ What specific tasks could be done to support students with weaknesses in the phonolological loop, including dyslexics?

☒ What activities can we design to help students mimic sounds successfully, thus helping them them to maintain an accurate version of words in phonological memory?

Further reading and viewing

☒ Baddeley, A., Gathercole, S. & Papagno, C. (1998). The Phonological Loop as a language learning device. *Psychological Review 105* (1) 158-173

☒ Service, E. (1992). Phonology, Working Memory and Foreign-language Learning. T*he Quarterly Journal of Experimental Psychology A*, *45* (1), 21-50.
Available at: researchgate.net/publication/21519743

☒ "Dyslexia Varies Across Languages". Science Daily, 13 October 2009.
Available at:
https://www.sciencedaily.com/releases/2009/10/091012121333.htm

☒ Paul Merritt gives a slide presentation about the Phonological Loop. Available at:
https://www.youtube.com/watch?v=ID1eflBu9u

Visuospatial memory

5

Key concepts

In this chapter we consider:

- ☒ **What is visuospatial memory?**
- ☒ **Individual variations in visuospatial memory**
- ☒ **The role of visuospatial memory in reading and writing**
- ☒ **The role of eye movements in reading**

What is visuospatial memory?

Humans have a remarkable ability to remember pictures. It was shown several decades ago that people can remember more than 2,000 pictures with at least 90% accuracy in recognition tests over a period of several days, even with short presentation times during learning (Standing, Conezio and Haber, 1970). Other studies have shown that this excellent memory for pictures consistently exceeds our ability to remember words (for example, Paivio, 1971).

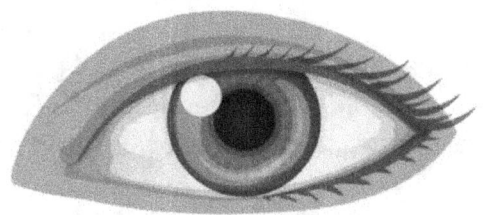

Imagine for a moment you had to describe an elephant. If you are doing it now, you'll be holding an image of an elephant in your mind's eye before thinking of the words needed to describe it. The *Visuospatial Sketchpad* is the term used to describe that part of working memory you used to visualise the creature. It handles images and spatial awareness. If the Phonological Loop is the 'inner ear', the Visuospatial Sketchpad is the 'inner eye'. Unlike verbal information, short-term memory for visuospatial material activates areas in the right hemisphere of the brain.

Not only can we hold images in our mind's eye, but also we have a keen sense of the space around us and the speed at which objects move (Logie, 1995). The Visuospatial Sketchpad allows us to move around a dark room from memory, navigate through a city or catch a ball. It gives us the ability to mentally rotate three dimensional shapes, presented from different angles, to see if they are the same (Shepard and Metzler, 1971).

When we hear speech, we process it sequentially, sound by sound, word by word, or phrase by phrase. Visual information, on the other hand, is what psychologists call synchronously organised. This means that when we look at a picture or diagram, the eye can take in and understand many elements at the same time. And it does so remarkably quickly. In one piece of research it was discovered that the human brain can interpret images in under 80 milliseconds (Potter et al., 2014). Imagine how long it would take to read a description of the same image.

Converting images to words

Images are a great resource for language teachers. Visually presented material can feed into the Phonological Loop if it can be named and pronounced. As we saw in the last chapter, when you see something nameable you can sub-vocalise it in the Phonological Loop. So you could look at four or five images and recall them by rehearsing them in your head as if they are words.

Visual and spatial memory have been studied less by language researchers than phonological memory, reflecting the dominant role that sounds play in processing spoken and written language. Phonological information is especially important in alphabet-based languages, but some research has highlighted the role of visual-orthographic skills in processing written Mandarin Chinese (for example, Tong and McBride-Chang, 2010).

There appears to be a relationship between visuospatial working memory and general academic performance at primary school level. Gathercole and Pickering (2000) found that poorer visuospatial working memory was associated with lower academic attainment for 6-7 year-olds.

This part of working memory, like the Phonological Loop, also has a limited capacity, able to process no more than a two to four images at the same time. It not only stores images, but also visual information derived from verbal descriptions, meaning that, just as we can create language from a picture, we can create an image from language.

Some psychologists (for example, Logie 1995) argue that, just like the Phonological Loop, visuospatial working memory comprises not only a short-term store (the *visual cache*), but also a mechanism for rehearsal of visual and spatial material (the so-called *inner scribe*). Just as you might rehearse words and tunes in your mind, so you can redraw and replay images.

So the Visuospatial Sketchpad holds the information gathered during initial processing, it may rehearse this and, if retrieved later from long-term memory, it produces the recollection of an image (a place, someone's face, etc.).

Given the power of images it's not surprising that they are used by teachers to reinforce memory for language. In the multi-component model of memory, through the Phonological Loop and Visuospatial Sketchpad, language and images are combined by the Episodic Buffer and Central Executive to reinforce learning and memory. This is known as the *dual coding effect* which we return to in Chapter 6.

Did you know...?

Humans have evolved to be particularly good at remembering faces. But the ability to pair faces with names gets worse after your 30s, according to a study by Laura Germine and colleagues from Harvard University. They found that our ability to identify faces peaks between the ages of 30 to 34, and slowly declines after that, until we can only recognise an estimated 75% of people in our 70s (Germine et al., 2010).

At the time of writing you can test your own ability to recognise famous faces at https://www.testmybrain.org/.

Individual variation

The use of the Visuospatial Sketchpad varies a good deal from person to person. Some people use it often while thinking; others use it very little. It can be developed with practice using visualisation techniques and conscious effort, though people have their own limits of patience and aptitude. As with all other aspects of memory, the more you try to use the Visuospatial Sketchpad, the easier it becomes. The mind can be 'trained' to strengthen the response, and by doing exercises of visual recall, you strengthen the Visuospatial Sketchpad to produce clearer images on demand. Over a period of time, the recollection of an image can change from general recall to one with crisp detail through practice and patience.

The role of visuospatial memory in reading and writing

Although the Visuospatial Sketchpad is less important than the Phonological Loop for language acquisition, it often plays a key role. Whether you're reading alphabetical symbols or images denoting words, as we've seen, the inner eye activates the inner ear.

Writing is a visual activity guided by the eyes where we put words we're thinking of into written form. But it's also a spatial activity in that it involves organising text by leaving a graphic trace on a page or screen. Furthermore, writing can involve translating visual and spatial mental representations into text and the written text may also be represented in a visuospatial format, such as graphs, tables or diagrams.

Writing has been described as an 'external auxiliary memory' (Olive and Passerault, 2012), in that once you have written down symbols they remain on the page, lightening the load on verbal working memory. This is one reason why it's useful to take notes when listening to a lecture of course.

When students are writing target language sentences they need not only to plan ahead, but to look back at what they've already written. Evidence has shown that, when writing at an advanced level, people are able to quickly localise previous words or sections, particularly those nearer the top of a page (Zechmeister and McKillip, 1972).

Dédéyan, Olive and Largy (2006) showed that, with novice writers, detecting errors in writing mainly uses verbal working memory. On the other hand, skilled writers use a visual search to identify word endings in their texts (Dédéyan, Largy, and Negro, 2006).

Useful takeaways here for language teachers are the importance for memory of using the written word to support other skills (external auxiliary memory), training students in the metacognitive skill of checking back and reviewing sentences and paragraphs, and, at more advanced levels, getting students to think about the spatial layout of their written work, in particular paragraphing.

Remember the picture

Display a picture such as a street scene or room in a house. It's best if students are already familiar with most of the vocabulary. Describe the picture, do some choral repetition work and questioning so that students are familiar with the vocabulary.

Then hide the picture and ask students in pairs to recall as many points as possible. With the right class, this whole activity could be done in pairs.

Spot the differences

This listening task grabs students' attention with a picture.

1. Display a picture, for example a beach or street scene. Pairs make sentences to describe the picture. Scaffold the task by separately displaying a bilingual glossary of words and phrases.

2. Read out three descriptions of the picture. Only one of the descriptions is correct while the others contain one or more inaccuracies, for instance about the appearance of the people in the image, their clothing, what they are doing, their location.

3. Students can be told in advance to look out for 'X' number of inaccuracies. They listen and note down the inaccuracies for the faulty descriptions.

Conti and Smith (2019)

The role of eye movements in reading

Eye movements play a critical role when reading. We have the impression that our eyes (and mind) sweep smoothly across the text, and it's only when we encounter difficulty and pause to consider what we've just read, or go back to reread earlier material that we are aware of our eye movements. In reality, the progress of the eyes across the page is not continuous. They remain relatively still for periods called *fixations*, which usually last an average of 200–250 milliseconds. Between fixations the eyes move rapidly in what are called *saccades*, after the French word for sudden movement.

Children with reading difficulties move their eyes differently and show greater pupil dilation when reading (Ozeri-Rotstain et al., 2020). In addition, they often demonstrate weaknesses in working memory. A research study by Andy Pham and Ramzi Hasson explored the relationship between verbal working memory (the Phonological Loop), visuospatial working memory and reading ability in a sample of school-aged children with a wide range of reading skills (Pham and Hasson, 2014).

Although the results indicated that verbal working memory was a stronger predictor of reading fluency and comprehension, visuospatial memory also significantly predicted reading skills and comprehension - more so than speed of reading. These findings suggest that visuospatial working memory may play a significant role in higher level reading processes than sometimes thought, particularly in reading comprehension.

Did you know...?

The brain can be extraordinarily adaptable.

Just in case you think that everything is neat and tidy about the role different areas of the brain play, don't forget how it can adapt in some amazing ways. Stanislas Dehaene, in his book *How We Learn* (2020) recounts the story of a boy whose right brain hemisphere was almost completely removed at the age of three, yet he was able to learn to draw, paint, understand computer science and wheelchair fencing, all by just using his left hemisphere, normally associated with language use. He is just one example of many people whose brains have shown a remarkable degree of adaptability and resilience.

Summary

- ✓ Although the Phonological Loop is the most important component of working memory for language acquisition, images have great power so are often used by teachers to help make language memorable.
- ✓ Input to the Phonological Loop and Visuospatial Sketchpad is thought to be bound together by the Episodic Buffer and Central Executive of working memory to reinforce learning and memory.
- ✓ As we saw in Chapter 4, when we see words, images or objects, our Phonological Loop is activated. We automatically turn images into language.
- ✓ Just as phonological memory varies to a degree from person to person, so does visuospatial memory.
- ✓ Visuospatial ability comes into play when reading and writing, with writing being extremely useful in helping working memory, for example when we take notes.

For reflection

- ☒ What use do you make of images in your lessons? Why do you use them?
- ☒ How many different ways can you think of for using pictures?
- ☒ What factors do you keep in mind when selecting images to use?
- ☒ How can you train students to monitor and edit their written work successfully?

Further reading and viewing

- ☒ Logie, R. H. (1995). *Visuospatial working memory*. Hove: Erlbaum
- ☒ McLeod, S. A. (2012). *Working memory*. Simply Psychology. Available at : https://www.simplypsychology.org/working%20memory.html
- ☒ In this presentation Paul Merritt explains how the Visuospatial Sketchpad works. Available at: https://www.youtube.com/watch?v=7ZQNLgtcPGU
- ☒ Maggie Shiffrar gives an illustrated talk about visuospatial memory. Available at: https://www.youtube.com/watch?v=qVaerZ434QM .

Cognitive Load Theory | 6

Key concepts

In this chapter we consider:

- **The idea of cognitive load**
- **Cognitive Load Theory**
- **Fluency**
- **Three types of cognitive load**
- **Schemas**
- **Desirable difficulty**
- **Principles for dealing with cognitive load**
- **Factors affecting cognitive load**
- **Cognitive load and growth mindset**
- **Learning styles and dual coding**

Cognitive load

Think about those training sessions you've attended as you try to take in new information, presented via overcrowded PowerPoint slides with spoken commentary. Unless we pick and choose what to concentrate on, our minds are quickly overloaded with information. It can be hard to take in.

A child in a languages classroom is confronted with a greater challenge still: an adult talking in a new language, a stream of slides to look at, text to read, other students to listen to and watch, instructions to process and an enthusiastic teacher waving their arms about and urging quick responses. Needless to say, some students cope with this input and memory burden more easily than others.

This is where the idea of **cognitive load** comes in. Cognitive load is the amount of information, in our case language, that we have to process in working memory at any one time. Put crudely, it's how hard we have to think. But as we've seen, working memory is fragile, has short duration and a very limited capacity. It's also hard to focus on more than one task at the same time. For example, it's known that language learners cannot focus simultaneously on both the form and meaning of a spoken message. If they are asked to concentrate on the form, they neglect the meaning and vice versa.

When a student is coping with both comprehending and responding to a complex message, monitoring their own performance as they do so, it puts a great strain on working memory and often leads to hesitation, errors or failure to retrieve the vocabulary needed. This is called **cognitive overload**.

Poorly designed resources, ill-conceived lesson planning and busy classroom environments can increase the chances of cognitive overload and its harmful consequences for learning. We can keep the load manageable through the way we design lessons and use teaching resources.

Cognitive Load Theory

A principled framework for managing the levels of cognitive overload in the classroom is provided by **Cognitive Load Theory** (CLT), developed by Australian professor, John Sweller (Sweller, 1988). Renowned educationalist Dylan Wiliam has described it (on Twitter, as it happens) as "the single most important thing for teachers to know".

We decided to feature CLT strongly in this book as we believe it provides a useful way to categorise the factors and contexts which can increase cognitive load and a range of strategies that language teachers can use to make learning as efficient and enjoyable as possible. In essence, if we can manage the cognitive load on students, they are much more likely to enjoy their work and remember more.

Fluency, every language teacher's Holy Grail, is achieved when the comprehension or production of language poses a light cognitive load on working memory. Fluency happens when students have automatised enough vocabulary and grammatical patterns to speak at reasonable speed without having to piece sentences together word by word.

Lack of fluency, on the other hand, typically marked by pauses, hesitations, errors, backtracking and self-repairs, is often caused by cognitive overload. In sum, having lots of language in long-term memory is the key to reducing cognitive load – the more students can draw on known language, the less working memory has to do.

What is fluency?

Retrieval from memory is a question of both access and speed. If we say that X is 'fluent in Spanish' we usually take it to mean that they can speak quickly, similarly to a native speaker of the language. In this sense fluent = proficient. Researchers take a much more nuanced view of fluency. Norman Segalowitz (2016) explains how fluency involves mentally assembling ideas into words, then being able to deliver them promptly without pauses or breakdowns. He refers to three aspects of fluency.

- *Utterance fluency* – the fluidity of speech as measured by temporal features, such as syllable rate, duration and rate of hesitations, filled and silent pauses, and repair fluency (how quickly you put things right).
- *Cognitive fluency* – the speed and efficiency of the thinking processes responsible for speech – assembling sounds, words, chunks and good grammar.
- *Perceived fluency* – subjective judgments of a speaker's oral fluency.

Paul Nation (as discussed in Nation and Yamamoto, 2012) argues, as part of his *four strands* (meaning-focused input, form-focused instruction, meaning-focused output and fluency development), that 25% of classroom time should be devoted to fluency development. What does a fluency task look like? Nation says:

- Is it message and meaning focused?
- Is it easy? (familiar material – nothing new)
- Is there pressure to go faster? (speed)
- Is there quantity of practice?

One of his best known examples of a fluency activity is the 4,3,2 task where students perform the same oral activity three times, each one in less time (four minutes, three minutes, then two minutes – you can shorten the timings).

For example, put students in groups of three. Student 1 speaks, Student 2 notes down the main points in the speech and Student 3 is a critical listener who gives feedback on specific features they are asked to pay attention to. The feedback session at the end of each of the three rounds can last around two minutes.

As an example, give students four bullet points to talk about, such as the following:

- *a past holiday*
- *a holiday you are planning to go on in the near future*
- *your ideal holiday*
- *what you usually do during the holidays when you don't travel anywhere*

During planning time allow students to write notes, ask questions or use online resources to help.

Three types of cognitive load

First of all, look at these three key points:

1. Some things are inherently harder to learn than others, for example forming the future tense in French is easier than forming the *passé composé* (perfect tense).
2. The way we present and practise new language affects how successfully it will be taken up. For example, simultaneously teaching a new grammatical structure with new vocabulary will make it harder for students to focus on one or the other.
3. Finding the right level of challenge for students is vital – we don't want tasks to be too easy or too hard. With a proficient intermediate class we would rarely teach new vocabulary via flashcard slides, for instance.

Corresponding to these three issues, a popular model of cognitive load claims it comes in three forms: **intrinsic, extraneous** or **germane** (Sweller, 1988). Psychologists argue about the precise definitions of these, and even whether it's possible to divide cognitive load into such neat categories (de Jong, 2010). However, this way of looking at cognitive load is useful to teachers who want to understand how working memory can be made to function efficiently and maximise long-term memory. Because this is such an important issue, we've decided to look at it in some detail.

Intrinsic cognitive load

This refers to the inherent complexity of the task or concept, and a student's ability to understand it. Technically speaking, it is a measure of how many new, interacting things a student has to do to simultaneously in order to complete a task. That's why, in the example above, the future tense in French is easier to work out than the perfect tense. Now, it's said that you cannot alter the intrinsic difficulty of a task (for example, understanding a text with unknown words is almost certainly going to be harder than understanding one with known words). But, as we'll see, you can reduce the *overall* load of a task by breaking it down into smaller steps.

Extraneous cognitive load

This is produced as a result of demands placed on students by the teacher through the way they choose resources, present information or design teaching activities. It is a measure of the load imposed by the organisation of the task.

This type of cognitive load falls outside (is extraneous to) the learning task, and is increased by teaching which may cause confusion through distracting information, or an over-complex set of procedures. For example, including unknown vocabulary in a drill which is aiming to practise a verb tense distracts from the main point of the task. Another example: explaining, entirely in the target language, the use of the imperfect to a class of intermediate learners of French will add an extra layer of difficulty to an already complex set of grammar rules. Similarly, trying to get the same students to master all at once the different uses of that same tense creates unnecessary cognitive load.

Effective teaching can help reduce the extraneous cognitive load imposed on students, freeing up enough space in working memory for the students to focus on the key point and remember it better.

Germane cognitive load

This is perhaps the hardest to grasp. Cognitive load is not a bad thing in itself. The word germane means relevant, so this gives a clue to its meaning here. In general, germane cognitive load refers to the right amount and type of load needed to build knowledge schemas in long-term memory and increase learning (see below for more on schemas).

In the case of language teaching, it refers to the process of linking new information with information already stored in long-term memory in order to create new schemas (for example, chunks of language). So when learning a new verb tense, you may call on knowledge of an existing tense. Germane load can be seen as a measure of the extra load imposed by the teaching activity which *supports* learning. It is where metacognitive strategies come into play; where students are aware of their thinking processes and able to adapt new information accordingly. In sum, you could say it's where the real learning happens!

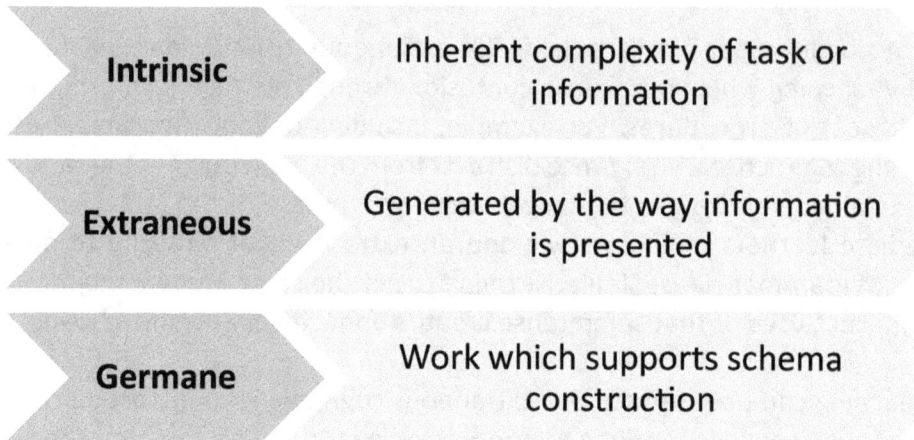

Figure 6.1 Three types of cognitive load (Sweller).

Schemas

Memories can be stored as episodes, concepts or facts, but we also chunk these together into what are called **schemas** (or *schemata*). The term was used separately by psychologists Jean Piaget and Frederic Bartlett. Piaget defined a schema as follows:

"... a cohesive, repeatable action sequence possessing component actions that are tightly interconnected and governed by a core meaning" (Piaget, 1952, p.7).

The term has taken on a broader meaning and been used, for example, in the study of second language reading. You might like to imagine an old-fashioned filing cabinet with drawers. The filing cabinet is the mind, and the drawers are schemas. Individual cards in the drawer are memories or bits of knowledge (Wadsworth, 2004). Alternatively, think of schemas as folders in your computer or your own personal Wikipedia.

Schemas bring together your bits of existing knowledge and influence how future knowledge will be stored. Once schemas are established in long-term memory, little effort is needed when they are combined with new information entering working memory. The more schemas you have, the easier the job becomes for working memory. Schemas tend to be long-lasting and hard to alter, for example, once we have an established view of something it's difficult to overcome it.

Interestingly, when new items are perceived which do not fit into existing schemas, they tend to be remembered less well, unless they are really distinctive. In one experiment, if a picture of a room is presented with a slightly unusual item in it, that item is more easily forgotten in memory tests. This is because the item doesn't fit into your existing schema of what rooms typically look like in your culture. However, if the unusual item is particularly distinctive, it will be remembered more easily.

For language learners, we can see schemas as ready-made chunks of the target language held in long-term memory that can be quickly brought into use when comprehending or speaking. Or they could be communicative functions such as knowing how to apologise or make a request. They are also, importantly, the schemas available from knowledge of the first language. For example, when trying to retrieve a target language word, knowing its cognate or similar-sounding word often helps.

A challenge for language teachers is to help students build up an increasing number of interconnected schemas which can be quickly retrieved from long-term memory.

Desirable difficulty

It's worth noting that linking old knowledge with new (***associative learning***) works best when it involves a level of ***desirable difficulty*** (Bjork, 2011). If work is just a fraction beyond a student's current state of learning it should produce the right amount of cognitive load. If the brain has to work a little harder to process information, memory becomes stronger. From the field of second language acquisition research, Stephen Krashen has called this i + 1. This means supplying language which is at or just above the student's current level of comprehension, any new words being worked out by the context, for example using other language, images, context, gesture and so on (Krashen, 1982).

Now, bear with us here as this gets a bit complicated! In CLT, the different types of cognitive load are said to interact. The higher the extraneous cognitive load, the lower the germane cognitive load and vice versa. If extraneous load is minimised, space is freed up in working memory for germane cognitive load. This is easier when students are more proficient, since the more schemas a student has in long-term memory, the lower the intrinsic load of a task becomes (see Figure 6.2). This means we need to be very careful about how we manage language input and the degree of difficulty in any classroom activity.

So, for instance, when producing or translating a sentence such as 'My mother is generous and thoughtful' into French, a beginner has to retrieve vocabulary and apply grammatical rules to do with adjectival agreement at the same time. What's more, learners with English as a first language do not consider adjective agreement to be salient and so do not always pay attention to it. This creates a high cognitive load. However, a more proficient student who has already automatised that sentence through use and/or has created a schema for the underlying pattern (i.e. my + noun + is + adjective) can produce that sentence with little or no cost in terms of cognitive load.

This comes down to something quite simple: how do we present and practise language in such as a way as to achieve just the right amount of cognitive load, so that extraneous cognitive load is reduced to the bare minimum, intrinsic load is kept at, or just beyond, their current competence and there is enough space in working memory for germane cognitive load (i.e. learning) to happen.

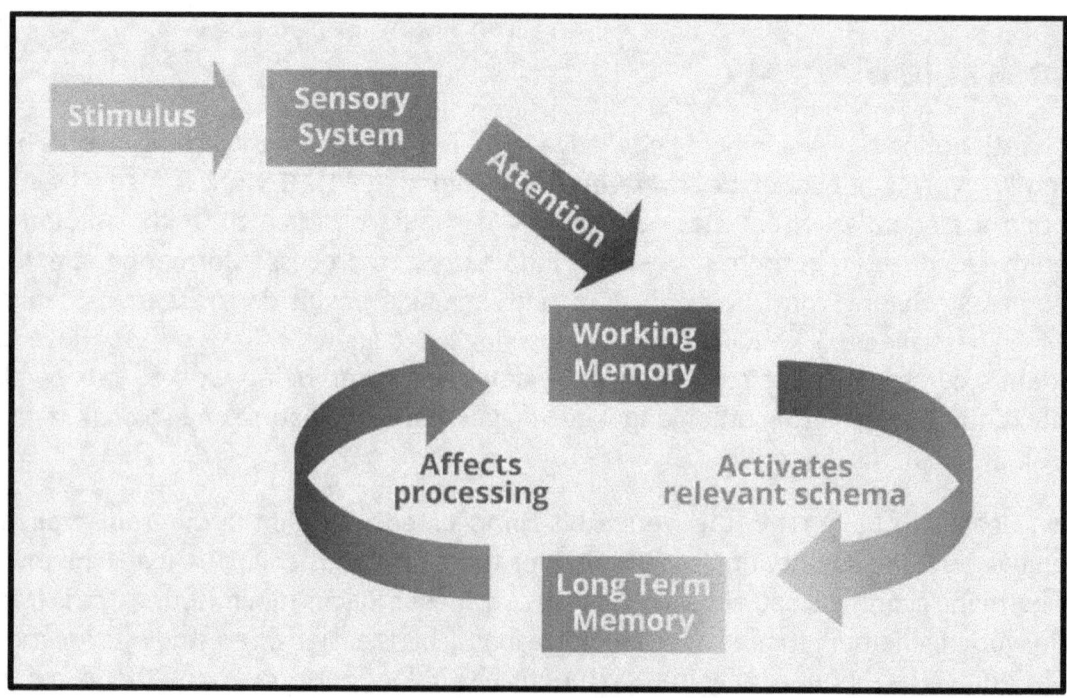

Figure 6.2 Schema activation and the relationship between working and long-term memory

Principles for dealing with cognitive load

The information store principle

Most of what we do is driven by information stored in long-term memory. When we are confronted with a task, as explained in Chapter 3, working memory retrieves the relevant information and skills needed, from long-term memory, to carry it out successfully. The ease of retrieval affects the cognitive load – the more effortless the retrieval, the greater the space available in working memory for germane load. Hence the importance of ensuring that our students create 'strong' memories and develop fluent recall of the target language through plenty of retrieval practice.

The borrowing and reorganising principle

Most of the information we store in working memory is borrowed from the long-term memory of other people. We learn by imitating other humans, by listening to what they say and by reading what they write. When we acquire this information, we reorganise and integrate it into our existing schemas in long-term memory. Our schemas may be different from the source's, as schema creation is affected by our personal biases and existing knowledge. Schema creation requires germane cognitive load, hence the importance of freeing up as much processing space as possible in working memory by limiting intrinsic and extraneous cognitive load.

The randomness-as-genesis principle

If we can't learn information from others, we need to generate it ourselves using problem solving strategies. We have evolved to use strategies whenever we're faced with new information or tasks. We generate these strategies randomly and test them for effectiveness. According to CLT, although this *randomness-as-genesis principle* is applied in important human activities such as research, its use in the classroom is harder to justify when students can obtain the information from the teacher. Since problem solving is inefficient in terms of cognitive load, it is mainly useful as a last resort.

But this principle has major implications for any form of inquiry-based learning, for example inductive grammar learning (working out rules), *flipped learning* (learning at home to be discussed in class) and student-led research projects. This suggests it might be less suitable for beginners than more advanced learners. The same is true of any task, such as homework, where students have to independently understand input, or produce output, beyond their current level. For instance, it is generally unwise to let students read and hear texts which contain less than around 95% comprehensible input since research suggests the language is just so hard to process that little learning happens (Hu and Nation, 2000). This is not to mention the fact that coping with work which is too hard is just dispiriting for students.

If you set tasks well beyond a student's current level, they have to apply problem-solving strategies and educated guesswork, for example, inferring meaning from context or using background knowledge. These strategies are no doubt useful, but create unnecessary extraneous load. Problems arise if you give students unscaffolded, open-ended tasks which may require vocabulary and structures that have not yet been taught or are well beyond their current level. The result is often word for word translation which may be difficult to understand. This is one reason students resort to online translators.

The narrow limits of change principle

Working memory, as we have seen, is severely limited both in capacity (3-5 items at any one time) and duration (roughly 20 seconds without rehearsal). When it comes to new information (which is not yet part of a schema), teaching needs to limit the number of elements students need to process at any time. This doesn't apply to information students are already familiar with and can recall effortlessly.

This means sticking to the essential points and matching them to students' cognitive capacity. For instance, imagine requiring an average learner of Spanish at the end of their first lesson on family members and personality adjectives to produce or translate the sentence below:

I like my parents because they are kind and generous

Asking a beginner of average ability to produce in Spanish a sentence of this length containing unfamiliar words which must agree in gender and number and the conjugation of an unfamiliar verb, flouts the 'narrow limits of change' principle. Why? Firstly, because it contains more than the 3-5 items working memory can handle at one time and, secondly, it involves a high degree of interacting elements (i.e. the words in the sentence affect each other in terms of number and agreement). The intrinsic cognitive load is high for a beginner. If students had had lots of practice using the words, structures and syntactic pattern in that sentence, the cognitive load would be much reduced.

The environmental organising and linking principle

While working memory cannot handle much new information, it has no known limits when dealing with organised information already stored in long-term memory (schemas). Thus, when we carry out a task, the more schemas we have available in working memory, the smaller the cognitive load will be. In other words, schema acquisition reduces working memory load. So our focus should be on building schemas in long-term memory.

By the way, if the term schema still seems a bit vague to you. Here are some more concrete examples of schemas in second language learning:

1. sets of multi-word phrases for specific communicative contexts, such as greeting someone, expressing a like or dislike, reserving a table at a restaurant ;
2. phrases for opening or closing an essay;
3. the set of grammar rules needed to produce *if* clauses;
4. sets of words or phrases for linking paragraphs;
5. rules of appropriacy for using slang.

While creating schemas is key to the efficient functioning of working memory, fluency in using language requires schemas to be automatised – instantly available for quick production. For instance, a student might want to produce under communicative pressure (for example, during a conversation with a native speaker or in an exam) the following target language sentence:

If I were rich I wouldn't need to work

Simply knowing the required grammar and syntactic rules (schemas) isn't enough to reduce working memory load. Only if the retrieval and application of those rules is automatised and fluent (i.e. fast and effortless) will the cognitive load be significantly reduced.

Disappearing text

A great way to manage cognitive load is to use the 'disappearing text' procedure during lessons. Once you have displayed and worked with a paragraph or set of sentences, gradually remove words or chunks from the text, one slide at a time. Each new slide contains more gaps, while students try to recall the missing language.

Factors affecting cognitive load

More practically speaking, let us now look at the factors that can reduce or add to cognitive load, what Sweller and other scholars (for example Mayer and Moreno, 2003) call *cognitive effects*. Although some of these are more relevant to the learning of concepts (such as how river valleys are formed or wave theory in physics) than language, we have included examples to show their relevance to your work as language teachers.

The worked-example effect

The widely studied *worked-example effect* is predicted by cognitive load theory (see the randomness-as-genesis principle, above). It refers to the learning effect when worked-examples are used as part of instruction, compared to other teaching techniques such as problem-solving and discovery learning where students figure out answers on their own.

What is a worked example? Just as in maths a teacher might work through a problem on the board to show how it is solved, a language teacher can work through how to solve a translation by applying grammatical knowledge. In a two-way process, suggestions can be sought, questions asked, prompts provided and explanations offered.

Sentence builders (also known as substitution tables) can be used as part of the process. These consist of multiple examples of one or more sentence patterns and can be used to model how the patterns operate. They can be manipulated by keeping the same sentence stem or sentence frame constant while changing the remaining building blocks. By breaking down a sentence pattern into a manageable number of chunks (consistent with the narrow limits of change principle) sentence builders help to limit cognitive load and promote the chunking process which is key to schema creation.

Guidance-fading, problem-completion and expertise-reversal effects

According to the *guidance-fading effect*, over longer courses, teaching methodologies should change. This is because, as a student gains in proficiency, they accumulate more numerous and complex schemas which can be used to carry out tasks, thereby requiring less support. So, while worked examples can be a more effective way to present information to beginners, they could demotivate more proficient students who may find them too easy.

One solution to this issue proposed by CLT research is the so-called *problem-completion effect* where parts of the worked example are removed. Students have to complete some information by providing a missing chunk. So, for example, take this sentence again:

> *If I were rich, I wouldn't work*

You could first provide worked examples illustrating the sentence pattern, then provide a set of gapped sentences from which the imperfect tense was removed. Later, a set of sentences from which the present conditional was removed. The next step could involve asking the students to translate another set of sentences independently and finally, they would have to produce their own sentences on a given topic.

In line with the guidance-fading effect, with more proficient learners, the worked example stage could be removed altogether, as they may have sufficient resources to apply problem-solving strategies. So, for instance, instead of explaining a grammar rule explicitly before practising it (deductive grammar teaching), you could provide a set of examples and ask the students to work out the rule by themselves, without support (inductive grammar teaching). According to CLT, with more proficient learners using worked examples can potentially have a negative effect on cognitive load. Sweller calls this the *expertise-reversal effect*. In simple terms, expert learners do not need as much direct instruction and structured support.

To give an example, you could ask an advanced class to read and summarise a text in the target language with little or no extra support, but with a less proficient group you would take the students through a text in detail, asking questions and doing controlled activities.

Experienced teachers will recognise what has been described above and may consider it common sense, but it's worth understanding these points explicitly as well as the underlying cognitive processes involved. It's also important to recognise that teaching needs to be adapted to the class; very high-achieving classes develop long-term memory much more quickly than a group of less proficient students.

Growth mindset and cognitive load

Researchers have looked into whether motivational factors can affect retention and perception of cognitive load. In a 2020 study Kate Xu and colleagues carried out a controlled experiment with 138 secondary school students. The effects of a growth mindset belief (created by the researchers during the learning phase of the experiment) were examined. Participants in the growth mindset group perceived a lower intrinsic load and extraneous load and performed better on retention and transfer tests (Xu et al., 2020).

We look into motivational factors and growth mindset in more detail in Chapter 14.

The element-interactivity and isolated-element effects

As mentioned above, the intrinsic load of a task is affected by how many interacting elements need to be processed in order to carry it out. Remember that any element for which there is an automatised schema available in working memory doesn't affect the load. One way to limit the number of elements is to teach vocabulary in multi-word chunks. So, for instance, look at this sentence:

I have a dog and a cat at home

There are nine elements if you take the words individually. However, if you teach the chunk 'I have + a(n) animal + and + a(n) animal + at home' the element count is reduced to five.

However, the number of elements in a sentence is not the only factor affecting cognitive load. The interactivity between those elements (the grammar) is another major factor. How do some words or phrases affect others? The higher the interactivity between the elements (the more complex the grammar), the higher the load. So, for instance, imagine translating this sentence into German:

I love German because it's interesting and fun

The interacting elements pose word order problems, namely the need to send the verb to the end of the sentence after *weil* ('because').

One way to lessen the cognitive load caused by high element interactivity is called the **isolated interacting elements effect**. This means making processing easier by dealing with each element in isolation before handling them all together. In the case of the sentence above, this would involve ensuring that the students are already able to apply correct word order automatically.

For example, when doing a simple drill worksheet based on sentence prompts, orally or in writing, the first time through you could focus on just one element, for example changing a tense. The second time you could combine changing the tense with altering another part of the sentence or adding a new element.

The redundancy effect

The element interactivity effect can also be reduced by removing from worked examples any extra information which is not essential. For example, when presenting a new sentence pattern to beginners, it makes sense to include in the example only the essential items so that students focus cognitive resources on those. Other elements would be irrelevant or redundant. At a later stage, when students are familiar with the pattern, additional items could be included, allowing more complex schemas to be formed.

Interestingly, the redundancy principle suggests we avoid presenting identical streams of printed and spoken words – in theory students cannot simultaneously pay attention to both sources. However, a word of caution is needed since, as we mention below, there are good reasons to show text while reading it out, to limit the load of listening or to develop phonics skill (relating sounds to spellings).

The split-attention and spatial-contiguity effects

CLT also suggests that teachers should remove competing stimuli in order to avoid the *split-attention effect*, allowing students to focus on a single visual source of information at any given time. The point here is that we cannot focus on two tasks at once. All we can do is switch from one to another.

This was demonstrated in a study which concluded that the learning experience could be improved when competing stimuli were merged into one source of information. By embedding a written explanation of a diagram within the illustration itself, they found that learners could understand the information presented to them better than if the diagram and explanation were provided separately (Chandler and Sweller, 1992).

The split attention effect can be exacerbated or reduced by the spatial distance of the two competing stimuli. The greater the distance, the greater the cognitive load. This would be a reason, for example, to show any glossed words alongside a text rather than below and further away. This sort of choice may seem of relatively little importance, but anything which encourages easier attention and better memory is worth doing.

The modality effect

The *modality effect* (the *dual coding effect*) was first described by Allan Paivio in 1971. As explained in Chapter 3, when images are linked to spoken language, working memory processes the information through the Visuospatial Sketchpad and Phonological Loop, aided by the Central Executive and Episodic Buffer, thus enriching learning.

The ability to code a stimulus in two different ways increases the chance of remembering that item. This combined use of visual and linguistic information is known as dual coding. In a sense, a double memory trace is formed, which strengthens the potential for later retrieval. Figure 6.3 shows that, for example, a student can store the concept 'table' as both the word *table* and as the image of a table. When asked to recall the stimulus, the student can retrieve either the word or the image individually, or both simultaneously. If the word is recalled, the image of the table is not lost and can still be retrieved at a later point in time.

A point to bear in mind here is that any imagery associated with oral or written input needs to be unambiguous, especially where non-concrete vocabulary is concerned. If the meaning of an image is not crystal clear it may be better to use translation.

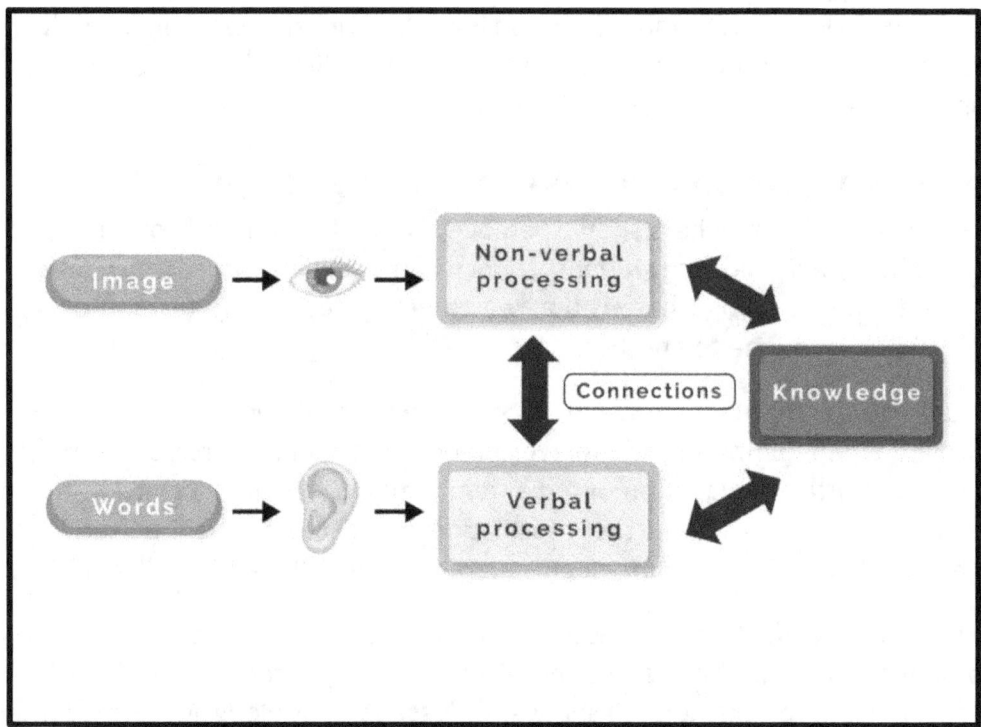

Figure 6.3 Allan Paivio's Dual-Coding Theory

Listen and draw

In this classic language learning task the teacher describes a picture while the class attempts to draw what they are listening to. The same activity can be done in pairs if the class has the necessary oral skills.

Beginners can play a variation of this called Listen and Colour In, where students are given a black and white line drawing of a simple scene, for example a room in a house, and have to listen to the teacher describe the colours of each item in the scene.

Alternatively, listeners can mark in places identified on a map or diagram.

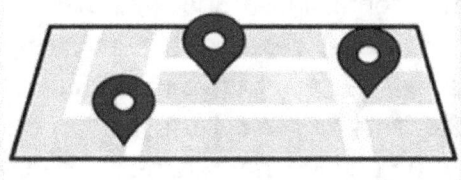

The transient information effect

Listening input is transient, it passes by quickly. As we observed in Chapter 4, it lingers in working memory very briefly and is erased by any new incoming sound. So when students are doing a listening comprehension exercise, much of the input is forgotten from one moment to the next. This makes it useful for students to record any auditory input in some form of written or visual form which can act as a kind of auxiliary memory store.

Even if students answer questions correctly, little of the input may be retained. One solution is to make students listen to the same text several times over, but each time with a different task focusing on a different levels of the input. For example, this might include the general meaning of the text, specific details, the meaning of specific word, sounds, grammar. Another strategy could involve relistening to the text with a transcript on the classroom screen and performing various comprehension tasks. This sort of intensive approach to listening is described in Conti and Smith (2019).

The temporal contiguity effect

CLT research suggests it is better to present narration and corresponding animations or images simultaneously to minimise need to hold representations in memory. As language teachers we are familiar with describing short scenes from films or picture sequences. But it's also worth noting that deliberately separating images from spoken or written text can present a worthwhile memory challenge for students. If you tell a class they will be tested on something they saw, read or heard, they may try extra hard to retrieve the language (creating germane cognitive load). No one should think these things are simple!

Disappearing picture

Show a picture containing a good number of elements, such as a beach or street scene, describe it, practise the language, then tell students to close their eyes as you hide one or more elements from the picture. Students must recall the missing elements. Eventually the whole picture can be hidden for students to describe from memory.

The segmentation effect

This suggests that we should break down teaching sequences into bite-sized segments, over which the student has some control. This becomes relevant when explaining grammar or through general lesson planning when you vary activities through a lesson but with a focus on the same target language. Learner control can come into play through skilled formative assessment techniques, such as checking if students have understood. Is the class ready to move on to the next part of the lesson?

The pre-training effect

The suggestion here is that if you pre-teach the names and characteristics of some components of a learning task, it becomes easier. This is relevant when we think of pre-listening or pre-reading tasks which may highlight key language to be encountered, or important aspects of the content of a listening or reading text. Pre-teaching of this type can even just arouse curiosity, thereby leading to greater attention and better subsequent memory.

The variability effect

This suggests, unsurprisingly, that varying teaching tasks has a positive effect on learning. However, research suggests (for example Likourezos, Kalyuga and Sweller, 2019) that the effect is greater once students become more advanced, or in our case proficient. For language teachers this might suggest that a narrower range of task types is advisable for beginners. It's worth bearing in mind here that beginners also appreciate being able to do familiar activities. Perhaps this is partly because their attention is not diverted by having to cope with a new set of routines.

Learning styles and dual coding

You may already be familiar with the term learning styles. *Learning style theory* claims that matching teaching tasks to a student's preferred learning mode (auditory, visual or kinaesthetic) will lead to better retention. There is little support for this i n the research literature (Rogowsky et al., 2015) whereas dual coding, exploiting both the visual and linguistic modes of learning, has been repeatedly shown to help build memory. One example is a recent study by Joshua Cuevas and Bryan Dawson which specifically pitted learning styles against dual coding and found that, whereas dual coding led to improved memory, matching the learning activity to students' stated preferred learning mode produced no gains (Cuevas and Dawson, 2018).

Research into language aptitude has suggested, however, that different pedagogical techniques may play to individual students' aptitude profile. For example, students with efficient working memory and phonological decoding skills may profit more from listening work. In contrast, students who find phonological processing hard, may benefit more when language is presented in written form. For them, holding and rehearsing language in working memory is more difficult. It's worth pointing out that in general, just like you, students may have stated learning preferences, but this doesn't necessarily mean that matching tasks to those preferences leads to better outcomes. Less able learners may be more comfortable than you might imagine with the support they can gain from reading and writing.

Concluding remarks

We've looked in some detail at cognitive load and CLT, since they are central to designing and delivering effective lessons. Some readers may feel we went too far! In sum, whatever the theoretical and technical details, when it comes to managing cognitive load with a class, a key element is our ***cognitive empathy*** with the class. This means that sense of what students, both individually and as a group, can handle at any moment. It is a subtle ability every teacher gets wrong from time to time, but which stems from both experience and sound formative assessment techniques. The latter include checking that meaning is understood, the use of mini-whiteboards and skilled use of questioning.

We have argued that a clear understanding of CLT can support the common-sense perceptions of teachers and standard good practice, and is useful for understanding the processes underpinning successful learning and memory building. Adjustments, even marginal ones, to a teacher's lesson plans, resources and procedures can add up and make a difference.

Summary

- ✓ Cognitive load is the amount of information we have to handle in working memory when we are doing a learning task.
- ✓ When the amount of information exceeds our capacity to process it, this is called cognitive overload. For language teachers this can mean, for example, supplying input containing too much unknown language.
- ✓ The popular Sweller model of cognitive load postulates three types: intrinsic, extrinsic and germane. The teacher has a degree of control over all of these.
- ✓ Schemas are knowledge structures in long-term memory. The more relevant schemas we have, the more likely it is that cognitive load is reduced during a learning task. Building long-term memory is always the main goal.
- ✓ The idea of desirable difficulty is that learning activities should not be too hard, but also not too easy. The brain has to do a certain amount of work for memory to be enhanced.
- ✓ A range of principles can be applied to help reduce undesirable cognitive load. Getting the balance right and using cognitive empathy are crucial elements of a teacher's skill. We need to be able to clearly sense what the class finds easy and hard. Formative assessment techniques help.
- ✓ We need to be aware of the whole range of cognitive load effects, including the well-known dual coding and worked example effects.
- ✓ There is little if any research which supports the idea that matching teaching to a student's expressed learning preference (for example, visual, auditory or kinaesthetic) will lead to better retention.

For reflection

- ☒ How might your knowledge of dual coding affect how you design learning resources?
- ☒ How could your knowledge of types of cognitive load influence your lesson planning?
- ☒ What strategies and techniques can be used to keep cognitive load manageable?

Further reading and viewing

- ☒ Mayer, R.C. & Moreno, R. (2003). Nine ways to reduce cognitive load in multimedia learning. *Educational Psychologist 38* (1), 43-52. Available at: https://www.researchgate.net/publication/253772914_Nine_Ways_to_Reduce _Cognitive_Load_in_Multimedia_Learning
- ☒ Paivio, A. (1969). Mental Imagery in associative learning and memory. *Psychological Review, 76 (3),* 241-263.
- ☒ Rogowsky, B.A., Calhoun, B.M. & Tallal, P. (2015). Matching Learning Style to Instructional Method: Effects on Comprehension. *Journal of Educational Psychology, 107* (1), 64-78. Available at: https://www.apa.org/pubs/journals/features/edu-a0037478.pdf
- ☒ Sweller, J. (2017). Cognitive Load Theory and Teaching English as a Second Language to Adult Learners. *TESL Ontario. Contact Magazine.* Available at: http://contact.teslontario.org/wp-content/uploads/2017/05/Sweller-CognitiveLoad.pdf
- ☒ David Hendricks explains Cognitive Load Theory and how you can apply it to PowerPoint presentations. Available at: https://www.youtube.com/watch?v=stJ-MkTgRFs

<table>
<tr><td>

Managing cognitive load in the classroom

</td><td>

7

</td></tr>
</table>

Key concepts

This chapter picks up on the previous chapter about Cognitive Load Theory and considers in more detail the pedagogical implications we believe stem from it. We consider:

- ☒ Building phonological memory
- ☒ The skilled use of questioning
- ☒ Working step by step
- ☒ Preventing divided attention
- ☒ The role of comprehensible input
- ☒ Chunking the input, including the use of sentence builder frames and knowledge organisers.
- ☒ Learnability and processability
- ☒ Preventing inattentional blindness
- ☒ Metacognitive strategies
- ☒ Managing cognitive load in Task-Based Language Teaching
- ☒ Cognitive fatigue
- ☒ The Rosenshine Principles of Instruction applied to language learning

Building phonological memory

For students to be able to pronounce accurately, listen and read successfully, then we need to help them establish clear phonological memory through appropriate pedagogy. In Conti and Smith (2019), we proposed a model for this as shown in Figure 7.1.

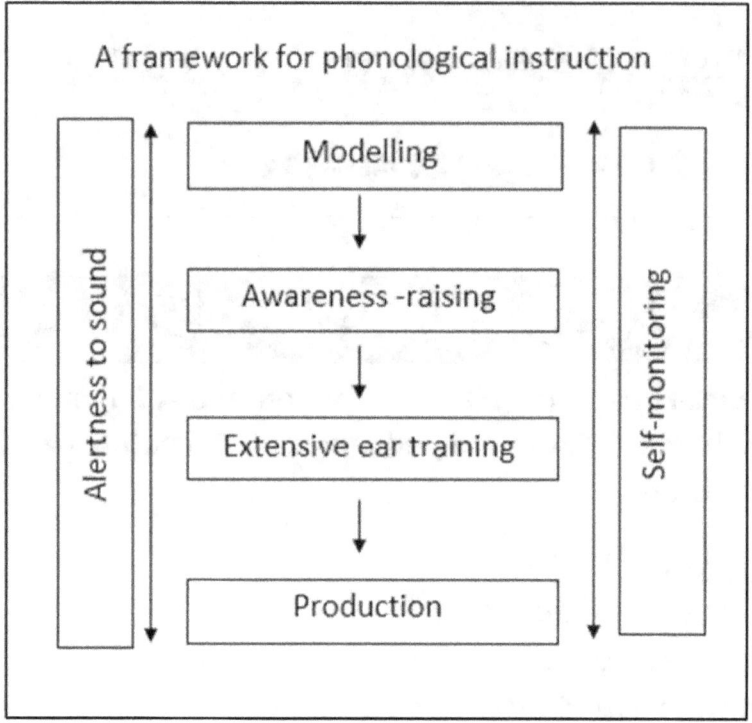

Figure 7.1 A model for building phonological long-term memory
(Conti and Smith, 2019)

Receptive processing of target language phonemes and syllables is best done before asking students to say too much. Why? Firstly, less confident students may find receptive practice less challenging and threatening than speaking. Secondly, it takes lots of receptive practice through recycling and spaced repetition before skills becomes internalised. The danger is that if students have to produce language too soon, they fall back on incorrect or incomplete knowledge, or on knowledge of the sounds of their first language. Moreover, if production is faulty, students will end up with inaccurate forms in long-term memory.

In short, it's a good idea to preempt phonological errors by doing lots of receptive practice first. Remember that words and chunks are stored in memory not just as meanings and spellings, but in their sounded out form. If vocabulary is not stored in this way, it is harder to identify in the stream of sound. Hence the focus in recent methodologies on phonology and phonics.

Identifying students with poor phonological memory is very helpful. A very simple 'oral ping-pong' activity, where you ask students to repeat unfamiliar words and phrases of increasing length, is a quick, but effective way to do this.

In Conti and Smith (2019) we provided a wide range of strategies and many specific activities with the aim of developing phonological and phonics awareness, briefly summarised below.

Explicit phonological awareness-raising activities. Activities designed to explicitly teach and practise phonology (both segmental – phonemes and syllables, and suprasegmental – intonation).

Scripted listening tasks. Activities where students listen to a text while reading the transcript. These tasks usually involve identifying differences between the spoken and written versions, for example extra words can be added in (*Spot the intruder)* or omitted (*Spot the missing detail*); different words are used in places (*Spot the difference*); the transcript includes grammar or spelling mistakes (*Spot the error*); the pronunciation is wrong (*Faulty echo*); word order is wrong in the transcript (*Sentence puzzle*).

Dictations. These included classic dictation tasks, gapped dictation, dictation puzzles (where the dictated language is provided in the wrong syntactic order), delayed dictation, running dictation and so on.

Read-aloud activities. These include traditional teacher-led reading aloud, shadow reading and delayed repetition.

Scaffolded dictation

You can reduce the cognitive load of dictation, by scaffolding the task in various ways.

1. Supply the first letter of each word.

2. Supply all consonants, but no vowels, or vice versa.

3. Provide a gapped version omitting chosen grammatical points such as articles, verbs or prepositions.

4. Provide a translation; give students a translation of the text you read. This allows them to focus on form (phonics) less than meaning, lightening the load on memory.

Conti and Smith (2019)

Shadow reading

In shadow reading, students read aloud a text as they follow a recording or reading of the text in order to imitate the speaker's rhythm, intonation and pronunciation.

Ghost reading is a shadow-reading technique which works particularly well with younger learners. Students to whisper like ghosts to make it more fun. Besides the enjoyment this produces, reading like ghosts forces them to slow down and enunciate more clearly the chunks of language.

Skilled questioning

Books about the pedagogical implications of cognitive science often mention the importance of questioning during lessons. Skilled, structured questioning can involve all students and engage thinking at various levels, from simple factual recall to deeper conceptual thinking.

Language teacher questions usually perform a rather different role. They are a tool we use for various purposes, including checking comprehension and getting students to think about grammar, but above all, especially for beginners, to recycle language in order to generate repetition of input and output. In this way we build memory and acquisition.

When leading classroom oral work, consider the range of questions and other interactions you can use to manage cognitive load. A yes/no question or either/or question is easier to process than a question using an interrogative word such as *when*, *why* or *how*. The latter require students to retrieve more language from memory. You can work through sequences of easier and harder questions, matching them to an individual's or class's current level. This is sometimes called ***circling***. An easy alternative to asking a question is to ask students to correct false statements. This incurs a relatively light cognitive load as students are able to repeat what they hear while making one change. Many examples of the use of questions and similar interactions set within lesson plans can be found in Smith (2017).

One further point about questions. When Communicative Language Teaching came to the fore in the 1970s, traditional question-answer sequences were criticised for being artificial in nature – not genuine communication. After all, why would you ask someone 'How old is Catherine?' (a so-called **display question**) if Catherine's age is clearly shown on a PowerPoint slide? We would argue that, despite its artificiality, there is a place for this type of questioning. A useful teacher skill is to make questions as naturally communicative as possible through facial expressions, emotional reactions and sheer enthusiasm! Beginners are very happy to engage in this type of classroom exchange, more experienced learners a bit less so. Just remember two things: the number of repetitions questioning generates and its role of keeping lessons in the target language.

Question types – easiest to hardest to process

1. **Yes/No**. Is Xavier a policeman?

2. **Either/Or**. Is Xavier a policeman or a taxi driver?

3. **Multi-choice**. Is Xavier a policeman, taxi driver or a firefighter?

4. **Question word question**. What does Xavier do for a living?

Working step by step

To limit extraneous cognitive load, when you explain how a structure is used model it carefully, step by step, to students, allowing each stage to be held in working memory and be processed. When introducing a new, complex verb tense with more experienced students, take it one step at a time. For example, with the perfect tense in French begin with regular *avoir* verbs. If students later over-generalise the rule and use *avoir* with *être* verbs and reflexives, this is not the end of the world and is something even native speakers do occasionally.

When introducing a new verb with near beginners, avoid introducing all its forms at once, for example stick to the first person of the present tense before showing other parts of the verb. Allow students to hear, see and use lots of examples of one form before introducing others. A student may be able to memorise a whole conjugation, but this doesn't mean they will then use a relevant form correctly in spoken or written output. Being able to conjugate a verb is a somewhat illusory form of mastery. How many students can rote learn a verb, yet still be incapable of using it correctly when they speak or write spontaneously?

For listening and reading tasks, pre-teach some key items in advance to lighten the load on working memory during the task (the pre-training effect). Allowing students to activate knowledge from long-term memory eases the load. Because beginner students don't have much knowledge of the target language to draw on, they can benefit from their knowledge of the first language, so exploit this when useful. Students have an awful lot of first language knowledge in long-term memory.

At novice level keep audio listening items and teacher talk brief, recycling the same language as much as possible. Avoid playing lengthy extracts which students will be unable to process.

Preventing divided attention

Cognitive overload is often caused by divided attention. This can be caused by environmental factors, poor design of resources, information overload, task complexity and by interference from the first language. But it can also be caused by time constraints, learnability issues and by anxiety (for example, exam-related stress).

Time comes into play if you try to cover too much material in one lesson. There is sometimes pressure to do this in order to show evidence of progress. The learnability of a structure may also play a role, for instance in a case where both the form and usage of a verb tense or mood have to be taught, it may be wiser to focus on one aspect at a time. Stress may cause a loss of attention during a listening or speaking assessment where there is pressure to perform quickly.

In the previous chapter we mentioned the example of confusing students by presenting too much information about a verb tense all at once. Think also about the implications of using digital technology in lessons. If a task requires a good deal of non-linguistic attention (for example, making a film or drawing pictures) weigh up the motivational gains this may bring against the distraction from the main goal of language learning.

Divided attention comes into play. It may be wise to maximise the brain's resources on language, rather than other non-linguistic activity. Some tech tasks may be superficially attractive, but don't necessarily help so much with language learning.

Developing phonological and phonotactic skills

Receptive processing: Phonics Bingo

1. Create bingo cards featuring individual letters or letter combinations. Hand out identical cards to all students or make, say, four different ones.

2. Either read out individual sounds or single syllable words containing sounds on the cards as students tick them off.

3. When a student thinks they have won they read out the sounds identified. The whole class can repeat for further practice.

Receptive processing: Same or Different?

Display and say a word to the class which features a sound you wish to focus on. Say the same word again, either the same or slightly differently. Students must spot whether your pronunciation was the same or different. Try saying the same pairs of words identically a few times to encourage really close listening.

Receptive processing: Faulty Transcript

The simple task of having students compare what they hear with a transcript including deliberate mistakes, sharpens their awareness of sound-spelling matches and phonotactic rules.

Comprehensible input

Cognitive overload easily occurs when there are too many unknown words in a spoken or written text. Research tells us that around 95% to 98% of words in a text should be easily comprehensible, otherwise the average language learner is unlikely to understand and therefore learn much from it. A study on extensive reading by Hu and Nation (2000) found that when 80 % of the words in a text are known, even more able learners had inadequate comprehension.

Although you'll no doubt want students to learn to make meaning from context, be aware of the cognitive challenges an inexperienced reader with a limited vocabulary faces when grappling with a text containing too many unfamiliar words. This is worth keeping in mind if you like to use authentic texts with classes. Weigh up their cultural and motivational value against their comprehensibility. With beginners this may mean using contrived texts in the interest of providing high frequency understandable language and the repetition needed to help it stick.

At advanced level, when large numbers of knowledge schemas are established, focus more on general comprehensible input to take advantage of natural language acquisition processes. By this stage students will have a large store of target language in their long-term memory and, with the aid of glossaries or a dictionary, can cope with lengthy authentic texts such as novels.

Chunking the input

We've seen that, in terms of working memory efficiency, it makes more sense to teach multi-word units of language rather than single words. Remember too that single words offer limited expressive power for a beginner because you can't actually say much with them. For instance, knowing that the French for 'dog' is *chien* isn't much use unless you can use or understand it in a sentence.

On the other hand, high frequency chunks such as *On a un chien* ('We have a dog'), *Je voudrais un chien* ('I would like a dog') or *J'aime les chiens* ('I like dogs') take up the same amount of working memory capacity as the single word *chien*, but which allow students to express a meaning. Chunks give you more memory 'bang for your buck'.

Imagine a beginner student of French has just been taught a list of words for clothes. After practising the words with repetition, flashcard games or other oral and written tasks, you then ask them to produce sentences where the new words must be used alongside colours (for example, *I wear a red dress, I wear a green tie*). This task may appear as a very simple one to the expert French speaker, but it requires the application of a complex set of rules:

- Students must link the gender of the clothing to the colour adjective.
- The word order is different from English (the adjective goes after the noun).
- French adjectives usually add 'e' to create the feminine form.
- If an adjective ends in 'e' already, an extra 'e' is not needed for the feminine form.
- Some adjectives have irregular endings, such as *blanc* which becomes *blanche.*
- Some adjectives don't change at all in the feminine form (for example, *marron*).

This all suggests that teaching single words and the grammar rules to string them together creates an unnecessary cognitive load. As mentioned previously, a 'words plus grammar' approach is less efficient than one which places chunking at the heart of language teaching.

An alternative approach is to model sentences, for example, in a text, via PowerPoint, question-answer sequence or sentence builder frame like the one in Table 7.1 which gives students the means to talk about pastimes and why they like them.

Once they have repeatedly heard, seen and read aloud multiple examples of the sentences, students should be able to use them comfortably at some point, without having to analyse how each sentence was formed. At a suitable moment (for example if someone asks) you can give a 'pop-up' grammatical explanation which some will be able to apply to new examples they wish to create. Many students will be happy to work with and combine their ready-made examples.

This approach lessens cognitive load at the presentational stage. A student repeatedly processing chunks containing the perfect tense of French verbs ending in '-er' will quite possibly remember and use them without even noticing or analysing how they were formed. Students with higher aptitude will do this more quickly, of course.

The chunk memorisation approach relies largely on implicit memory – students 'pick up' patterns rather than analyse them. To repeat, it's faster, lighter on working memory and less vulnerable to error than an approach involving learning vocabulary and making it fit grammatical rules. It also produces longer-lasting retention. If you feel that this smacks too much of rote learning, keep in mind that over time creativity becomes possible as students are able to marshal lots of known chunks, while adapting them to create new ones. Students cannot be expected to be spontaneous speakers in the early stages of language learning. Indeed, as we explain in Chapter 14, demanding too much can lead to feelings of failure and anxiety.

Don't forget, though, that some inquisitive classes may be keen to know rules quite early on. If the class is ready for this and a rule can be simply given, then that shouldn't be a problem, provided the emphasis remains on *using* the language in comprehensible input, via chunks and whole sentences, not *talking about* the language.

Je joue (I play) **Je fais** (I do) **Je regarde** (I watch)	**au football** **au rugby** **au cricket** **au tennis** **au tennis de table** **aux jeux vidéo** (computer games) **du judo** **de la gymnastique** **de la danse** **des randonnées** (walking) **la télé** (TV) **des films** (films) **des dessins animés** (cartoons)	**avec mes parents** (with my parents) **avec mes amis** (with my friends) **avec ma mère** (with my mother) **avec mon père** (with my father)	**à la maison** (at home) **à l'école** (at school) **dans un club** (in a club) **dans ma chambre** (in my room)	**le weekend** (at the weekend) **le soir** (in the evening) **de temps en temps** (occasionally) **souvent** (often) **quelquefois** (sometimes)
J'aime (I like) **J'adore** (I love)	**ça** (that)	**parce que** (because)	**c'est** (it's)	**amusant** (fun) **intéressant** (interesting) **relaxant** (relaxing)

Table 7.1   A French sentence builder frame for chunking input and output

Another way to chunk language is by means of a ***knowledge organiser*** consisting of sentences with their translation in a parallel text format. Look at the brief example for French in Table 7.2. Verb chunks are highlighted. A table like this can be exploited in many ways: choral reading aloud, individual reading aloud, rote learning, replacing chunks with other chunks, adding new elements to the base sentence. The same sentences can be recycled in mini listening tasks such as transcription correction, dictation, tense spotting or aural translation into English.

Je vais **au cinéma** souvent avec mes amis	I often go **to the cinema** with my friends
Je préfère les films d'action et de science-fiction	**I prefer** action movies and science fiction
Je regarde souvent des films en ligne	I often **watch** films online
Nous avons Netflix à la maison. C'est super.	**We have** Netflix at home. It's great.
Samedi dernier **j'ai regardé** le nouveau film de James Bond	Last Saturday **I watched** the new James Bond film
Le weekend prochain **je vais aller** au cinéma avec mes parents	Next weekend **I'm going to go** to the cinema with my parents

Table 7.2 Part of a French knowledge organiser

Once you know students are secure in their receptive knowledge, you can do highly controlled activities, practising the language repeatedly via questions, oral drills or games. This could include structured writing tasks first and, later, when the students are working faster and accurately, a series of oral tasks. It often makes sense to put writing first, especially in all ability classes, because it poses a lower cognitive challenge than speaking and allows more thinking time. (It is sometimes suggested that you should avoid writing with lower-attaining students, but these students cope least well with just listening and speaking.)

In line with the ***narrow limits of change*** principle described in Chapter 6, sentences used to drill new patterns ought to include highly familiar language and a low level of element interactivity in order to reduce extraneous load. Before doing any writing, students could brainstorm (individually or in pairs) the errors that negative transfer might cause. Another way to preempt transfer errors is to give students a checklist reminding them of the errors to look out for.

Learnability and processability

Intrinsic cognitive load is influenced by a range of factors. How similar or different is it from the first language equivalent? How complex is it? How 'ready' is a student to process it?

The learnability of an item is often connected with its processability - the number of cognitive steps needed to understand or produce it and the challenge each step poses. (Production is harder than understanding.) Unless each step has been fully automatised, the average learner may not be ready to acquire the item. The more steps that need to be fluently carried out, the higher the cognitive load. Think of driving a car without having properly learnt how to change gear, use the indicator and to brake. Each of these tasks competes for attention.

We return to this in more detail in Chapter 13, but for now keep in mind that any aspect of language you teach, whether it be phonological, lexical, morphological or syntactic, has its own degree of difficulty.

Cognitive empathy with students is key when tackling the issues of learnability and processability. We need to anticipate which steps our students are going to find the most challenging and devise ways of managing the cognitive challenge they are likely to pose. Our own experience as language learners can be helpful in this regard.

Blind mimes

This is a great task to build memory for verbs in particular.

1. Prepare an easy story to tell students, containing the verbs you want to focus on. The story could be something very mundane, such as what you did yesterday, or something more creative and elaborate, depending on the class.

2. Mime the story as you relate it. Students mime along with you. You may display the story on the board. Do not be afraid to occasionally use the first language with near beginners.

3. Retell the story without acting it out. Students use the gestures you used the first time or their own. The text can still be displayed on the board.

Preventing inattentional blindness

As we saw in Chapter 6, inattentional blindness is caused by divided attention, which may result in students failing to notice and remember linguistic features, because of the competing demands of paying attention to both the meaning and form (known as *parallel processing*). So, for instance, a student asked to note down the main points of a text is unlikely to notice an interesting new phrase or grammatical construction because their attention is focused on meaning (locating the information needed to answer questions).

On the other hand, if you get students to do exercises which make them focus solely on the vocabulary or grammar of the text, they are not likely to gather the gist of the text. Beginners are more vulnerable to divided attention as they are less practised in parallel processing.

To maximise learning from a text, it is advisable to exploit texts intensively in different ways, each exercise eliciting a different level of processing (phonological, lexical, grammatical). This kills two birds with one stone. First, it gets students to process the same text repeatedly, increasing familiarity with it, which decreases cognitive load. Second, it means that the students' limited attention is used more efficiently, with more potential opportunities for deeper processing of the text and, consequently, learning.

The same applies to speaking and writing. If, for instance, we want to develop spoken fluency, it makes sense to train students to prioritise hesitation-free, fast and effective communication and not to worry too much about accuracy. This minimises divided attention caused by worrying about accuracy while speaking.

As far as editing written output is concerned, divided attention is often the reason for students failing to identify errors. Conti (2004) found that many lower intermediate writers edit their written output by translating into their first language - focusing on meaning. The effect is that they usually fail to spot the large majority of spelling and grammar errors. By looking for mistakes without having a specific goal in mind, students are unable to focus their attention efficiently. Training them to check several times, each time focusing on a specific problem, leads to more errors being identified (Conti, 2004).

Metacognitive strategies

Metacognitive knowledge refers to what learners know about learning. It's often described as 'thinking about thinking' or 'thinking about learning'. When metacognitive knowledge is used, memory encoding and retrieval can be improved (Bransford et al., 2000). Teachers can help students develop their metacognitive knowledge, which comes in three forms (Flavell, 1985).

1. **Personal knowledge**: students' knowledge of their own cognitive abilities (for example, 'I have trouble remembering how to use verb tenses').

2. **Task knowledge**: the students' knowledge what is needed to carry out particular tasks (for example, 'To get the highest marks I need to show examples of different tenses').

3. **Strategic knowledge**: students' knowledge of strategies available to them and when they are appropriate to the task (for example, 'If I look for the endings on verbs this will help me recognise the tense being used').

Managing cognitive load in Task-Based Language Teaching

If your syllabus is designed around learning through meaningful tasks, for example as opposed to a topic or grammar-based syllabus, then it's wise to keep cognitive load in mind when planning tasks.

As we explained in Chapter 6, any task has an intrinsic cognitive load. This is influenced not just by the difficulty of the language, but by the very nature of the task – how complex it is to explain, set up and carry out. Familiarity with the type of task is one factor, with unfamiliar tasks requiring more cognitive steps to complete them. In addition, greater complexity in each individual step means higher cognitive load.

As we have seen, we know that for a student to effectively learn from a text they need to understand almost all of it unaided. Having to resort to external sources, such as the dictionary or vocabulary lists, divides attention, with a potentially disruptive effect on memory, learning and motivation. This is why one of the principles of task-based learning is that students should work with language they already know.

Task repetition is one way not only to strengthen learning but also to create task-familiarity, thereby lowering cognitive load (Bygate et al., 2015). Each time a task is repeated, it becomes easier and more fluid. In Conti and Smith (2019) we list several fluency-building activities such narrow reading/listening and fluency cards which involve task repetition. With younger learners, we recommend activities which motivate students to repeat the task with a well-defined purpose.

To reduce cognitive load, a student-led preparatory phase is advisable when setting up a task which is likely to pose a significant cognitive load. In this phase students can be asked to:

- plan the task (for example, brainstorm ideas, evaluate them and generate new ideas);
- retrieve useful language items (for example, based on task-knowledge, the title or other information given by the teacher about the task - the kind of vocabulary and structures they expect to hear or use);

☒   identify potential problems and generate solutions (for example, predict the kind of mistakes they are likely to make and generate a list of items to double-check).

This is particularly advisable in the case of challenging listening and speaking tasks. Research suggests that pre-task planning helps with oral and written performance and fluency. Table 7.3 lists some types of oral and written tasks. Those on the right pose a higher cognitive load.

Lower cognitive load	Higher cognitive load
One way. One person only has the information.	**Two way**. Each person has unique information that has to be shared to complete the task.
Open. No one has the answer (for example, ranking tasks such as deciding which items to take to a desert island).	**Closed**. Students must find a solution (for example, finding the way to a destination on a map).
Convergent. Students reach agreement on a solution to a problem (for example, a profile of a person, who has to choose from six different holidays).	**Divergent**. Debates or arguing the merits of different sports teams.
Here and now. Students derive information from available sources such as texts.	**There and then**. Sources are removed so students must retrieve language for themselves.
Structured. Best used mid-way through a teaching sequence.	**Unstructured**. Best used later in a teaching sequence.
Familiar. Good for consolidating fluency.	**Unfamiliar**. Requiring more spontaneity so best used later in a teaching sequence.
No time limit. Useful at the start of a teaching sequence.	**Time limited**. Useful later on when you are focusing on fluency (speed of comprehension or production).

Table 7.3 Task types classified with cognitive load in mind

A pre-task, teacher-led practice phase can also help reduce cognitive load. This may involve:

1. activating prior linguistic knowledge (intensive targeted drilling of specific challenging language items) or metacognitive knowledge (knowledge of task-related strategies), and
2. a series of pre-tasks which require repeated processing of vocabulary and structures likely to be needed. The repetition needed for this has been shown to make it easier to retrieve language duing the task. This is an example of priming (see Chapter 9).

The P.I.P.O. reading/listening for writing/speaking sequence integrates all the above strategies.

- **P** Pre-task teaching and planning
- **I** In-reading/listening tasks (texts are exploited intensively at many levels)
- **P** Post-task consolidation (the key linguistic features found in the text are revisited and consolidated through retrieval practice)
- **O** Output (written and/or oral input is produced based on the knowledge acquired in the previous phases)

When setting up more challenging listening tasks, it's useful to do pre-tasks based on written texts similar to those students are about to listen to.

Cognitive fatigue

Cognitive fatigue is the technical term for feeling mentally tired out! You will probably have noticed students seem less motivated and more tired in the afternoon. Research shows that the time of day affects test performance because, over the course of a regular day, students' mental resources are taxed. Sievertsen et al. (2016), for instance, found that for every hour later in the day, test scores decrease by 0.9%. They also found that a 20 to 30 minute break improves average test scores. The implication is that higher cognitive load tasks or high amounts of sustained concentration may be better done in the morning or after a break.

Ways to combat cognitive fatigue include:

- alternating long focus (for example, looking at the classroom screen) and short focus (such as looking at the exercise book, textbook or digital device);
- alternating sitting down and moving around activities;
- alternating easier and harder tasks;
- using a variety of activities tapping a range of skills;
- using 'quieter' listening and reading activities in the afternoon.

Rosenshine's Principles of Instruction

Educational psychologist Barak Rosenshine's *Ten Principles of Instruction* (2012) are becoming more familiar to teachers. One of the main points behind them is to help manage cognitive load to allow learning to happen efficiently. We list them below and suggest brief examples of how they can be adapted to language teaching.

1.   Begin the lesson with a review of previous learning

Lesson starters can include entry and register routines, quick translation, 'do now' tasks on the board, snappy oral drills (for example changing a tense or one element of a prompt sentence) or conversational routines such as 'What did you do last weekend?'

2.   Present new material in small steps

When presenting a new tense, avoid teaching all parts of a conjugation at once and explain and practise regular forms before irregular ones. Build on previous knowledge. With new vocabulary use choral repetition and reading aloud first with beginners, before moving on to individual repetition or reading aloud.

3.   Ask a large number of questions (and to all students)

Use the full range of questioning types to recycle patterns as much as possible. Use other interactional formats such as 'Correct my sentence', 'Change one element in my sentence'.

4.   Provide models and worked examples

Model target language structures and vocabulary in comprehensible texts, teacher demonstration and picture sequences. Model how you would go about doing tasks such as translation, role play and essay writing.

5.   Practise using the new material

Do intensive and extensive listening, reading, speaking and writing – recycling the same language in several different ways. Use a mixture of teacher-led, pair and group work to re-use language. Use purposeful games. A key lesson planning skill of any language teacher is to find different ways of rehearsing the same language, so that work seems fresh to students and lessons move on at a suitable pace.

6. Check understanding frequently and correct errors

Monitor comprehension using formative assessment techniques, cold-call (no hands up) questioning, mini-whiteboards etc. Sensitively correct where needed (see Chapter 15).

7. Obtain a high success rate

Use highly comprehensible language and enjoyable activities which are readily accomplished. Use your skilled questioning technique to ensure students can all answer. Provide wait time where needed to allow students to silently rehearse answers. Plan tests so that students can achieve good scores.

8. Provide scaffolds for difficult tasks

For writing tasks, model good examples, provide templates and gap-fill versions of tasks. 'Structure strips' are popular – strips of paper which students stick in their exercise books as a reminder of the elements to include in a written composition.

9. Independent practice

At a later point in your teaching sequence, after a good deal of receptive input and controlled practice, give students opportunities for less guided conversation, information gap tasks and free writing.

10. Monthly and weekly reviews

These may consist of end of unit tests or more informal reviews of what you have been practising.

Summary

- ✓ Phonological memory is crucial for language learning. For students to be able to pronounce accurately, listen and read successfully, we need to help them establish clear phonological memory through appropriate pedagogy.
- ✓ Skilled, structured questioning involves all students and engages thinking at various levels, from simple factual recall to deeper conceptual thinking.
- ✓ In terms of working memory efficiency, it makes more sense to teach multi-word units of language rather than single words. Teaching single words and the grammar rules to string them together creates unnecessary cognitive load.
- ✓ The learnability of an item is often connected with its processability - the number of cognitive steps needed to understand or produce it and the challenge each step poses.
- ✓ To maximise learning from a text, exploit it intensively in different ways, each exercise eliciting a different level of processing (phonological, lexical, grammatical).
- ✓ To limit extraneous cognitive load, in explaining how a structure is used model it carefully, step-by-step to students, allowing each stage to be held in working memory and be processed.
- ✓ Keep in mind the divided attention effect, including when using digital technology. If a task requires a good deal of non-linguistic attention weigh up the motivational gains against the distraction from the main goal of language learning.
- ✓ Improving students' metacognitive knowledge and training them in metacognitive, cognitive and affective learning strategies can help reduce cognitive load.
- ✓ When working with a Task-Based syllabus, as opposed to a topic or grammar-based syllabus for example, keep cognitive load in mind in planning tasks.
- ✓ Consider ways to mitigate cognitive fatigue, including how to time and vary different language learning tasks.
- ✓ The Rosenshine Principles of Instruction provide a useful framework for lesson planning.

For reflection

- To what extent do you make it a priority to teach phonological awareness and phonics to beginners?
- Do you plan carefully for the use of questions and other interactions with students?
- To what degree do you favour chunked language over isolated words and grammar rules?
- What advantages does digital technology offer?

Further reading and viewing

- Rosenshine, B. (2012). Principles of Instruction. Research-Based Strategies that All Teachers Should Know. *American Educator*. Available at: www.teachertoolkit.co.uk/wp-content/uploads/2018/10/Principles-of-Insruction-Rosenshine.pdf
- Smith, S.P. (2017). *Becoming an Outstanding Languages Teacher*. London: David Fulton, Routledge.
- Teacher and teacher educator Martina Bex explains the value and limitations of questioning (circling). Available at: comprehensibleclassroom.com/how-to/essential-strategies-for-tprsci-teachers/how-to-circle/
- Rod Ellis (in 2020) talks about Task-Based Language Teaching. Available at: youtube.com/watch?v=jsBTQgE8uhw&t=115s

Long-term memory

8

Key concepts

In this chapter we consider:

- **What is long-term memory?**
- **Bjork's Theory of Disuse**
- **Chunking and background knowledge**
- **The role of chunking in reading**
- **The role of synapses**
- **Forgetting**
- **Paying attention**
- **Multi-tasking**
- **The role of noticing**
- **Distractions**
- **Failing to encode properly**
- **Decaying from memory, the Ebbinghaus forgetting curve and serial position curve**
- **Interference**

What is long-term memory?

Learning has been famously described as a change in long-term memory (Kirschner, Sweller and Clark, 2006). In second language acquisition research the term for this acquired knowledge of a language is often called *mental representation*. The aim of all teachers is to build long-term memory. We need students to be able to recognise and retrieve a huge amount of language.

Long-term memory is where we store information over a long period of time. It is the means by which the brain's neural networks can reactivate information on a permanent basis. It has been defined as follows:

> *All of the knowledge we have of the world, of our experiences, of our learning in specific disciplines, of our lexicon, of our tacit (implicit) knowledge, and of our internalized procedures and habits we have in navigating our world are aspects of long-term memory* (Grabe and Stoller, 2019 p13).

Despite our everyday impression that we forget things, it's likely that long-term memory actually decays very little over time, and can store an apparently unlimited amount of information. Indeed, there is some debate about whether we actually ever 'forget' anything at all, or whether it just becomes increasingly difficult to access certain items from memory (for example, Robert Bjork's **theory of disuse**).

Bjork's theory of disuse

This modifies Thorndike's (1914) original law of disuse. The original law proposed that without continued use, memory traces decay over time. Later theorists showed that it is not the passage of time itself that causes forgetting, but rather the interference of other information. As Robert Bjork (2011) puts it succinctly, learning leads to forgetting.

In Bjork's theory, any item you encode in memory is said to have two characteristics: **storage strength** and **retrieval strength**. Storage strength is a measure of how *well learned* an item is, whereas retrieval strength measures how *accessible* the item is. The more you are exposed to an item, the stronger the storage strength gets (repetition). But storage strength does not have a direct effect on memory performance; reproducing something from memory (for example, a phone number) depends almost entirely on how easily it is retrieved, that is, its retrieval strength.

Storage strength cannot decrease, but retrieval strength can vary.

When thinking about long-term memory, you might recall that bottle we mentioned back in Chapter 2, with its large, potentially leaky body, since long-term memory is subject to **fading** (or, in Bjork's view interference with competing memories) as we naturally forget things over time. Maintenance rehearsal (several recalls or retrievals of memory) may be needed to preserve long-term memories. Individual retrievals can take place in increasing intervals by using **spaced repetition**. This can happen naturally through reflection or by deliberate recall (**conscious retrieval**), often dependent on the perceived importance of the material. Using tests as a form of recall can lead to the **testing effect**, which aids long-term memory through information retrieval and feedback. See Chapter 10 for more about this.

Chunking and background knowledge

As we saw in Chapter 3, the phenomenon of tying together different bits of information to form knowledge schemas is called *chunking.* A way to increase the capacity of working memory is to *chunk* the information being learned. To recap, this means collapsing into manageable units a number of items which would normally be too big for working memory. Look, for example, at these two lists of 16 letters and numbers and see how many you could memorise. Try it!

List one: XCA2PLO3B1FJZ4DH

List two: 1FBI2BBC3CIA4SKY

Most people would have trouble remembering all the letters and numbers in the first list. As we saw previously, psychologist George Miller came up with the figure 7 plus or minus 2 for what most people would remember from a list of digits. (The engineers at Bell Labs in the USA made use of Miller's research when they decided that seven numbers would be good for phone numbers.)

The second list of the same length would be remembered in full by most readers. Why? Because it's possible to impose some meaning on the list. In this case the items can be chunked (put together in meaningful groups) as a sequence 1-4 and the names of well-known institutions. Put another way, for the first list we had to remember 16 items, whereas for the second it was only five – four chunks of three letters (FBI, BBC, CIA, SKY) and a sequence of four numbers (1,2,3,4). Can we take advantage of this to make language learning easier? More of this later.

The example above demonstrates how we use prior knowledge of the world (famous institutions and number sequences) to chunk information and make it easier to remember things. If we apply this to spoken or written language, a good example of chunking and world knowledge playing a role is in listening and reading comprehension.

Now read this: *Anderson trundles in from the pavilion end and, from around the wicket, bowls an off-cutter to Smith, who glides the ball down to fine leg. The fielder returns with a fast low throw taken by the keeper just above the bails.*

It is possible to decode these two sentences and derive some meaning from them, but you have to be a cricket fan to really understand what is meant. A poor reader who watches a lot of cricket would understand the sentences more than a good reader who knows nothing about the sport.

This is a case of where background knowledge (in this case a set of schemas about cricket) is required to make meaning from language. The cricket fan is able to chunk their knowledge, for example, by knowing that *trundles in* is often used to describe a bowler's approach, the phrase *pavilion end* indicates that bowlers can begin their approach from one of two ends in cricket, *around the wicket* only makes sense as an idiom if you know that a bowler can launch the ball either from the left or right side of the stumps and so on. This background knowledge is also known as ***top-down*** knowledge, whereas when we decode a message by using only the sounds we hear or marks on a page we are engaging ***bottom-up*** knowledge.

The role of chunking in reading: key points

- Being able to chunk is a crucial skill for fluent reading (Samuels, 2006).
- Chunking skills allow "the reader to see larger sentences and phrases as wholes, **a process which assists in reading more quickly**" (Hudson, 2007, p. 80).
- Readers who don't know how to chunk often read **in a word-by-word manner** which is less conducive to understanding and learning from a text.
- **Less skilled readers often group words inappropriately** in ways that deviate from the type of phrasing that occurs naturally in oral language (Kuhn and Stahl, 2003).
- **Chunking and intonation are closely linked** because intonation can provide clues to where a reading text should be segmented (Schreiber, 1991).

The role of synapses

Most researchers believe that memory creation is associated with the strengthening of existing connections or the growth of new connections between neurons (brain cells). These connections are called synapses. They allow information carried in the form of nerve impulses to travel from one neuron to the next.

When two neurons communicate repeatedly the efficiency of the communication between them increases. This process is called *long-term potentiation*.

In the human brain, there are trillions of synapses which form a complex, flexible network which allows us to feel, behave, and think. It is the changes in the synaptic connections in areas of the brain such as the cerebral cortex and hippocampus that are associated with the learning and retention of new information.

You don't need to make many new synapses and get rid of old ones when you learn or memorise. You just need to modify the strength of the existing synapses. However, it's likely that few synapses are made or eliminated to achieve long-term memory.

With age synapses falter and weaken for a number of reasons. First, the hippocampus loses 5% of its neurons every decade. Second, the number of neurotransmitters produced in the brain drops over time. Third, as we age we find it harder to pay attention, so synaptic connections form less readily.

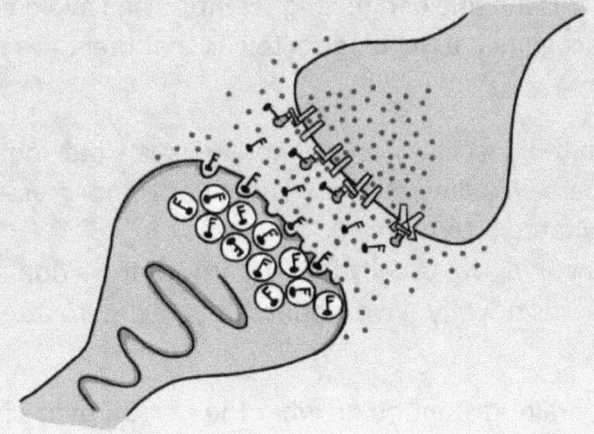

In sum, we can say that background knowledge facilitates chunking, which creates room in working memory, making it easier to link ideas and understand. The more background knowledge we can help students build, the more effective will be their use of long-term memory. The more you know already, the easier it is to learn new things.

Forgetting

Understanding why students forget is important if we want language to stay in long-term memory. We can design individual lessons and a whole curriculum with this understanding in mind.

The first thing to say is that students forget what they have been taught for a number of reasons:

- Not paying attention in the first place.
- Not encoding information properly.
- Losing information from memory through decay.
- Interference from other stored memories.
- Not using the same cues when trying to retrieve an item as when first learning it (known as *cue-dependent forgetting*).

We next look at each of these in turn, except the last, which we return to in Chapter 11.

Paying attention

What's called *attentional control* is considered to be part of working memory. In Chapter 3 we pointed out that, in the multi-component model of memory, it's the Central Executive which performs the role of directing attention and avoiding distractions. When it comes to attention, cognitive psychologists tell us that there are three key aspects we need to keep in mind:

- Attention is limited, just like working memory span, but some learners have a bit more than others. Working memory is about both processing new information and deciding what to attend to.
- It's selective, meaning we usually fail to learn what we don't pay attention to.
- It's biased towards novelty – we instinctively pay more attention to what's new or unexpected.

Attention focuses the brain's attention on what the person thinks is important. Clearly, if you aren't paying attention to something you tend not to remember it. In addition, humans can only pay attention to one thing at a time. That said, psychologists and applied linguists have also shown that people can learn things implicitly, i.e. without conscious awareness or the intention to learn. Much of the language we acquire and use can be 'picked up' without us really noticing - although we must have heard or read that language, even if we were not intending to learn it.

The pre-frontal cortex is the part of the brain at the front of the head which is critical for paying attention. It receives the information from other areas of the brain associated with vision, hearing and feelings. What psychologists call *executive attention* focuses on a particular task or multiple tasks at hand. It has been shown that children with ADHD have reduced blood flow in their pre-frontal cortex.

Did you know...?

If you close your eyes you might remember more of what you previously saw. One study by Vredeveldt, Baddeley and Hitch (2013), in the journal *Legal and Criminal Psychology,* found that when people closed their eyes, they were able to answer 23 percent more questions correctly about a film they had just watched. By closing your eyes, you remove outside distractions and allow your brain to focus on the recollections at hand.

As the authors put it in their abstract "eye-closure instruction constitutes a simple and time-efficient interview tool for police interviewers".

The average person has an attention span of 40 minutes, depending on the complexity of the task - a good reason for suggesting to students that they take breaks between revision sessions of no more than 40 minutes.

If we don't pay attention to information, it is not consciously available, so it can't enter working memory at all and cannot pass into long-term memory by that route. To reiterate, however, some of the information we don't pay attention to may potentially pass directly into long-term memory through implicit (unconscious) learning. One famous second language acquisition scholar, Stephen Krashen, called this *acquisition*, as opposed to *learning* (Krashen, 1982), though many writers are now reluctant to make this clear distinction.

But remember that working memory is also able to draw on information we already possess in long-term memory. In this way, as mentioned previously, working memory and long-term memory combine to help us carry out a learning task. The more information we have stored in long-term memory, the less we have to depend on new information in working memory, and the easier the task becomes.

Multi-tasking

While we can't properly attend to two tasks at once because of the *divided attention* effect (think of the dangers of using a mobile phone while driving), we can switch from one task to another. However, this comes at a cost. Studies have shown that students who are heavy multi-taskers (those who keep screens open on their computer and mix study with social media use) are more susceptible to false memories, are more easily distracted and even have less grey matter in the pre-frontal cortex of the brain – that part which is associated with executive attention. Rubinstein, Meyer and Evans (2001) hypothesise that there are two stages to this process:

1. **Goal shifting**: deciding to do one thing rather than another.
2. **Role activation**: changing from the rules for a previous task to a new one.

Moving through these stages repeatedly adds to the time taken for tasks and impairs thinking, particularly for teenagers, it seems. In one study, Ophir et al. (2009) found that people who were considered heavy media multi-taskers were worse at sorting out relevant information from irrelevant details and were easily distracted. It would seem that heavy multi-taskers are not very good at it!

The implications for learners and teachers seem clear. Students need to be fully focused on learning tasks and avoid jumping around from one task to another.

Noticing

Paying attention is also associated with the concept of *noticing* which has been much discussed in second language acquisition literature. One very influential hypothesis put forward by second language acquisition researcher Richard Schmidt is that for language patterns to be internalised in long-term memory, you have to notice their form. This is called Schmidt's *Noticing Hypothesis* (Schmidt, 1990; 2001). These are its key features:

1. Attention is crucial for *input* (what students are exposed to) to become *intake* (what they actually take in for processing) and therefore learning.

2. Focusing attention on the input is accompanied by awareness at a low level.
3. What is noticed becomes intake.
4. Intake cannot happen without some level of awareness at an early stage in the learning process (when you are trying to understand).
5. Awareness becomes less important during subsequent processing of input.

It's worth noting that there remains a good deal of debate about what 'noticing' actually means and that students seem to be able to pick up new language without appearing to have noticed it at all (implicit learning). As researcher Lourdes Ortega puts it, "the jury is still out on the question of whether learning can happen without attention" (Ortega, 2013, p. 96). Nevertheless, an important role for language teachers is to get students to notice patterns in the language during work focused on meaning and communication.

For example, one approach to introducing grammatical forms is to do some work with a text containing examples of language you wish to target. After a full range of activities – repetition, reading aloud games, question-answer and listening/reading comprehension exercises – you can ask students to notice patterns, or simply point them out. Evidence suggests that unless you deliberately get students to notice patterns, only a minority will do so themselves.

One repeated finding from research is that students naturally tend to focus on the meaning of language rather than its form, for example morphological features such as agreements. Meaning is usually more interesting after all. If we wish students to notice grammatical features, it has been suggested that the input can be manipulated to achieve this. Bill VanPatten has called this **Input Processing Theory** (VanPatten, 1996). Here is an example. Compare these two sentences students hear:

1. *Last weekend I went to the restaurant with my boyfriend.*
2. *I went to the restaurant with my boyfriend.*

For the first sentence the presence of the time marker *last weekend* right at the start of the sentence means that students are less likely to attend to the form of the verb than in the second case. In other words, the verb form is redundant. In the second sentence the only clue to time is in the form of the verb so students have to process it to work out the full meaning of the sentence. You could keep this in mind when preparing oral grammar drills, for example. In a 'spot the tense' aural drill it would be better to omit time expressions and just let students process the verb form. As Benati (2017) puts it: "Processing instruction helps learners to process input correctly and efficiently and therefore increases learners' intake of the target language" (p.391).

VanPatten recommends structuring input in the above way, as well as explaining rules to raise awareness and enhancing input by any means (using so-called **input-flooding** and **text enhancement**). Input flooding means including many examples of the pattern you want students to notice and use. Text enhancement means, for example, using colour to highlight key points such as adjective agreements, verb endings or sound-spelling correspondences (phonics). In classroom oral exchanges input enhancement may involve exaggerating stress or intonation to get students to notice, or using gestures to indicate accented letters. Many teachers are familiar with these techniques. Striking examples of how to use text enhancement to highlight phonics can be found in the PowerPoint resources on the ncelp.org website based at the University of York.

Distractions

Students would be wise, when studying or revising, to avoid distractions such as a phone, background speech or some types of music.

As far as music is concerned, the literature is a bit inconclusive. Although some research has suggested that listening to calming music may be beneficial for some aspects of learning, for example, Hallam, Price and Katsarou (2002), other research is less positive about listening to music *while* studying. Some types of music take away attentional resources from the learning task at hand. Music may have a restful effect, but students who listen to music with lyrics while completing reading or writing tasks tend to be less efficient and come away having absorbed much less information.

In one study (Perham and Currie, 2014), students who revised in quiet environments performed more than 60% better in an exam than their peers who revised while listening to music with lyrics. Loud music can also have adverse effects on reading comprehension and on mood, making focus more difficult. Other studies, for example, Jäncke and Sandmann (2010), found that listening to music while you learn makes little difference to outcomes.

Failing to encode properly

Even if you pay attention to something and *notice* it you may not end up storing it properly in memory. As far as language teaching is concerned, language has to be transferred from working memory to long-term memory. For this to happen a process of **maintenance rehearsal** is needed – reviewing material over and over again. This takes time and effort. As we have seen, conscious retrieval from memory and testing can assist the encoding process. Making links (cues) with previous knowledge helps with encoding. The greater variety of cues you can establish, the more likely it is that information will be remembered.

For example, if a student wanted to remember in French which perfect tense verbs are conjugated with the auxiliary *être*, they could use various cues, such as the idea that these verbs usually involve motion, that they don't take direct objects or that they can be recalled with a mnemonic such as MR DRAPERS MT VAN. (A mnemonic is a system such as a pattern of letters, ideas, or associations which helps you to remember something, for example that the letters stand for particular words.) Other cues might include associations with a story worked through in class, personal descriptions of past activities or a set of pictures depicting the verbs in question. This combination of cues results in elaborate processing, which helps embed memories.

Decaying from memory

Unfortunately, even if you have paid attention and encoded information successfully, it can seem to disappear, i.e. we forget it. Back in Chapter 3 this was also described as decaying from memory. You know the feeling! In 1885 the German psychologist Hermann Ebbinghaus famously did experiments with short nonsense words of three letters, which he attempted to remember at various time intervals after the initial learning. The results of his experiments were clear and have been replicated since. People forget things really quickly! His famous forgetting curve, shown in simple form in Figure 8.1, reveals the rate at which people forget.

Information apparently fades or decays from memory, therefore. An alternative view, as we saw earlier, is that memories are always there, but just hard to retrieve (Bjork, 2011). It seems that people tend to forget more recent things faster as they are constantly learning masses of new trivial information.

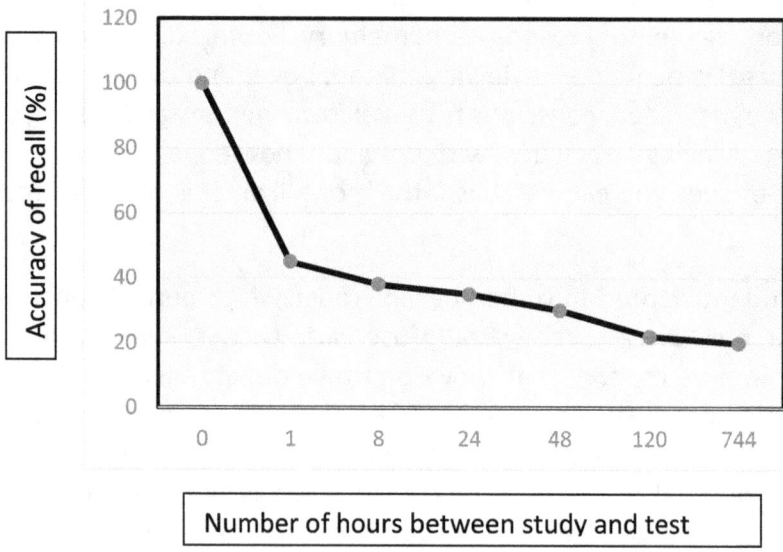

Figure 8.1 The Ebbinghaus Forgetting Curve

The serial position curve

Ebbinghaus also discovered that when people have to learn a list of items, they tend to remember those at the beginning and end better than items in the middle. This **serial position curve** is a U-shaped learning curve that is normally obtained in word recall experiments. It is produced by more accurate recall of words from the beginning and end of the list than words from the middle.

So imagine that you've been given a list of random words and have two minutes to try and memorise. When you try to recall the words in any order, you will most like begin with items that were last on the list. This is known as the **recency effect**. The next items will probably be the first few on the list, a tendency known as the **primacy effect**. You might like to explain this to students and try the same experiment with them. Or observe what happens when you play a well-known cumulative language game such as *I went to the market and I bought...*

Two working memory games

I went to the market and bought.... This is an example of a popular classroom games which requires students to use their short-term memory. When playing, you may observe the recency and primacy effects in action. As a whole class or in groups, one student begins by saying, for example, I bought some bread. The next says I bought some bread and some apples. The next adds a third item and so on. In theory students should only be able to hold a limited number of items in working memory. But associating words with those who said them, including their position in the classroom or group, acts as a memory aid. The game also produces lots of repetition, of course.

Kim's Game. This is where you show a grid of slides, often images depicting vocabulary items such as places around town. Real objects can be used if you lay them out on a table visible to the class. Students are asked to close their eyes as you remove an item from the set. As the game unfolds and students have heard the words used many times, you can remove more than one item. The name of the game is derived from Rudyard Kipling's 1901 novel Kim, in which the hero, Kim, plays the game during his training as a spy.

Forgetting is good

Another of Ebbinghaus' findings was that when we forget something, the next time we learn it the process is easier and leads to greater retention. It's as if the information was there all along, but hiding, and reactivation left a more permanent trace.

In other words, the act of trying to recall information increases storage strength. Forgetting doesn't undo learning, it creates the chance to reinforce learning. As Robert Bjork put it, "...retrieving information from memory is a learning event, and the more involved or difficult the act of retrieval, provided it succeeds, the greater the learning benefit" (Bjork, 2011, p.9). Long-term memory storage is probably limitless, but retrieving that information is often hard. Forgetting bits of information may help with its subsequent learning and improve retrieval.

What's more, Bjork claims that the stronger the storage strength is (for example, how interconnected a piece of information is with other information, how elaborately it was processed during learning), the stronger retrieval is likely to be. If storage strength is very high, then an item can be retrieved instantly and there is no point in teaching the same item again, at least not in the same way. So, for example, if an individual word is instantly and quickly retrieved, the best way of recycling that word would be to place it in new contexts which can involve new connections and new learning.

Interference

Forgetting is also caused by interference from distracting items, which were either presented prior to learning, known as *proactive interference,* or after learning, during memory consolidation (see above), known as *retroactive interference*. The effects of interference are thought to be greatest when the memories are similar. So we can say:

- Proactive interference is where knowledge you already have negatively affects how you learn new information.
- Retroactive interference is where new information you receive disrupts your existing knowledge.

Proactive interference happens in a case, for example, where students have learned a set of German verbs in the perfect tense, which are all conjugated with the auxiliary verb *haben* ('to have', as in *Ich **habe** gelernt* – 'I have learnt'), then they are taught that some verbs require the auxiliary *sein* ('to be', as in *Ich **bin** gegangen* – 'I have gone/been'). As a result they may over-generalise and forget to use the auxiliary *sein* for those verbs that need it. Their previous knowledge has interfered with new learning.

In contrast, in the case of retroactive interference, an obvious example is where students begin a second modern language at school which may adversely affect their knowledge of the first. So students who learn Spanish after French may make mistakes in French owing to their new knowledge of Spanish.

To give a more specific example, in an experiment, students had to learn pairs of words (German-Japanese), then they were given another set of German-Japanese paired words to learn (the *interfering* words). Another group only had to learn the first set of word pairs. The first group did up to 20% worse on the test of the first set of words since, the researchers concluded, retroactive interference had not allowed enough time for the memory of the first list to be consolidated (Sosic-Vasic et al., 2018).

A message for the classroom here is that vocabulary needs to be introduced in limited doses, allowing enough time for it to bed in, before too many new words are introduced. Text books often introduce too much language at once. The temptation to 'finish the book' needs to be resisted!

Summary

- ✓ Long-term memory is where/how we store information over a long period of time. It is the means by which the brain's neural networks can reactivate information on a permanent basis. A main goal for language teachers is to build long-term memory.
- ✓ Some psychologists believe that we don't forget information; it is displaced or interfered with by new learning. Indeed, it is even claimed that we need to forget in order to remember new things.
- ✓ We cope with the vast amount of information we receive by chunking it. This means organising a number of items which would normally would be too big for working memory to hold into manageable units. Chunking and world knowledge play a role, for instance, in listening and reading comprehension.
- ✓ Background knowledge is known as **top-down** knowledge, whereas when we decode a message by only using the sounds we hear or marks on a page we use **bottom-up** knowledge.
- ✓ The more background knowledge students have, the more effective long-term memory will be. The more language they have already, the easier it will be to learn new language.

✓ Understanding why students forget is important if we want language to stay in long-term memory. We can design individual lessons with this in mind.

✓ A teacher's main focus has to be on getting students to pay attention. Attention, like working memory, is limited, selective and biased towards novelty or the unexpected.

✓ Language passes into long-term memory both via working memory (conscious learning) and through implicit learning (picking up language without any particular focus on its form).

✓ We can't properly focus on two tasks at once, but we can switch our attention from one to another. Multi-tasking tends to result in poorer learning and memory.

✓ The Schmidt Noticing Hypothesis claims we usually need to notice patterns in the language to internalise them. Research suggests that students can also pick up patterns implicitly.

✓ Students find it very hard to focus on the form and meaning of language at the same time. We cannot assume students will notice patterns unless we get students to look for them or point them out.

✓ Input can be manipulated to encourage students to notice patterns.

✓ On balance it seems that listening to music with lyrics while studying is distracting, but research supplies mixed messages on this subject.

✓ For memories to become more permanent, maintenance rehearsal is needed.

✓ The Ebbinghaus Forgetting Curve is a clear reminder of how quickly students can forget language. Regular distributed practice is usually needed for memories to stick.

✓ There is a positive side to forgetting. Forgetting language may help with its subsequent learning and improve retrieval.

✓ Interference between bits of information can disrupt memory. Proactive interference is where knowledge you already have negatively affects how you learn new information. Retroactive interference is where new information you receive disrupts your existing knowledge.

✓ When neurons communicate via synapses repeatedly, the efficiency of the communication between them increases. This process of 'long-term potentiation' builds schemas.

For reflection

- How could the idea of chunking influence the way you present and practise language with students?
- When planning lessons, how can you take advantage of previous knowledge in long-term memory to advance current learning?
- How can curriculum and lesson planning discourage language decay from long-term memory?
- What strategies and techniques can be used to hold students' attention and help them maintain attention when working independently?
- How can lessons be planned to stop interference affecting later recall?
- How can we get the right balance between routines and novelty?

Further reading and viewing

- Anderson, R. C. (1984). Role of the Reader's Schema in Comprehension, Learning, and Memory. In *Learning to Read in American Schools: Basal Readers and Content Texts,* ed. Richard C. Anderson, Jean Osborn, and Robert J. Tierney. Hillsdale, New Jersey: Erlbaum.
- Baddeley, A.D. (1997). *Human memory: Theory and Practice (Revised Edition).* Hove: Psychology Press.
- Bjork, R. A. (2011). On the symbiosis of learning, remembering, and forgetting. In A. S. Benjamin (Ed.), *Successful remembering and successful forgetting: a Festschrift in honor of Robert A. Bjork* (pp. 1-22). London, UK: Psychology Press. Available at: https://bjorklab.psych.ucla.edu/wpcontent/uploads/sites/13/2016/07/RBjork_2011.pdf
- Robert Bjork explains his theory of disuse in this interview: Available at: gocognitive.net/interviews/theory-disuse-and-role-forgetting-human-memory
- Brown, J. (1958). Some Tests of the Decay Theory of Immediate Memory. *Quarterly Journal of Experimental Psychology, 10*: 12-21.
- Murre, J. & Dross, J. (2015). Replication and Analysis of Ebbinghaus' Forgetting Curve. *PLOS One.* Peer-reviewed open access journal. Available at: https://www.ncbi.nlm.nih.gov/pmc/articles/PMC4492928/
- Pooja Agarwal talks about spaced practice in this short video: Available at: https://www.retrievalpractice.org/spacing
- Andrew Luttrell gives an illustrated talk about schemas. Available at: https://www.youtube.com/watch?v=WB9raKI-cJY

Declarative and procedural memory

9

Key concepts

In this chapter we consider:

- **What are declarative and procedural memory?**
- **The protégé effect**
- **Auitomaticity revisited**
- **The processing of vocabulary and grammar**
- **The role of priming, including phonological, lexical and structural priming, along with implications for the classroom**
- **The role of sleep in consolidating memory**

What are declarative and procedural memory?

You'll remember that at the start of the book we referred to two types of learning, *explicit* and *implicit*. Explicit learning is usually intentional and conscious. Implicit learning happens 'beneath the radar', sub-consciously as we perform tasks. When we learn our first language(s) we do so implicitly. It's just natural, what Geary (2008) calls biologically primary. With second language learning there is a much greater role for explicit learning, but the jury is still out to what extent implicit or explicit learning processes dominate.

Nick Ellis (2017) points out that:

- implicit and explicit learning are distinct processes;
- humans have separate implicit and explicit memory systems;
- there are different types of knowledge of and about language;
- these are stored in different areas of the brain;
- different educational experiences generate different types of knowledge.

This ties in with what cognitive psychologists call **declarative memory** and **procedural memory**. Broadly speaking, explicit learning tends to produce declarative knowledge ('knowing *that*', for example, knowing the endings of a verb), while implicit learning tends to produce procedural knowledge ('knowing *how* – being able to use those verb endings without having to think about it). It's not quite that simple, of course, but more of this below! The place of these two parts of long-term memory are illustrated in Figure 9.1, based on the work of Larry Squire.

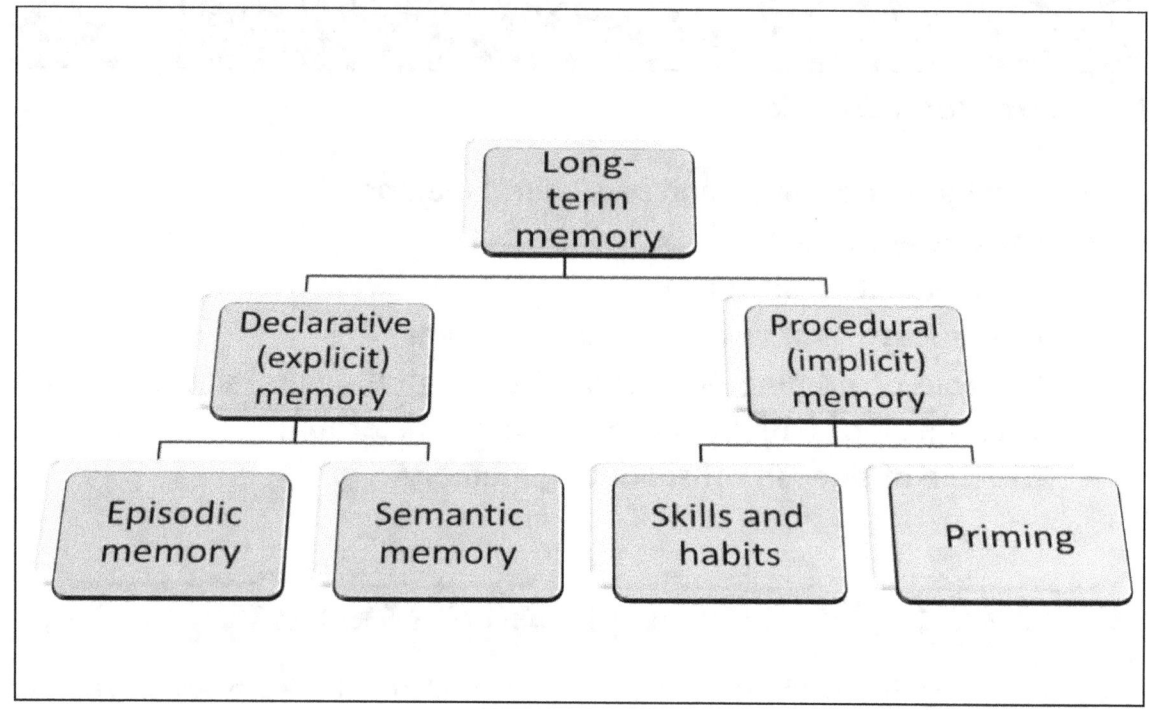

Figure 9.1 Components of long-term memory based on Squire (1992)

Declarative (or explicit) memory refers to those memories you experience consciously. As we saw in Chapter 1, some of these (known as semantic memory) represent factual knowledge: things like the capital of Spain (Madrid), the number of days in a year (365) or the fact that verbs have different endings in the present tense of Spanish. Others, known as episodic memories, consist of past events you've experienced, such as a wedding.

Implicit memory, also called procedural memory, builds up unconsciously. It uses different memory systems from declarative memory, which rely on other areas of the brain. Implicit learning includes **priming** (see below) as well as procedural memories, which your body uses to remember the skills you've learned. If you play an instrument or ride a bicycle, those are your procedural memories at work. We build up knowledge of our first language(s) through implicit learning. Procedural memory also shapes your body's instinctive responses, like salivating at the sight of your favourite food or tensing up when you see something you fear.

Characteristics	Implicit (procedural) knowledge	Explicit (declarative) knowledge
Awareness	Student has no conscious awareness of linguistic rules but knows instinctively what sounds right	Student is consciously aware and can explain rules
Type of knowledge	Procedural, namely available for automatic processing	Declarative – facts about the language which are only available through controlled processing
Systematicity	Variable but systematic	Often inconsistent since students may only have a partial understanding of a linguistic feature
Use of second language knowledge	Only evident when students use it for communication	Used to monitor production; it is used when students lack implicit knowledge
Self-report	Consists of internalised constructions and procedures which may not easily be reported	Can be reported using metalanguage (grammatical terminology)
Learnability	There may be age limits on learners' ability to acquire knowledge implicitly (for example grammatical rules)	Explicit knowledge is learnable at any age (but older learners have greater world knowledge)

Table 9.1 The nature of implicit and explicit knowledge (adapted from Ellis and Shintani, 2013)

Did you know...?

The ***protégé effect*** is the term used to describe the fact that we remember information better when we know we'll have to teach it to someone later (even a virtual tutee). In 1980 John Bargh and Jaacov Schul found, in a study of 42 undergraduates, that those who were told they would have to learn information to teach it to another person did better in a subsequent recall test than those who had to just learn for themselves.

Other papers have also suggested that the very act of teaching (and the interactivity involved) reinforce memory, for example, Kobayashi (2018).

Procedural memory is frequently not available to your consciousness; it is implicit or 'tacit', meaning you can do something, but are unable to explain how to do it very easily. This would be the case for, say, putting on your clothes, or explaining the rules of your native language, for example, why 'b' at the end of the word *bomb* is silent. In the latter case, you know how to say *bomb* correctly, but are highly unlikely to know why. Neuroscientists believe that procedural memory is controlled by the striatum, an area on top of the hippocampus (see Figure 9.2). Procedural memories are encoded and stored by the cerebellum, putamen, caudate nucleus and the motor cortex, all of which are involved in motor control.

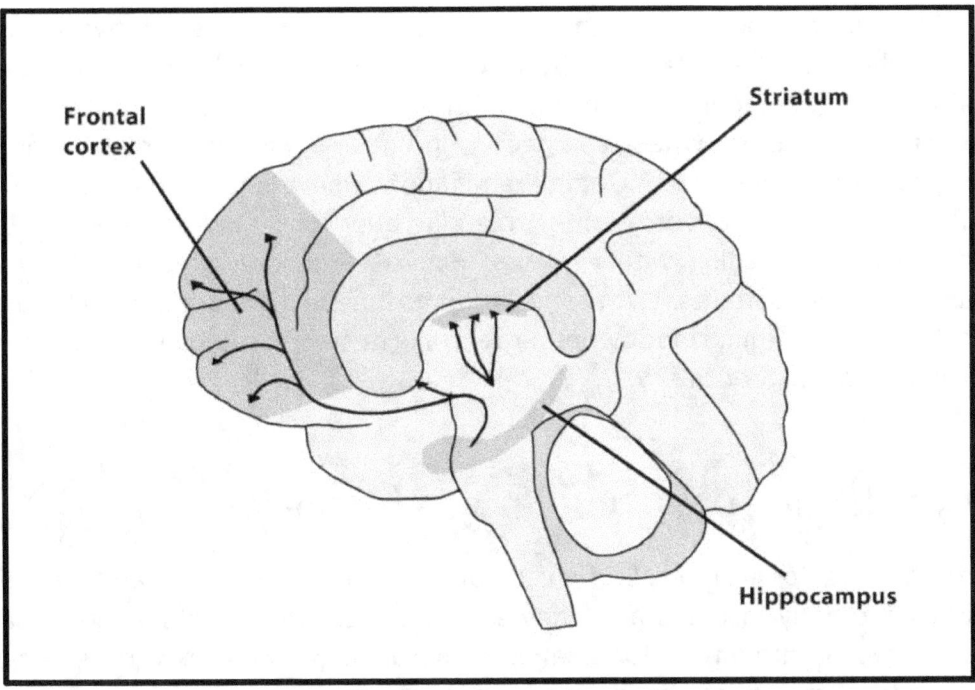

Figure 9.2 Location of the hippocampus and striatum

Automaticity revisited

We noted above that the relationship between explicit/declarative and implicit/ procedural knowledge may not be simple. An interesting question is whether, in second language learning, knowledge which is declarative can *become* procedural, in other words if it can become **automatised**, or **proceduralised.** This is of great interest to language teachers who wish to know whether knowing the facts about language helps students become better users of the language. With most learning tasks it seems that consciously learned skills can become proceduralised (like learning to drive a car or play a computer game), but with language learning there is a good deal of debate between scholars about whether consciously learned information can be become proceduralised.

In the literature about second language acquisition, the term **interface** is used to denote the potential barrier between declarative and procedural learning. Researchers disagree about the extent to which the interface can be crossed, with most believing that it can, under certain conditions, for example, N. Ellis (2005) and Ullman (2006). These conditions could include how **developmentally ready** a student is (older students may be able to cross the interface more readily than younger ones) or even the nature of the individual language items being taught (Han and Finneran, 2014).

There's little doubt that for students in schools, memorised declarative knowledge (language which has been learned by rote, but the rules of which have not been internalised for spontaneous use), can be of great use in some contexts. These include specific real-life situations where you need to produce a learned formulaic chunk (for example, 'Where are the toilets?'), or in examinations where you can benefit from having memorised answers to conversation or role-play questions. Our own belief is that by combining explicit teaching with repeated implicit exposure, students do gradually internalise language patterns. With some students it happens more quickly than others and teachers need to think about whether teaching declarative knowledge is likely to be helpful in developing proficiency.

The processing of vocabulary and grammar

Some researchers (for example, Ullman, 2006) believe that vocabulary and grammar are processed differently in the brain. They say that vocabulary is stored in declarative memory, whereas grammar (for example, morphology such as verb endings and adjectival agreements) is stored in procedural memory. This may explain why grammar is harder to master for classroom second language learners, since procedural memory takes longer to establish and they receive relatively little input. Another way of putting this is to say that the *system* (grammar) is harder to acquire than its *components* (vocabulary).

Teachers should not be surprised, therefore, that students seem to remember vocabulary more easily than they are able to apply grammatical rules. Even if they appear to 'know the rule' (from declarative memory), they find it hard to actually use it (procedural memory). So patience is needed with grammar and we'd advise teachers to limit the amount of grammar covered, but to do it repeatedly and extensively, with the focus on use rather than explanation.

Priming

This brings us to a really important concept for language learning. Speaking our first language at normal speed seems pretty effortless. We're able to do this because every time we utter a word or phrase we are sub-consciously associating it with previous and possible future words or phrases. Our vast experience with the language gives us a huge range of possibilities since we've heard or read a myriad of possible combinations. So when we're about to utter the next word or phrase, in a fraction of a second (around 50 milliseconds to be precise), we subconsciously choose the right one from the range of possibilities. This subconscious process of words affecting the following ones is called *priming*. One word or phrase primes the next.

In general terms, priming is about unconscious triggers which get you to remember or act in a particular way. For instance, you might happen to see a commercial for a product, then the following day end up buying the same product without even remembering that you had seen the advert. You were primed to carry out an action.

There are two main types of priming which have powerful learning effects:

- *Perceptual priming*. When you see or hear something for a second time you process it more quickly.
- *Conceptual priming*. Where you hear or see a second item related in meaning to the first you also process it more easily.

Psychology describes other types of priming; an interesting one is *emotional priming*. We often have emotional experiences: moments of pleasure when reading a good book or being frightened when seeing a spider. In these cases, we're consciously aware of the emotion and, usually, its cause. But emotions can also be implicit and subconscious – we may not consciously feel or be aware of what triggered the emotion.

In everyday dealings with colleagues and students we can prime their reaction to what we say by couching it in positive or negative terms, or even by a facial expression such as a smile. So, as students enter the classroom, we might say, "Good to see you! Did you have a good last lesson?" instead of "Don't talk when you come in!" So we can prime positive language and attitudes by projecting them ourselves. This is a powerful teacher tool as we try to build a positive learning environment which will encourage learning and memory.

In second language learning priming takes the form of *semantic (lexical) priming*, *phonological priming* and *syntactic priming*.

1. **Semantic or lexical priming**. This is when a listener, hearing the word *bread* will recognise words like *baker, butter, knife* more quickly than unrelated words like *chair, cement* or *lightbulb*. For example, if you present the word *transport* a second time, a student processes it faster (perceptual priming). Subsequently, if you present the word *train* it is processed more quickly because it is related to the topic of transport (conceptual priming). Priming is known to activate the brain areas in the cortex associated with the thing being primed. So priming the word *transport* causes all the areas of the brain associated with transport to become active for a brief moment. This extra bit of activity makes it easier for additional information to be activated fully. This is known as *perceptual fluency*.

Michael Hoey's (2005) *Lexical Priming Theory* maintains that each time we encounter a word we make a subconscious note of the words which could occur alongside it (*collocations*) and of any associated grammatical pattern (*colligations*). Through multiple encounters with that word we become primed to associate it with the most commonly recurring elements. Think of how, when you enter a word in Google other words immediately appear after it, based on frequency of search or your own previous searches. As mentioned elsewhere, this suggests we should consider teaching vocabulary in chunks and sentences to encourage the lexical priming effect. In this way, retrieving chunks from memory becomes more fluent and effortless.

2. **Phonological priming.** When one word primes another which sounds similar, such as rhyming words. *Light* primes *night* and *bite*. Any teaching which encourages students to notice phonological similarities will help students remember words and phrases. Rhymes are a good example.

3. **Syntactic priming** (also known as *structural priming*). This is when speakers have a tendency to use the same grammatical structures as ones they have recently heard or read (Bock, 1986). Short term syntactic priming is thought to involve explicit memory (re-using an expression just heard), whereas long-term syntactic priming is thought to be the result of implicit learning (Bock and Griffin, 2000). The evidence that the learning is implicit is that it occurs in brain-damaged speakers who have no explicit memory of the prime sentence (Ferreira, Bock, Wilson and Cohen, 2008).

Manipulating the language input is likely to lead students to use and remember structures more successfully. That's why it's a good idea to repeatedly use high frequency grammatical patterns in the expectation that students will pick them up both in the short and long term. This can be done, for example, by means of sentence builders, question-answer sequences or audio-lingual style drills, as well as flooding input language with the patterns you want students to pick up. Sets of short paragraphs, each one containing examples of the same grammatical structure, when worked on intensively with a range of exercises, can supply the input and interaction needed to encourage syntactic priming. This is known as *narrow reading* or *narrow listening* (for example, Smith and Conti, 2016), based loosely on an idea by Stephen Krashen

Interestingly, there is also a phenomenon called *cross-linguistic priming.* This is when, say, the French word *chat* ('cat') primes both the English words *cat* and *chat* (conversation). Bilinguals are constantly priming both first and second language words. Think of your own experience when speaking your second language. In the classroom you need not shy away from encouraging comparisons between the first and second language. This can give you a reason to highlight so-called false friends (words which look the same across two languages but have different meanings).

The power of priming in marketing

Sales people are well aware of the power of priming.

In 1999, Adrian North and colleagues carried out a fascinating experiment in a grocery store. For two weeks, French and German music were played on alternating days and the amount of French wine versus German wine sold was measured. Purchasers of the wine were asked to fill out a survey, the results of which revealed that they were unaware of the effects of music on their choice. More French wine was sold on days when French music was played and more German wine was sold on the German music days. A simple, auditory prime had a significant effect on buying behaviour (North et al, 1999).

Staying on the wine theme, in another study by North (2012) it was found that participants described the taste of wines differently, depending on what type of music was being played. Participants drank the same wine while one of a number of pieces of music with different emotional characteristics were played in the background. Those who heard Carmina Burana were more likely to describe the wine as powerful and heavy, those who heard Waltz of the Flowers were more likely to describe it as subtle and refined, and so on.

Guess what comes next

This activity develops lexical priming.

Write a narrative of a past event or series of events. Produce a gapped transcription (see the example below). Scaffold the activity by displaying a set of words from which students can choose.

On Saturday morning I decided to go into town with my (pause) friend. We took the bus and arrived in the city centre just opposite the (pause) supermarket. First we walked to the café. I ordered a (pause) coffee and my friend ordered a (pause) coffee too. We stayed in the café for fifteen minutes. We talked about my (pause) dog and our school work. We left the café and crossed the (pause) street. We entered the (pause) bank because I had to get some money from the cash dispenser...

1. Slowly recount a story. Pause every now and again, as shown above.

2. During this pause students should write on a mini-whiteboard their best guess at the next word then hold it up.

3. Ask a few students to say their word.

4. Reveal the actual word you wrote. Any student who guesses the right word gets a point.

Conti and Smith (2019)

Rhyming pairs

This activity develops phonological priming.

1. Give students a list of five words all with different endings, chosen based on difficulty or simply because they contain sounds students may need to pronounce during the rest of the lesson.

2. Read out six or seven other words (the extra one or two are distractors), five of the words rhyming with the five words provided initially (see French example below). Students cannot see the teacher's words.

3. Students identify which words rhyme with which.

Students' words: *moi – ville – famille – travailleur – brillant*

Teacher's words: *bois – mille – peur – soleil – ailleurs – dur – jouet – cédille – mer – souriant*

Conti and Smith (2019)

Implications of priming

We have seen that priming means repeating the presentation of something affects the way it's processed a second time. If students are frequently exposed to a repertoire of chunked language it is more likely that one word, phrase or sentence will prime the next, allowing fluency to develop. In time-poor classroom settings, to achieve the amount of recycling needed for priming effects to develop, it's wise to limit the amount of language input. You might like to think of it this way: at the start you have a small snowball of language. Over time, as new language is added, the snowball gets larger and larger as you add new language to the existing repertoire.

One alternative, teaching through the explanation of grammatical rules and lists of single words, is likely to be less successful and more stressful for most students. It is far less likely to build implicit memory and promote priming.

The role of sleep in reinforcing memory

As we explain in Chapter 10, the brain remains very active at night and sleep helps learners embed memories through a process of consolidation. There are competing theories about how and the extent to which declarative or procedural memory are consolidated. Many researchers think that specific characteristics of brainwaves during different stages of sleep are associated with the formation of particular types of memory.

If people are deprived of sleep, they learn and remember less well. But researchers have found that the influence of sleep on procedural memory is much stronger than on declarative memory. Sleep also aids the retention of emotional memories.

Teenagers should get at least nine hours of sleep each night – significantly more than adults. In reality, they often get around seven (Gradisar et al., 2013). Inadequate sleep results in problems with attention, memory, decision making, reaction time and creativity, all of which are important in school.

Summary

- ✓ There are two types of knowledge referred to by psychologists: declarative ('knowing *that*') and procedural ('knowing *how*'). The latter is much more important for us than the former, but most researchers believe declarative knowledge can become procedural in some circumstances.
- ✓ There are two types of learning happening in language lessons, implicit (unconscious) and explicit (conscious). The more comprehensible language that students hear and read, the more chance there is for implicit learning to occur.
- ✓ Priming is a type of implicit learning where previous learning events affect those in the future, or one word or pattern influences the next. It has important implications for language teaching.
- ✓ When we know we'll have to teach something after learning it, we tend to remember the information better. This is called the *protégé effect*.
- ✓ Sleep plays an important role in embedding both declarative and procedural knowledge, though more strongly in the case of procedural.

For reflection

- In your own teaching experience, to what extent do you think it's possible for consciously learned language to become part of procedural memory?
- How helpful is to explain grammatical rules to students? If it is useful, when and how should it be done?
- What is the right balance between explicit teaching of language and simple exposure to, and interaction with, comprehensible input?
- What behaviours could you model to prime the way students act and think?

Further reading and viewing

- Anderson, J. R. (1982). Acquisition of a cognitive skill. *Psychological Review (89/4)*: 369-406. Available at: https://pdfs.semanticscholar.org/eb32/4f42d42dc29d9f89e044a76516227e4e2c66.pdf
- DeKeyser, R. M. (1995). Learning Second Language Grammar Rules: An Experiment with a Miniature Linguistic System. *Studies in Second Language Acquisition. 17* (3): 379–410.

- Leow, R.P. (2015). *Explicit Learning in the L2 Classroom*. New York: Routledge.
- Mitchell, R., Myles, F. & Marsden, E. (2013). *Second Language Learning Theories*. London: Routledge.
- Rasch, B., & Born, J. (2013). About sleep's role in memory. *Physiological reviews*, *93* (2), 681–766. Available at: https://www.ncbi.nlm.nih.gov/pmc/articles/PMC3768102/
- This video presentation summarises the interface debate, based on an article by Han, Z. and Finneran, R. (2014). Re-engaging the interface debate: strong, weak, none, or all? *International Journal of Applied Linguistics (24/3)*: 370-389. Available at: https://www.youtube.com/watch?v=jfaDjYbZE78

Making it stick

10

In this chapter we consider:

- **Memory consolidation – how memories are stored**
- **Restructuring of memory**
- **Retrieval practice (the testing effect)**
- **Using apps for retrieval practice**
- **The pre-test effect**
- **Vocabulary learning**
- **The difference between performance and learning**
- **What makes ideas 'sticky'**

Consolidation

The brain's main function — processing and transmitting information through electro-chemical signals — uses a surprising amount of energy. For the average adult in a resting state, the brain consumes around 20% of the body's energy. Even when you are asleep at night, the brain consumes roughly as much energy as it does during the day. While you rest, your roughly 100 billion neurons capable of transmitting a thousand trillion connections, are constantly communicating, updating each other on what is happening. It's believed that this process is to do with reinforcing the brain circuits associated with memory. We learn and remember while asleep. This energy-intensive process of storing memories in the brain is called *consolidation*.

Consolidation modifies the information from your perceptual system and combines its features to fix it into memory. This often takes a long time for all learning, notably language learning, but the process can be speeded up. For example, drugs which stimulate the central nervous system or sleeping after study both enhance consolidation.

But, as we mentioned in Chapter 9, sleep seems to consolidate procedural memory more than declarative, which, in theory, should be a good thing with language learning in mind. Remember that it's procedural long-term memory we're trying to build.

Now, conscious *retrieval* of information (bringing a memory back into working memory) alters that memory slightly and allows it to be *reconsolidated*. Neuropsychologically speaking, compared with when you first learn something, the difference is that the pattern of brain activation starts with the cortex (where memories are stored), moves to the hippocampus (where memories are consolidated) and then to the sensory cortex (where the item was earlier perceived). On initial learning the process works in reverse.

Neuroscientists say that retrieval doesn't produce the same pattern of brain activation as during learning, because learning requires more processes and some information may not have been stored properly. Conscious retrieval is directed by the frontal lobes of the brain, the areas which control attention, thinking and deliberate behaviours (as opposed to non-thinking behaviours such as walking or picking up an object). Thinking back to Chapter 3 on working memory, it's the Central Executive which is doing the job of controlling attention.

Did you know...?

You've probably heard of power-napping, but it seems that a nap can also help you remember better.

When Suzanne Diekelmann and colleagues in Germany asked two groups of subjects to memorise the location of pairs of cards, they found that the group who took a 40-minute nap remembered 85% of the cards, while the group who stayed awake remembered just 60% of them.

It seems that the learning had gelled during sleep, but less so during wakefulness. It appears that in some circumstances staying awake can destabilise memories (Diekelmann et al., 2011).

During sleep are our memories just consolidated or do they actually change? Some neuropsychologists (such as Paller and Voss, 2004) believe that during sleep our memories are not just consolidated, but *restructured*. Imagine it as the same cards being shuffled to produce a different combination. Other researchers have even suggested that this restructuring of memory occurs most during certain types of sleep, when brainwaves are at a certain amplitude (Cowan et al., 2020).

General advice for helping to consolidate memories

Avoid Stress. Research has found that extended exposure to stress can inhibit the function of neurotransmitters (molecules which send signals from neuron to neuron). Other studies have found that stress shrinks neurons in the prefrontal cortex and hippocampus.

Avoid drugs, alcohol, and other neurotoxins. Drug use and excessive alcohol consumption have been linked to synaptic deterioration. Exposure to dangerous chemicals such as heavy metals and pesticides can also cause synaptic loss.

Exercise. Regular physical activity helps improve oxygenation of the brain, which is vital for synaptic formation and growth.

Stimulate the brain. Researchers have found that elderly adults who engage in mentally stimulating activities are less likely to develop dementia and people with higher educational statuses tend to have more synaptic connections in the brain. *Use it or lose it.*

Restructuring

In one view of learning from cognitive psychology (Rumelhart and Norman, 1978), there are three stages in the acquisition of knowledge:

1. **Accretion**. Where a student acquires facts and information, adding more structures to existing schemas. This phase only works when the material being learned is part of a previously understood topic.

2. **Restructuring**. A student develops new memory structures to interpret the material that is to be learned. This is the most difficult and significant form of learning, since it marks the acquisition of new ways of thinking.

3. **Tuning**. Students refine their learning. This stage of learning does not increase the amount of knowledge, but it makes using the knowledge more efficient.

If we look at the second of those stages, what could restructuring mean in language learning terms? McLaughlin (1987) describes an example of restructuring as a sudden realisation that you have made a leap forward or gained a sudden insight, possibly after a frustrating feeling of stagnation. You will be aware of this feeling yourself, no doubt. Psychologists tell us, therefore, that learning happens in a discontinuous, non-linear way, with times of forgetting and quantum leaps forward.

This is why progress with acquisition usually feels more like B, than A, in Figure 10.1.

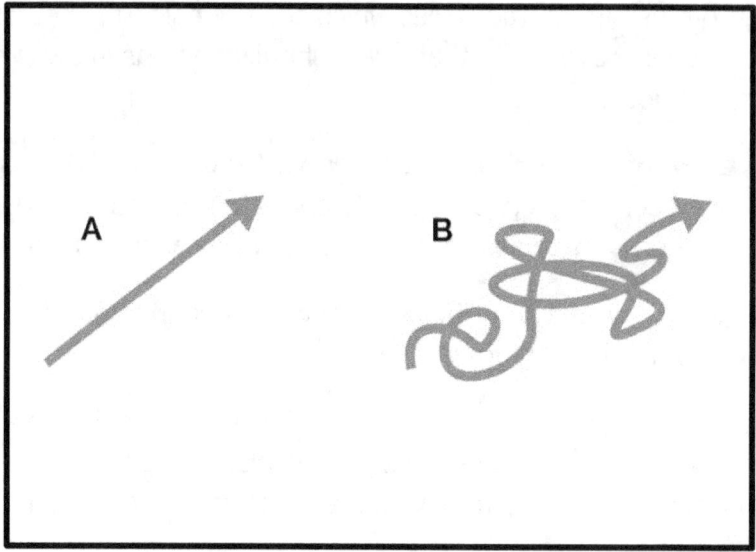

Figure 10.1 How we imagine progress and what it is really like

Retrieval practice (the testing effect)

You may understandably think that children are tested too much, but the ***testing effect*** is the clear finding that long-term memory is increased when learning time is devoted to consciously retrieving the information to be remembered. When an effort has to be made to recall information, it is better retained later (Bjork, 2011). Since an early seminal study by Edwina Abbott in 1909, hundreds of experiments have shown that practice testing enhances learning and retention. Essentially, when students are actually tested on material, rather than just practising it, the learning gains are far greater.

The testing effect is also sometimes referred to as ***retrieval practice, practice testing***, or ***test-enhanced learning***. We're not talking here about high-stakes summative testing, by the way, but the day-to-day low-stakes recall tests which language teachers are familiar with – vocabulary quizzes, quick translation, 'do now' tasks which require students to retrieve language from previous lessons. This research has led some schools to insist on starting every lesson with 10 minutes of retrieval practice. We wouldn't advocate such a prescriptive practice for language departments, but in general retrieval has to happen.

The testing effect is so powerful that research has even shown that students who revise by testing themselves in stressful situations, such as prior to exams, recall information better than those who simply re-read material in a non-stressful situation (Smith et al., 2016). Stress is known to impair memory owing to an increase in cortisol being released in the brain. This blocks pathways near the hippocampus, making it harder to recall things. However, retrieval practice is thought to offer a way around this, as the act of having to generate an answer creates alternative routes, circumventing the 'stress blockade'.

Contrary to what some might imagine, in general the sequence study-test-test-test is more effective than study-study-study-test. But the very nature of language lessons means that students are constantly having to retrieve language, a process which resembles ongoing self-testing. This is another reminder that language learning is not the same as that in some other subjects.

In addition, the research is clear that 'Goldilocks tests' (not too hard, not too easy) help build memory (think back to germane cognitive load, as described in Chapter 6). If you set a test at a suitably challenging level, and test in varying ways, learning will be stronger and memories will stick better. With this in mind, teachers should look at tests not just as *assessment* tools, but as *learning* tools. As Busch and Watson (2019) strikingly put it, you can tell students that studying isn't something you do in order to do well at tests but, rather, you do tests to study more effectively.

Using apps for retrieval practice

Language teachers are familiar with apps and programmes which enable students to practise vocabulary, either at the single word level or in whole sentences. Quizlet, Memrise, Duolingo and Busuu are just four of the numerous apps available to supplement teaching.

A 2018 study by Fernando Rosell-Aguilar surveyed users of the Busuu app. The researcher found that most users are at beginner level and learn for personal interest. These users reported that the app helped them improve their knowledge of the language, with vocabulary as the main area of improvement. The study concluded that a large proportion of users consider apps a reliable tool for language learning.

The popular app Duolingo, which presents vocabulary in sentences with sound, can be quite addictive for motivated adult learners, but a common frustration is that there is insufficient explanation of grammar. The app uses adaptive learning technology, adjusting examples to take account of previous success rates, and clearly takes advantage of the spacing effect. A study by Loewen et al. (2020) of nine students learning Turkish found a positive, moderate correlation between the amount of time spent on Duolingo and learning gains. The participants in the study generally viewed the app's flexibility and gamification aspects positively, but variability in motivation to study and frustration with the learning materials were also expressed.

There's no doubt that apps can help reinforce memory of target vocabulary. At the time of writing (2021) teachers report that retrieval practice is supported by the use of Quizlet, Memrise, Kahoot!, Quizziz, Flippity, Socrative, Wheel of Names, Glisser, ClassroomQ, Goformative, Plickers, NearPod, Mentimeter, Wooclap and Spiral. In general, we believe it's advisable for teachers to plan any vocabulary being retrieved to support other, more communicative work using the same language. Topic-based lists of isolated words may be helpful but are likely to be less effective and efficient for building memory than language presented in chunks. Using chunks means students get to retrieve not just meanings and spellings, but deeper knowledge involving collocations, morphology and grammatical patterns. We'll consider this in more detail in Chapter 11.

As with all language learning activities, the **_surrender value_** of any task has to be weighed up. Is it possible that 30 minutes spent on a vocabulary app could be better spent engaging with that same vocabulary more communicatively and using a wider range of skills? Apps and programmes which allow for deeper processing of language at text level include _Textivate_ (a text manipulation programme which can be authored by the teacher, therefore permitting closer alignment with other teaching), _TeachVid_ (which allows parallel reading and listening while watching video clips), _The Language Gym_ which includes gamified listening, reading and writing and the popular free website _Languages Online_, which has a greater emphasis on grammar, alongside vocabulary.

The power of the testing effect

In a famous experiment in 2008, Jefferey Karpicke and Henry Roediger asked participants to try learning 40 Swahili-English word pairs (for example, *mashua-boat*). Four groups were set up and the one group which had to continue practice in recalling the pairs remembered twice as many a week later as the groups which only had to re-read words or be re-tested on those they got wrong the first time (Karpicke and Roediger, 2008).

We remember words or chunks of language much better when we are repeatedly asked to retrieve them from memory.

It may surprise you to know that memory is reinforced on a topic even if you fail on a pre-test of the information. It appears that getting a wrong answer in a multi-choice quiz, then having it corrected, or just guessing the answers to questions on a topic before you have even learned it, improves memory. In one study researchers found that generating an answer yourself produces better answers than just being tested. The theory is that having to generate answers, even guesses, leads to greater curiosity and attention and therefore learning (Potts and Shanks, 2014). This is known as the **generation effect**. People tend to remember things better when they participated in their generation, rather than just passively hearing or reading them. See Chapter 15 for more about how generating wrong answers can enhance memory. Similarly, carrying out pre-listening and pre-reading activities is likely to raise interest, promote deeper thinking and better memory

Performance versus learning

One rather counter-intuitive finding from cognitive psychology is that student performance may be a poor indicator of deeper learning. When a student gives a fluent presentation or completes a drill or comprehension task accurately, this reveals superficial achievement at a point in time, but not necessarily deeper understanding. Why is this the case? Current performance may be heavily influenced by the cues available. For example, if you ask a student *What did you do last weekend?* they may be able to give a reasonable answer, but only because they have heard the same question (the same cue) repeatedly, or recently did lots of practice with high-frequency verbs in the past tense. Does this mean they could cope with talking more generally about past events? For language teachers this suggests that a suitable balance needs to be found between using pre-rehearsed material or routines with novel ones, allowing students to build new schemas.

So performance is easy to observe, deeper learning not so much. This implies that genuine progress is not easily observable in a single lesson, as the skill and knowledge displayed in that lesson may be forgotten next time. Repeated performance over time gives a clearer indication of understanding and fluency. Remember to point this out to anyone observing your lessons!

Three zero prep retrieval starters

Students write responses on paper, mini-whiteboards or answer orally.

Quickfire translation. Give words or phrases to translate either into English or into the target language. The latter is more challenging.

Complete the sentence. Give a sentence starter to which students have to supply the end, with a word or phrase, for example, *I went to the baker's and bought _____?* Or: *Last weekend I went into town and _____.*

Change one element. Give a sentence and tell students they must change one word or phrase, for example, *Tomorrow night I'm going to go to the cinema* (Possible responses: *Next weekend I'm going to go to the cinema/Tomorrow night I'm going to go to the restaurant.*)

What makes ideas *sticky*?

Chip and Dan Heath studied for many years the factors which make ideas or stories memorable in the context of marketing and advertising. They came up with an acronym for six criteria which should facilitate the process of making learning material 'sticky': **SUCCES** (Heath and Heath, 2008). We've added our own gloss to these.

Simplicity. Keep presentation of activities clear and simple. Don't include unnecessary extra information. Short and to the point is often best. When presenting new grammar, don't confuse the issue by including new vocabulary at the same time.

Unexpectedness. Material which arouses curiosity because it goes against expectations is effective. For example, choose texts with surprising, distinctive content. (We return to the important principle of unpredictability as a driver of learning in Chapter 14.)

Concreteness. Concrete language is more sticky than abstract. Use concrete mental imagery when explaining grammar, for example use the hamburger simile to explain the positioning of *ne* and *pas* in French negation (the verb being the burger in the bun).

Credibility. Students need to know material is believable, such as from an authoritative source or related to personal experience. For example, use your own experiences to talk about culture.

Emotions. There is a powerful link between emotions and memory, to which we return in Chapter 14. Material which arouses an emotional reaction is more likely to stick in memory. If we care about something we're more likely to recall it. Select texts about issues of interest to students.

Stories. We are more likely to recall information via stories than facts. This principle is exploited a good deal by teachers who use the TPRS approach (Teaching Proficiency through Reading and Storytelling).

Summary

- ✓ Consolidation is the process whereby memories are embedded in memory during rest, for example sleep. The effect is thought to be stronger for procedural memory than for declarative memory.
- ✓ Restructuring of memories occurs between learning events. This can lead to new insights or improved task performance.
- ✓ The retrieval practice (testing) effect is a powerful driver of learning and memory building. Lessons need to incorporate opportunities for students to deliberately retrieve previously practised language from memory.
- ✓ Pre-testing students on a topic is thought to enhance later memory.
- ✓ Apps can reinforce learning, but we should recognise their limitations. Other activities may bring greater memory benefits.
- ✓ We need to avoid confusing current performance with deeper learning. Second language development takes time.

For reflection

- What types of classroom activity constitute retrieval practice?
- How can you be sure that students' *performance* is a fair reflection of their proficiency?
- What type of tests are most likely to build memory?

Further reading and viewing

- Butler, A.C. (2010). Repeated testing produces superior transfer of learning relative to repeated studying. *Journal of Experimental Psychology: Learning, Memory, and Cognition 36 (5)*: 1118-1133.
- Roediger, H.L. & Karpicke JD (2006). Test-enhanced learning: taking memory tests improves long-term retention. *Psychological Science 17*: 249-255.
- Robert Bjork talks in 2015 about the testing effect. Available at: youtube.com/watch?v=gkJz0PpvGf4
- Henry Roediger gives a lecture in 2012 on the subject of retrieval practice. Available at: youtube.com/watch?v=oqae85jbfbE

Remembering vocabulary 11

Key concepts

In this chapter we consider:

- **Transfer-Appropriate Processing**
- **Levels of Processing**
- **The role of repetition**
- **The production effect**
- **Spacing, interleaving and blocking**
- **Depth of processing for vocabulary learning**
- **Thematic versus semantic clustering of words**
- **Intentional versus incidental vocabulary learning**
- **Using texts for deep processing**
- **The Keyword Method**
- **Learning from lists**
- **A summary of useful vocabulary acquisition tasks**
- **The power of gestures**

Transfer-Appropriate Processing (TAP)

When you teach a class of beginners to recite the alphabet to a tune, they are likely to remember it successfully. If you then ask them to recite the alphabet without the same tune, they will find it harder. What does this tell us?

Edward Thorndike's **Theory of Identical Elements** (Thorndike, 1914) stated that transfer of learning from one context to another depends on the level of similarity between the environment of the training and performance. When we learn something, our memories record not only the information learned, but the cognitive and perceptual processes that were involved when the learning took place. Subsequently, when we try to retrieve the information from memory, we also recall aspects of the learning process.

In more recent times, research going back to Donald Morris and colleagues in 1977 has supported Thorndike's view. The greater the similarity between processing types used in learning something and those activated in our later efforts to retrieve that knowledge, the greater the chances of successfully learning it. This means that, since memory retrieval is affected by the context of the initial learning, students can learn in one context and fail to transfer it to another. Think, for instance, of a student who was able to perform a verb tense drill repeatedly and accurately, yet failed to write verbs correctly in a written composition.

The theory of **Transfer-Appropriate Processing** (TAP) states, therefore, that memory performs best when the processes engaged in during the encoding process match those engaged in during retrieval. In particular, retrieval is better when you supply the same cues present when the initial learning took place. If those cues are missing, for example the tune accompanying the alphabet, memory is weaker.

This was exemplified in a study by Morris et al. (1977) in relation to semantic and rhyming tests. When people were asked to remember the meaning of words, memory was better for those who focused on meaning rather than rhyme. However, for those who were asked to remember words which rhymed, memory was better if they had used rhyme to process the words rather than meaning.

Put simply, learners do best when they are asked to retrieve words in a fashion and/or context most similar to the way in which they learned them. If you fail to provide the same cues on retrieval as were given during the initial learning, then memory will be more likely to fail. This is known in the jargon as **cue-dependent forgetting.** If we take the classic activity of memorising words from a bilingual list, students will appear to remember the words better if you test through translating with words in the same order as in the original list. If you suddenly test students on that same vocabulary in a different way, for example in a gap-fill task, they are likely to recall the words less well.

The link between memory and language

TAP is one example of the so-called **encoding specificity principle**, according which memories are more successfully retrieved if they are recalled in the same context as when they were originally encoded.

Cognitive psychologists Viorica Marian and Ulric Neisser (the so-called father of cognitive psychology) found that autobiographical memories are more accessible when retrieved in the same language in which they were originally encoded or learned. They asked Russian-English bilinguals to recall specific life experiences in response to word prompts. Participants retrieved more experiences from the Russian-speaking period of their lives when interviewed in Russian and more experiences from the English-speaking period of their lives when interviewed in English (Marian and Neisser, 2000).

The researchers suggest that language is encoded as part of episodic memory (an autobiographical event) which makes the memory trace stronger, and that language at the time of retrieval, like other forms of context, plays a significant role in determining what will be remembered. Memory is tied up with language.

Further research has suggested that when grammar is taught separately from its context, that is, not within the framework of communicative tasks, students recall it better when tested in the same non-communicative fashion. On the other hand, grammar taught communicatively will be better recalled when tested in the context of a communicative event. If you teach by drill, then test by drill and students will perform better. This is what is meant by teaching to the test, so it's pretty clear that tests need to be well designed to match best teaching practice.

An interesting research finding is that if students are prompted that they will need to transfer information to a new situation, they are more likely to do so successfully (Woolridge et al., 2014). So, in general, while it's wise for tests to resemble classroom teaching tasks, if you deliberately create an unfamiliar task and warn students what they will have to do they may well do it better. There is an interesting conundrum here: if you want knowledge to be flexible, it needs to be used in new contexts, but if you make that new context too unpredictable memory performance may be weaker.

Levels of Processing (LOP)

Alongside TAP, there has been a great deal of research for a few decades into **Levels of Processing** (LOP). Unlike TAP, which emphasises type and context of learning, LOP focuses on **semantic processing** of information (processing of meaning) – for example, how superficially or deeply information is learned.

Both approaches assume, as we saw when describing working memory in Chapter 3, that the human mind has a limited capacity for processing information: we cannot notice, pay attention to, process, or remember everything we are exposed to. Thus, in a learning situation, we encode (store in long-term memory) some information, while other information goes unencoded or is encoded less effectively, making it less available for retrieval. Some of what we encode is what we intended to learn. However, other information is encoded incidentally, while our deliberate, intentional focus is elsewhere. Students may or may not, therefore, internalise what the teacher sets out to teach. Every teacher knows this to be true.

LOP researchers have been interested in these various levels of processing and encoding, believing that meaning is even more important than frequency when it comes to memory. In other words, the more meaningful and interesting we can make language, the better it will be recalled. Hundreds of research studies have produced findings on those factors which make encoding more likely. Some of these are described below.

Match up

1. Write a numbered list of twelve words (including two distractors) on the board and read out the definitions of ten of them in random order.

2. Students match the definitions with each item on the board, by writing down the numbers, until only the two distractors are left unmatched.

(Conti and Smith, 2019)

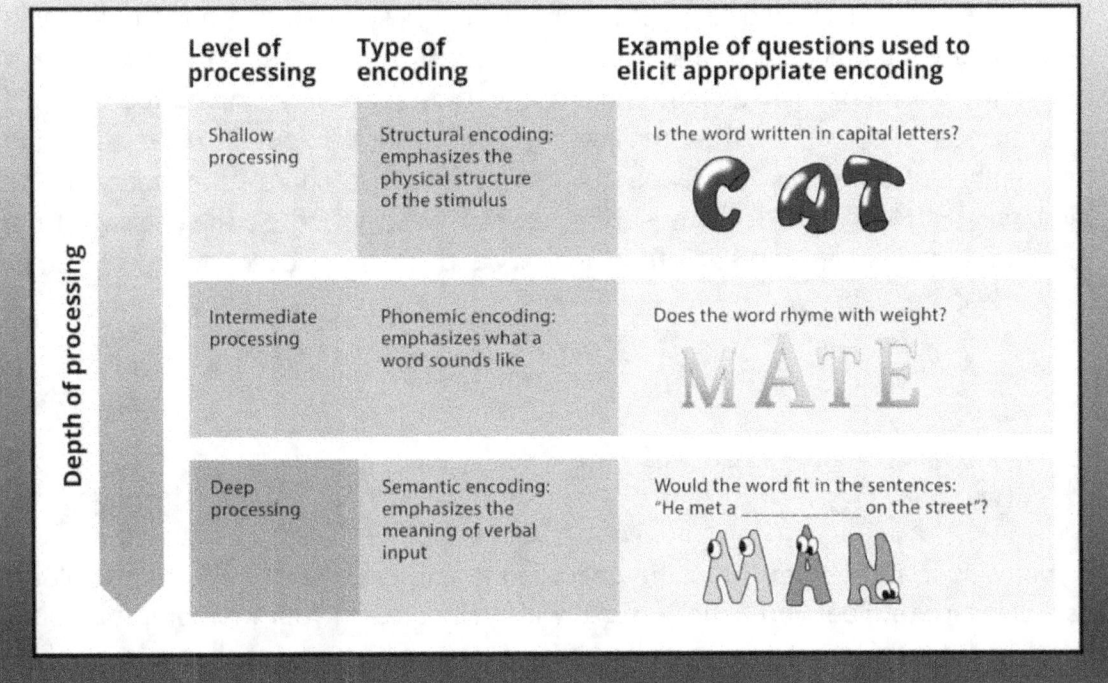

Figure 11.1 Depth of vocabulary processing from Craik and Lockhart (1972)

Repetition

Repetition is one of the fundamental necessities for learning. As Nick Ellis wrote: "the more times a stimulus is encountered, the faster and more accurately it is processed" (Ellis, 2006, p.5). Multiple encounters with language features are almost always required for effective memory encoding. One highly distinctive encounter might stick in long-term memory, particularly if a student thinks back to it a number of times after. Paul Nation has suggested that between 5 and 16 encounters are necessary for a word to stick. Can you think of language you instantly remembered following a distinctive encounter with it? As Nation puts it:

> ...repetition is essential for vocabulary learning because there is so much to know about each word that one meeting with it is not sufficient to gain this information, and because vocabulary items must not only be known, they must be known well so that they can be fluently accessed (Nation, 2001, p.77).

Little and often

With all learning, including language learning, it's best to spread out the learning encounters over time. 'Little and often' works well, as opposed to trying to learn everything in one go. What's more, in a 1970 study Arthur Melton showed not only that repeated encounters with words improved their retention, but also that increasing the number of other words between two study attempts improved memory of the target words (Melton, 1970). This is the concept of interleaving. So the message from this is to spread out encounters with vocabulary and structures over time, mixing other language in between.

The production effect

Do you want to remember the name of someone you just met? Say the name aloud - "It's a pleasure to meet you, Jean" - and it will stick better in your memory. It is usually helpful for learners to *produce* as well as hear or see an item during the learning phase, especially if they are later to retrieve it from memory, using it to express their own meanings. This is called the ***production effect***.

Research shows that learners retain lists of words better when they have read them aloud (for example, Forrin and MacLeod, 2018). It is thought that memory is strengthened since speaking involves three elements: auditory, motor/articulatory (the physical act of speaking) and what's called a self-referential component. The latter is the idea that we process our own voice differently from other people's.

Note, however, that in the classroom this doesn't mean forcing students to say too much before they are ready to do so confidently, but giving them success in producing language in a controlled manner through structured games, question and answer, or drills. It's clear that the act of speaking builds memory.

A production effect experiment

In a study by Rosner, Elman and Shimamura (2013), individuals were presented with pairs of words with the second word gapped (for example, GARBAGE-W_ST_) and asked to generate the second word (for example, WASTE). For another group, individuals simply read word pairs (for example, QUARREL-FIGHT).

Neuroimaging scans showed there was greater brain activation for word pairs where there were gaps than for the word pairs without gaps. The brain areas activated during the generation of completed words included the pre-frontal cortex, medial temporal lobe, and regions in the back of the brain known to be involved in thinking and imagining. This activation led to better performance later when memory was tested.

Spacing, interleaving and blocking

Research is clear that memory encoding happens more effectively when encounters with the information are spaced out over time (for example, Carpenter, 2017). This is called the *spacing effect* or *distributed learning effect.* Between each learning episode the brain has a chance to consolidate the learning (see Chapter 10).

Is there an ideal way to space out learning encounters? It's been suggested that the optimum time lag between learning episodes might be just as a learner is about to forget it (for example, Bjork, 2011), but of course this would be impossible to predict for any or every student in a class. In general, research is not clear about this, particularly when spacing intervals are tested outside laboratories in real classrooms (Rogers and Cheung, 2018). Perhaps the best we can say is that spacing is important (for example, Bahrick et al., 1993), but so is the memorability of each encounter and the depth of processing involved.

Interleaving is used in two senses. On the one hand, it refers to spreading out the repetitions, interspersing new material with old. This has a bearing on curriculum design (see Chapter 16). It also refers to studying different concepts by frequently alternating between them, for example, in the course of one language lesson you might combine the practice of one tense with another.

When you think about it, in terms of curriculum design, interleaving is an inevitable outcome of spacing. If you space out encounters with the same language over a period of weeks, in between these encounters new learning has to take place. To make sure students have enough encounters with words you'll almost certainly need to slim down text book content if there appears to be too much to get through. Students will benefit in the long run. Think in terms of mastery rather than coverage.

Massed practice, is when you study a topic intensively for a limited period, test it, then move on without reviewing it. The research is clear that massed practice without subsequent learning encounters, while useful for last minute exam revision, is not desirable for long term learning. This applies not just to vocabulary learning, but to the acquisition of morphology and syntax.

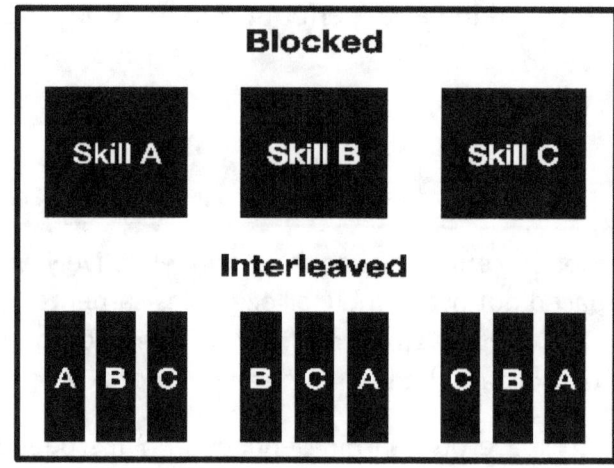

Figure 11.2 Blocking versus interleaving

Blocked study involves studying a particular knowledge point or skill before moving on to another. Technically speaking it's not quite the same as massed practice, because the latter doesn't have to focus on one particular skill or area of knowledge. For example, blocked practice might be focusing only on adverbs, whereas massed practice could focus on a range of language areas over a limited time.

There is a plenty of evidence supporting interleaving over massed practice or blocking in some subject areas, for example maths, but actually very little related specifically to language learning. One recent study by Pan et al. (2019) suggested better retention of verb conjugations when learning was interleaved with other activities. It is reasonable to assume, in general, that the 'little and often' principle applies.

The power of immersion for memory

Although in general learning, the importance of spacing is well known, it's worth mentioning also the power of *immersion* when it comes to language learning. Second language acquisition researchers Laura Collins and colleagues studied the learning outcomes in two versions of a massed (immersion) programme compared with a distributed programme of English as a Second Language (ESL) for French-speaking students of the same age (Collins et al., 1999).

In the immersion programmes, students completed the regular curriculum in French in five months and spent the remaining months learning English. In the distributed programme, the intensive ESL teaching was spread across the full ten months of the school year.

Confirming other studies, they found that the immersion groups achieved better outcomes than the distributed programme group. A clear takeaway is that if students are able to have an immersion experience, their learning will be significantly improved.

Depth of processing for vocabulary learning

Knowing words and chunks of language is the key to success in second language learning (Alderson, 2007). This is more important, for instance, than knowing the rules of grammar. As second language acquisition researcher David Wilkins famously wrote: "Without grammar very little can be conveyed, without vocabulary *nothing* can be conveyed." (Wilkins, 1972). Students often say that lack of vocabulary is the main reason for their difficulty in understanding and using the language (for example, Nation, 2013).

Therefore a prime goal for language teachers is to help students build their *mental lexicon* so they can remember words and phrases for fluent recognition and production.

Norbert Schmitt (2008) explains that to function competently in a language a large vocabulary of 8000—9000 word families is needed for reading, and perhaps 5000—7000 families for speech. But for school students following a four or five year course (for example, the GCSE syllabus in England, Wales and Northern Ireland) a reasonable aim would be between 1000 and 2000 words (Milton, 2006).

Much research into vocabulary learning has shown that vocabulary sticks more easily when it is processed in more elaborate ways. This means not just by knowing what a word means, but knowing what it sounds like, its written appearance, the company it keeps (collocations) and its various forms and meanings. An example of this is the fact that the word 'play' in English can mean various things, and occurs in various forms and contexts (*play, plays, playing, player, played, playful, role-play*, etc.). If we process words 'shallowly' we remember them less well than if we process them 'elaborately' (for example, Craik and Lockhart, 1972 – see Figure 11.1)

'Knowing a word' may be more complicated than you think. Table 11.1 shows how Paul Nation sums up the different dimensions of knowing vocabulary.

Form	☒ spelling
	☒ pronunciation
	☒ morphological knowledge (knowledge about affixation)
Meaning	☒ word-meaning
	☒ the role of context in defining meaning
	☒ synonyms and antonyms
Use	☒ understanding correct usage
	☒ collocations (knowledge of how words combine in natural usage)
	☒ when to use and not use a word

Table 11.1 Nation's (2013) three dimensions of knowing a word

The more connections we can help students to hold in memory, the easier is it for them to understand and generate more words. This is a long term, incremental process. We can't expect students to retain words and chunks with limited exposure.

In addition, some research suggests that when learning conditions are made harder retention can be better. For example, if words are presented in blocked topics, for example, *dress, shirt, shoe, hat*, they are retained less well than when presented in an unthemed fashion, for example, *shoe, apple, radio* and *black*. This is sometimes used as evidence that we should avoid teaching vocabulary from topic lists (see the following section). The concern here is that words from the same topic may interfere with each other in memory.

The research suggests that vocabulary learning needs to include both explicit, intentional learning ('teaching the words') and implicit, incidental learning from comprehensible input. Reading and vocabulary specialist Paul Nation's **_four learning strands_** are a good basis for building vocabulary learning into a curriculum.

1. Meaning-focused input – providing large amounts of comprehensible input in speech and writing.
2. Meaning-focused output – providing opportunities for students to speak.
3. Language-focused learning – getting students to think about the form of the language, for example how verb endings work, how plurals are formed or how nouns are related to verbs.
4. Fluency development – giving students the chance to build up speed of retrieval.

(Nation, 2008)

Did you know...?

Studies show that when we write something down by hand we recall it better than when we type it. For example, in a 2009 study of 61 adults, Timothy Smoker and colleagues found that those who hand wrote a list of 36 words remembered them better after five minutes than those who typed them.

The authors concluded that "...due to the additional context provided by handwriting, we remember target words more accurately when we take the time and effort to write them out than to type them" (Smoker et al., 2009, p. 1746).

More recently, scans have shown that the brain is more active when writing than when typing (Askvik et al., 2020).

Thematic versus semantic clustering of words

Researchers have sought more efficient ways of learning vocabulary from lists. One popular comparison has been made between semantic (topic) and thematic vocabulary clustering types. **Semantic clusters** provide students with groups of words that are related by their meanings. For example, parts of the body, such as *eye, head, ear* and *mouth*. The argument for semantic clusters is appealing. Firstly, the similarity between the words should ease the learning task and secondly, the student should become aware of slight distinctions between the related words. In addition, most of us have been used to learning and teaching words in this way.

Nation (2001) argues that:

1. It requires less effort to learn words in a set.
2. It is easier to retrieve related words from memory.
3. It helps learners see how knowledge can be organised.
4. It reflects the way such information is stored in the brain (so-called **semantic fields**).
5. It makes the meaning of words clearer by helping students to see how they relate to, and may be differentiated from, other words in the set.

But the downside of teaching in this way is that words of similar meaning may cause interference effects in memory. The closer two words are in meaning or association (including synonyms and antonyms), the greater the risk of interference and forgetting.

On the other hand, **thematic clusters** refer to the arrangement of a group of words that belong to a specific knowledge schema. The advantage is thought to be that memory is activated more powerfully when words are related to lived experience or episodes (knowledge schemas). So if you teach a group of words in the context of a lived experience the words should be easier to recall later. Tinkham (1997) suggested that arranging words by general theme in this way can limit the effects of interference between similar words. An example of a thematic cluster would be *sweat-shirt, changing room, tries on, wool* and *salesperson*.

What is the evidence? On the whole, researchers now favour thematic word sets to semantic. Some studies report that semantic grouping is actually worse than presenting lists of totally unrelated words. So if your textbook presents words as semantic clusters you should at least question the validity of this approach, which may just stem from tradition. As Dronjic (2019) points out, thematic clustering is better on the whole than semantic clustering and better also than just listing words randomly.

Does this mean you should stop playing Simon Says to teach parts of the body? Not at all. Don't forget the importance of motivation, distinctiveness and gesture in forming memories! In any case, all researchers agree that learning from lists, although apparently efficient, is a very small part of what learning vocabulary is all about.

Intentional versus incidental vocabulary learning

Intentional learning means deliberate attempts to learn new words. This can be through direct instruction such as call and response flashcard work, matching tasks, gap-fill, or through personalised learning from lists. There is research to suggest that intentional learning is more efficient than picking up vocabulary as you go along (incidental learning) (for example, Webb, 2007). Laufer and Rozovski-Roitblat (2011) found that intentional exercises (for example, practising words out of context, synonym and antonym work, selecting the right meaning from options, writing the words in sentences) led to better recall, both short and long term, than incidental approaches. Meaning-focused output, for example writing new words in sentences, is also a good technique, according to research.

In general terms, intentional, explicit vocabulary learning is most useful in the earlier stages of learning a language and will result in better short and long term retention.

Fluent vocabulary retrieval

Most teachers think of fluency in terms of speaking naturally or smoothly, but in the research it is also used about the other skills of listening, reading and writing. Retrieval of vocabulary from memory needs to be fluent (fast), especially when students are speaking. This takes time, but you can devote lesson time to tasks specifically aimed at developing fluent retrieval. Nation (2014) suggests these principles when planning fluency tasks:

1. The focus should be on receiving or conveying meaning.
2. There is no unfamiliar language, and content is largely familiar (thus limiting extraneous cognitive load).
3. There is some pressure or encouragement to perform at a faster than usual speed.
4. There is a large amount of input or output.

The overriding principle for maximising vocabulary learning is to increase the amount of engagement students have with words and chunks. Add in the role of repetition, spacing, interleaving, retrieval (through repeated recycling of words and chunks) and memorability, then you have the basis for a vocabulary curriculum. A curriculum in which students get regular exposure to texts containing high frequency language will allow students to remember, recognise and use the words they need.

As mentioned elsewhere, a good general principle is the idea that 'less is more'. In a school setting with limited time, for most students it's wiser to recycle a relatively limited repertoire of high frequency vocabulary than attempt to 'cover' a much larger repertoire superficially. This is why it is sometimes advised to avoid a topic-based approach to curriculum design since this might result in the important recycling of high frequency words and chunks being sacrificed to the teaching of more obscure topic-specific vocabulary.

Spot the nonsense

Absurd content amuses students, arouses attention and potentially makes language more memorable.

1. Tell the class they are going to listen to sentences in which you planted words that do not fit the context, as they verge on the absurd: statements like, *This morning I showered in the car* or *Last night for dinner I ate my homework.*

2. As the text is read, students write on mini-whiteboards P for Possible or I Impossible.

3. Say each sentence again as students note down a/the better alternative.

Conti and Smith (2019)

Using texts for deep processing

Depth of processing is encouraged if students get regular opportunities to hear and see vocabulary in meaningful texts. These could be encountered during lessons with the teacher or through personal listening and reading. This type of ***incidental learning*** of vocabulary is vital for building long-term memory. A study by Arndt and Woore (2018) demonstrated the value of students reading blogs and watching videos for enlarging the breadth and depth of their vocabulary. Glossing texts (i.e. adding some new words in the margin) is a useful aid to personal reading, reducing the cognitive load associated with the task. Research suggests that the nearer any translation can be to the glossed words, the better (thus avoiding the divided attention effect).

When working orally with texts take every opportunity to recycle chunks through question-answer routines and other oral drills, linking to written practice of the same chunks. Tasks such as gap-fill, translation, matching words to definitions, making up definitions and summarising all encourage deep processing. At more advanced levels, morphological exercises perform the same role, such as relating verbs and nouns with similar roots.

Sight words

These are what you might call the service words in a language, roughly 200 in number. They often perform a grammatical role and can easily slip below students' attention if you don't focus on them adequately in lessons. Below are some points about sight words.

- They appear frequently, making up around 50 % of the words in a typical text.
- They are mostly adjectives, adverbs, pronouns, prepositions, conjunctions and the most common verbs.
- They are usually skipped when reading in your first language as they are recognised automatically. When two of them occur together (for example, *I go **to the** cinema with my mum)*, they are both skipped.
- Are not easily represented by pictures, for example, *the* and *or*.

The Keyword Method

The so-called **keyword method** for learning vocabulary involves thinking of a first language word which has a similar sound or an image associated with the new word being learned. This engages knowledge schemas from long-term memory, so students and teachers can make use of as many connections as possible when new vocabulary is introduced: cognates, similar-sounding words or visual associations.

There are two stages to the keyword method:

1. Link the target language word with an English one (for example, the Spanish *carta* sounds like the English *cart*). *Cart* is the keyword.

2. Link the keyword with the English meaning of the target language word by forming an interactive image (for example, *carta* means *letter*, so you could visualise a letter inside a cart).

Other examples: the French for swimming pool is *piscine* – imagine what an unsociable person might do in the pool. Sometimes people are encouraged to remember the Japanese word *arigatou* ('thank you') by thinking of an alligator.

Studies have shown that the keyword method significantly aids retention (for example, Pressley et al., 1982; Sommer and Gruneberg, 2002), but we would suggest that, while it may be useful at the margins, it should not be relied upon to a great degree. Other principles such as repetition, spacing, distinctiveness, depth of processing and regular exposure to comprehensible input are far more significant.

Learning from lists

When you learned a new language did you keep a vocabulary book? Did you have lists of words to memorise? Setting words to memory from a bilingual list of so-called paired associates has often been frowned upon by teachers using communicative approaches, yet remains common practice in modern language classrooms and in countries where rote learning is the norm, for example China. It doesn't seem to align with how we learn languages naturally, but actually there is research support for the practice (for example, Lessard-Clouston, 2013).

Note that accepting the use of bilingual word lists assumes it's useful to bring in first language translations to help students remember. This may seem to go against the view that it's better to avoid using the first language in lessons at all costs. But we would argue that you sometimes need to use the first language to clarify meaning, and doing so allows students to notice similarities and differences between the two languages. In addition, showing examples of the first language helps develop general literacy.

Beginners with little knowledge to draw on are those most likely to benefit in learning from lists. The availability of vocabulary apps has made the task more appealing for many. The question still arises, however, to what extent students are prepared to spend time learning vocabulary and which other language tasks this displaces. Is twenty minutes spent in rote learning words better spent doing something else?

Summary of useful vocabulary acquisition tasks

This list is based on a chapter by González-Fernández and Norbert Schmitt in Loewen and Sato (2017).

- ⊠ Provide rich and varied language experiences through the four skills, including through independent work beyond the classroom.

- ⊠ Provide multiple encounters with words, compensating for any lack thereof in textbooks.

- ⊠ Provide instruction of words using clear explanations, explicit methods, simple definitions, then make sure words are recycled in various contexts. Different words may require different teaching methods, for instance flashcards work well for simple concrete nouns, collocations for adjectives.

- ⊠ Teach strategies for independent learning, for example explain how students can use morpheme clues, infer from context and use dictionaries.

- ⊠ Promote the interest and involvement of students in vocabulary learning, for example by keeping a tally of test scores or using a competitive element.

- ⊠ Extensive reading and listening help develop vocabulary. Use graded readers if you can find them.

- ⊠ For collocational knowledge and restrictions on use, massive exposure is needed. Provide as much as possible at higher levels.

- ⊠ Consider setting awkward words to learn before class so they are better understood when seen in context.

The power of gestures

Research has repeatedly shown that when we use bodily actions or gestures with words we are more likely to recall them (Macedonia, 2014). Psychologists call this the *enactment effect*. For example, German researchers conducted a laboratory experiment with 21 subjects using an invented language. They heard concrete and abstract words and their translations under one of three conditions:

1. with a video showing a symbolic gesture of the word's meaning, which they imitated;

2. with a picture illustrating the word's meaning, which they traced in the air;

3. with no gestures or pictures.

The subjects did paper and pencil translation tests two and six months after learning. These showed that learning with gestures was significantly better than the other conditions (Mayer et al., 2015).

In technical terms, it seems that multi-modal encoding during enactment establishes deeper memory traces, which benefits long term retrieval performance.

Even watching a teacher make gestures is an aid to memory (Hall, 2020). Gesturing is a fundamental part of the AIM language learning method used by some teachers, particularly in Canada.

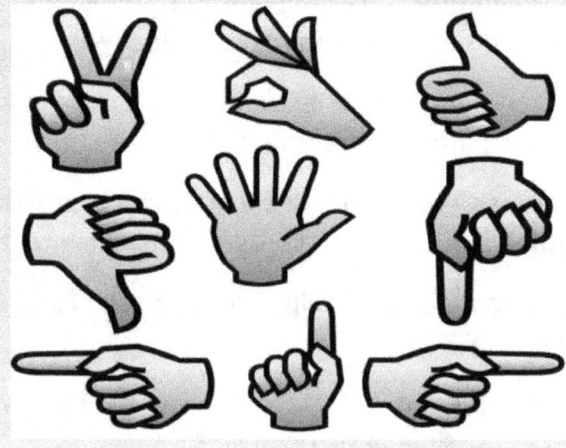

Summary

- ✓ When we learn something, our memories record not only the information learned, but the cognitive and perceptual processes that were involved when the learning took place. If we recreate the cues at the time of learning, recall will be better.
- ✓ If we don't supply the opportunity to retrieve memories in new contexts, learning will be inhibited. But on the whole it's wise to match tests to the activities carried out previously in class.
- ✓ Spaced repetition of vocabulary is vital.
- ✓ Levels of Processing research suggests that meaning is even more important than frequency when it comes to memory. The more meaningful and interesting we can make language, the more deeply it will be processed and subsequently better recalled.
- ✓ Vocabulary will be better recalled the more elaborately it is processed. Learning from lists is far from enough. Better to practise vocabulary in texts and meaningful activities.
- ✓ The keyword method is a well-known memory technique which can enhance vocabulary recall.
- ✓ Vocabulary learning happens gradually, both via intentional and incidental routes. For beginners, explicit teaching of vocabulary is important, using a variety of means.

For reflection

- What factors should you take into account when designing an assessment?
- What is the value of having students read aloud during lessons?
- How can we get students to process vocabulary more deeply to build memory?
- To what extent does your textbook or curriculum plan take account of spaced learning principles?
- What issues need to be kept in mind if you set vocabulary to learn at home?

Further reading and viewing

- Craik, F. I. M., & Lockhart, R. S. (1972). Levels of processing: A framework for memory research. *Journal of Verbal Learning and Verbal behavior, 11*, 671-684. Available at:
  wixtedlab.ucsd.edu/publications/Psych%20218/Craik_Lockhart_1972.pdf
- McLeod, S. A. (2007). *Levels of processing*. Available at:
  simplypsychology.org/levelsofprocessing.html
- Nation, I.S.P. (2015). Principles guiding vocabulary learning through extensive reading. *Reading in a Foreign Language, 27* (1), 136-145. Available at:
  nflrc.hawaii.edu/rfl/April2015/discussion/nation.pdf
- Robert Bjork talks (in 2012) about spaced practice. Available at:
  youtube.com/watch?v=TTo35X2rqls
- Amy Hogan talks (in 2017) about LOP. Available at:
  youtube.com/watch?v=TTo35X2rqls
- See ncelp.org and search for their presentations about vocabulary learning.

Prospective memory and metamemory | 12

Key concepts

In this chapter we consider:

- **Three types of prospective memory**
- **How prospective memory is thought to work**
- **Two processes in prospective memory performance**
- **Metamemory - do metamemory strategies help you remember more?**

What is prospective memory?

It's an area of memory research not very familiar to teachers, but one which has significant implications. Up to now in the book we've been talking about what psychologists call *retrospective memory*. This is what we normally think of when referring to memory – encoding, storing and retrieving thoughts from the past. *Prospective memory* has been described as 'remembering to remember' or, to put it more technically, the 'realisation of delayed intention'. It's when you think ahead or make a plan for the future – when you make a mental note to remind you to do something, if you like. When prospective memory fails, you forget to carry out what you had planned to do.

Laboratory research suggests that children and young adults are better at remembering to remember than older adults. In children, poor prospective memory can cause problems in school, for example when a child forgets to give their parents a permission slip for a school trip, fails to turn up to a detention or bring homework to class (Kvavilashvili et al., 2001). It's up to the teacher to decide when these omissions are down to prospective memory failure or something else!

According to a study by Uttl et al. (2018) both prospective and retrospective memory correlate moderately highly with intelligence, working memory and processing speed.

Lower-achieving students are likely to be more forgetful. So we could say that people with good memories tend to be less forgetful!

Why is prospective memory important?

Most human behaviour is **_goal-directed._** This means that we perform actions in order to achieve an objective at an appropriate time. For instance, we mark a set of exercise books on Sunday, knowing that we intend to hand them back on Monday morning, or we do those last minute photocopies in the knowledge that the next lesson is about to start.

So prospective memory tasks are part and parcel of daily life. They may be relatively mundane, but in some cases they create life-or-death situations. For example, a patient may forget to take medication or an airline pilot fail to perform safety procedures. So failure of prospective memory may have fatal consequences, or it may just be embarrassing, for example when you fail to carry out a promise, or forgetting to attend a parents' evening.

Interestingly, our reaction to failures of prospective memory in others varies. If an elderly person forgets to carry out a goal you might just put it down to age-related forgetfulness, whereas with a student we are perhaps justified in being more suspicious.

Deadly failures of prospective memory

In the book _Memory_ (2020), Michael W. Eysenck points out that nearly 40 children a year die of heatstroke in cars in the USA because of prospective memory failures by parents or carers forgetting to take their child out of the car.

Advice for avoiding prospective memory failures includes:

- Use external memory aids such as mobile phone alerts.
- Avoid multitasking when one of the tasks is critical.
- Carry out crucial tasks now instead of putting them off until later.
- Create reminder cues that stand out and put them in a difficult-to-miss spot.
- Link the target task to a habit that you have already established.

Three types of prospective memory

A big difference between retrospective and prospective memory is that the former usually focuses on what we know and may contain a lot of information, whereas the latter is usually focused on *what* we intend to do and *when* we intend to do it.

This is why psychologists sometimes refer to three types of prospective memory: ***event-based*, *time-based*** and ***activity-based*** prospective memory. Event-based prospective memory involves remembering to perform certain actions when specific circumstances occur. For example, seeing a student in the corridor reminds you they have to hand in their work at lunchtime. Time-based prospective memory involves remembering to perform an action at a particular point in time. For example, noticing that it's 10:30 a.m. reminds you of your meeting with the head teacher in 15 minutes.

For language teachers it is activity-based prospective memory which is of greatest significance – remembering to do something after completing an activity, for example attaching a file to an email message. For a language student it might be remembering to check written accuracy after completing a paragraph, remembering to use a model template provided for a written task or to write a plan for starting an exam essay.

How does prospective memory work?

Because prospective memory involves remembering to carry out an intention, it requires three elements:

- Episodic memory. Remembering when and how you were told to carry out a task. For example, when the teacher said you had to write down key phrases before starting to write a short essay.
- Declarative memory. Knowledge of the task to be done. For example, being clear what is needed for the essay to be successfully completed.
- Retrospective memory. Being able to recall what the task was exactly. For example, knowing that the oral presentation has to be a minute long.

These are supplemented by what psychologists call ***supervisory executive functions*** (think of the Central Executive we discussed back in Chapter 3) – bringing all the elements together. All of these are controlled by the frontal lobe of the brain. We know this because brain scanning reveals a slight increase in blood flow to the frontal lobe in participants completing prospective memory tasks which involve recalling a planned action, while performing other tasks.

Evidence suggests, perhaps unsurprisingly, that having to think about a future task interferes with ongoing activity, especially if the future intention is not totally clear in a person's mind (Hicks et al., 2005). You can imagine the confused, perhaps poorly-organised student with a range of different intentions interfering with their current task.

A debate in the research literature on prospective memory surrounds the extent to which it's possible to monitor a planned intention before it is carried out. Can students do anything to keep the intention in mind? Or is this beyond their control and they just have to hope the planned intention pops into their minds every now and again?

Two processes in prospective memory performance

The so-called **Preparatory Attentional Memory** (PAM) theory suggests there are two types of processes involved in successful prospective memory performance. The first involves a monitoring process that begins when a person constructs an intention which is then maintained until it's performed. For example, a student may intend to check they have conjugated a verb correctly in writing when they get to the end of a sentence or paragraph. Keeping that intention in mind takes up attentional resources which may compete with other priorities at that precise moment, such as spelling a word correctly.

The second process involves using elements of retrospective memory. This involves differentiating between the desired intention (wanting to check that verb later) and unwanted thoughts, in an attempt to keep focus on the goal and not the other distracting thoughts. Retrospective memory is needed in order to recall the need to use the monitoring process to be able to perform the planned action.

According to this theory, prospective memory should be enhanced when complete attention is given to the desired task. When attention is divided among multiple tasks original intentions may be forgotten. This suggests that anything we can do to help students focus on fulfilling their planned intention should be valuable. This could mean quite formal reminders built into lesson plans, or just subtle ones for students who are less likely to remember what they have to do. Especially for more forgetful students, we should try to avoid giving them competing tasks which may distract them from their intended goal at the time.

The importance of importance

Psychologists have researched the degree to which the perceived importance of something affects how likely it is you will remember to do it. One way to increase perceived importance is to offer a reward for doing a task. Meacham and Singer (1977) found that fellow researchers were more likely to return letters if they were told they would be paid to do so.

Sommerville et al. (1983) manipulated importance by varying the attractiveness of the intention to be remembered. They told young children to remember either to buy sweets (candy) or clean the dishes. The children remembered the more attractive task, suggesting that the attractiveness of the task increased its importance.

Getting students to believe a task is important is clearly an important factor in whether the work will be done, in class or at home. A simple "this is really important" can help, but ultimately a student's perception of importance comes down to a variety of factors – perceived attractiveness of a task, a reward associated with it (a sticker, prize or merit), how much the subject and teacher are valued, not to mention the general culture of the school.

Prospective memory in everyday life

One reason why people tend not to forget future intentions is that they spend so much time thinking about prospective memory. In a study Anderson and McDaniel (2019) found that prospective memory occupied our thoughts 13-15% of the time. Of these thoughts, 39% were 'externally cued' by something in the environment, while 61% were internally cued (meaning they just popped into people's heads).

A practical takeaway here is the common scenario of asking students to check their written essays for errors, range of language and coherence. If they attempt to do all these things at once they will be less successful than the student who systematically focuses on one task at a time. It's a good idea, therefore, to advise students to re-read repeatedly, each time focusing on one aspect. In this way they are more likely to improve their work and remember accurate forms, effective language and essay structure. Advice is not really enough, though. Students need training and practice on this in class, just as they do with so many activities.

Another way to help students use prospective memory successfully is to get them to make of use of their 'auxiliary working memory' – make notes! In practical terms, this could mean requiring students to write down at the top of the first page of their essay a number of reminders. These could include language expressions they intend to use, the aspects they need to check at the end (accuracy, range, coherence) and even time prompts, such as "only spend one hour on the essay". Each time a goal has been achieved, the reminder note can be ticked off.

Metamemory

The next part of this chapter concerns the concept of *metamemory*, an area which has been increasingly studied by psychologists in recent years. Metamemory is a branch of metacognition. Just as metacognition is 'thinking about thinking', metamemory can be described as 'thinking about memory' or even 'knowing about memory'. The term was first coined by John Flavell in 1970. It's about being aware of how your own memory operates, along with strategies you can use to help you remember better. For example, when a person says they are good at remembering maps and directions, but poor at remembering faces, that person is making a statement concerning metamemory knowledge. Just as metacognitive strategies can help make students better listeners or readers, could metamemory strategies help students remember more effectively?

In everyday life we use metamemory a lot. For example, you might believe you can remember all ten items you need from the supermarket without writing a list. Another person will believe they need to write down the items in case they forget. For students in school, metamemory plays a role when weighing up how well they think they will recall what they have learned.

As two researchers in this field put it: "...people's memory monitoring plays a pivotal role in the effectiveness of their self-regulated learning and retrieval" (Dunlosky and Thiede, 2013, p.283). In other words, students who are aware of and monitoring what they can remember are more likely to carry out tasks successfully. Language learners like this know how much they can rely on memory and how much they need to look up.

In addition, people's behaviour is influenced by feelings about their mental abilities (Tulving and Madigan, 1970). This could mean, for example, that a student who has an inflated view of their memory may decide to work less. Conversely, a student who doubts their memory ability may over-rely on outside sources.

The research on metamemory has produced four significant findings:

1. Younger children up to the age of 10 or so have poor metamemory. They find it hard to monitor the contents of their memory, estimate the resources needed to carry out

a task, select suitable strategies and monitor their own learning (Schneider and Pressley, 1997). With age metamemory improves, and people deliberately make greater use of memory techniques (Flavell, 1979), but even adults tend to suffer from illusions about the capacity of their memories. So language students may overestimate what they will recall in a test situation.

2. Metamemory develops continuously and by increments with age, from pre-school through to puberty and beyond. It is not clear whether this continues through adulthood, but it seems that improved metamemory is associated with increasing skill in a particular area. For example, as students develop language proficiency, it is likely they become more aware of how their memory works.

3. Metamemory can develop both through individual, self-generated problem solving and explicit training. Self-generated feedback, along with feedback from others, increases knowledge of the contents of memory and tasks they need to do. Modelling by the teacher allows students to emulate how an expert works. Just as with metacognitive training, by getting students to think like you they will become more expert and aware of how to exploit memory. In practice, this could mean modelling how you deliver an oral presentation, explaining how you drew on language and content from memory.

4. The more students know about memory, the more likely it is that they will be able to regulate their performance. So we suggest you share this sort of information with classes – tell them about issues such as working memory, cognitive load, declarative and procedural memory, and so on (not necessarily using that terminology!). A better understanding of how memory works may improve students' study techniques, performance and memory.

Sharing memory strategies

This is an idea from Bilbrough (2011). Give students a list of about 10 target language words or chunks with their English translation. Tell students to study them individually for five minutes, then move on to another activity. Later in the lesson, show the English translations and ask students to recall the target language vocabulary.

Then move on to another activity. A bit later, get students in pairs to remember as many words as possible and discuss any strategies they used to remember them. Did they, for example, say them out loud or in their heads, create an image, put the word in context, link it to another word or personalise it in some way? Then discuss strategies as a whole class.

Metamemory takeaways

What other practical implications can we draw from this? First, as language teachers, we can encourage students to think about what strategies and techniques help them remember language. This is bound to involve teaching traditional study techniques, for example memorising vocabulary using the Write-Look-Cover-Repeat method or using mnemonics. Students can be encouraged to think about what works for them. Do they enjoy memorising from lists? Does rote learning help them use the same language in other contexts later? How successful are they at estimating what score they'll get in a test?

Second, we can help students have a realistic view of how good their memories are. The research shows clearly that people overestimate their memory performance (Kornell, 2011). This means giving students regular opportunities to use their memories in tests. If tests are too easy and don't require students to revise they will not learn about the limitations of their memories. In addition, spontaneous on-the-spot tests of retrieval will let students see how good their memories are. You could consider assessing students' oral abilities without any prior warning. What can they really remember without special revision?

Do metamemory strategies help you remember more?

Research in this area suggests they do (for example, Schneider, 2017), although it seems that older learners are able to use metamemory strategies better than younger ones. Put another way, what people know about their memory frequently influences how they try to remember and how well they do so. However, although older school children know a lot about common strategies, there is evidence that many adolescents and adults (including university students) have little knowledge of some more complex, important, and powerful memory strategies such as those related to the processing of written text. The classic case in point is that self-quizzing on textual information is more productive for retention that just rereading or highlighting key passages.

Summary

✓ Prospective memory is when you make a mental note to remind you to do something. When prospective memory fails, you forget to carry out what you'd planned to do. Failures can lead to consequences of all sorts, some of them dire.

✓ Psychologists sometimes refer to three types of prospective memory: event-based, time-based and activity-based prospective memory. The latter type has most significance for language learning.

✓ The perceived importance of a task affects the likelihood it will be done. Teachers can manipulate how students perceive tasks.

✓ Guidance can be given to students to help them improve their prospective memory, get tasks done successfully and learn more.

✓ Metamemory is a branch of metacognition. It can be thought of as 'thinking about memory' or even 'knowing about memory'.

✓ Metamemory improves with age, up to adolescence at least. Whatever the age, people tend to overestimate their memory abilities, which can have side-effects if students fail to do enough work, for example.

✓ Metamemory can be improved through self-generated activity and with the help of teacher explanation and modelling. Specific techniques can be taught, just as with metacognitive strategies. These can help students remember more.

For reflection

- What mnemonics have you found useful when learning or teaching a language?
- What strategies could you employ to support more forgetful language learners?
- To what extent do you think it's useful to get students to explore the topic of memory in general?

Further reading and viewing

- Dunlosky, J. & Thiede, K.W. (2013). Metamemory. *The Oxford Handbook of Cognitive Psychology,* 283-298. Available at: scholarworks.boisestate.edu/cgi/viewcontent.cgi?article=1145&context=cifs_fa cpubs
- Walter, S. & Meier, B. (2014). How important is importance for prospective memory? A review. *Frontiers in Psychology*. Available at: frontiersin.org/articles/10.3389/fpsyg.2014.00657/full
- Paul Merritt gives a presentation (in 2018) about metamemory. Available at: youtube.com/watch?v=zWDNIsfpKcY&t=325s
- Rebekah Smith talks (in 2015) about her work on prospective memory. Available at: youtube.com/watch?v=akE90omC4K0

Learnability

13

Key concepts

In this chapter we consider:

- **Developmental readiness and natural orders of acquisition**
- **Processability**
- **Transfer effects from one language to another**
- **Pienemann's Processability Theory**
- **The learnability of different words**
- **The relative learnability of phonology, vocabulary and grammar**

Developmental readiness

Experienced teachers are well aware of the fact that students pick up some vocabulary and grammatical structures far more easily than others. Some language just sticks more easily. Why might this be? One thing the research literature on second language learning has shown is that the language we remember depends in part on how *learnable* it is. What does this mean?

To start with, research evidence suggests that the sequence in which humans acquire the morphemes in their first language is predictable (for example, verb endings like *-ed* on the end of past tense verbs in English) (Brown, 1973). From the 1970s research was carried out to show that the same applied to second language learning (for example, Dulay and Burt, 1974). This became known as the *Natural Order Hypothesis*, the idea being that learners acquire grammar at their own rate and in a similar order. It is sometimes said, therefore, that language learners have an *in-built syllabus* which affects what they can and can't easily acquire.

But this is a much debated and messy area of research and more recently doubt has been cast on the extent to which natural orders apply in second language acquisition (discussed in Kwon, 2005). Perhaps other factors such as frequency, inherent difficulty of grammar and differences between the first and second language come into play (see below). Others have pointed out that the social context may have an effect on sequence of acquisition, for example whether the language being learned is in a formal classroom or in other social settings (Ellis, 2015).

However, it is safe to say one thing: teaching can only have at best a partial effect on the order in which learners acquire grammar. Remember that by *acquire* we mean possess the internalised (automatised) ability to use grammar, not just explain it. In other words the grammatical system needs to be in procedural long-term memory and this takes time.

In sum, whether students are immune to the order in which you teach grammar or not, it's important to have a sense of whether students are ***developmentally ready*** to acquire new grammar.

Processability

How easy it is for students to consciously process a grammar point also depends on the number and complexity of mental operations needed in understanding and applying it. We considered how the number and interactivity of elements affects ease of learning in Chapter 6.

For instance, adjectival use in French requires four steps: (1) knowing the gender of the noun; (2) knowing if it's singular or plural; (3) knowing the adjective endings and (4) knowing the position of the adjective in relation to its associated noun (which also means knowing which adjectives are regular or irregular).

On the other hand, forming *si*-clauses in French takes more steps and requires more complex knowledge. You need to know the acceptable combination of tenses, the verbs being used (for example, do they have regular or irregular stems) and the verb endings required for each subject pronoun. This calls on a great deal of prior knowledge, so requires far greater mental processing.

In terms of vocabulary learning, some words are harder to process than others. They may be difficult to perceive in the continuous stream of speech, carry less obvious meaning (sight words), be short or be misleadingly similar to first language words ('false friends'). Research suggests that if some items are not brought specifically to learners' attention, they are not acquired.

So natural, communicative approaches to language teaching may not create the context for sufficiently deep processing of some language items. Specific research studies have shown that concrete words are easier to learn and less easy to forget than abstract words (for example, Walker and Hume, 1999). This is because it's thought to be easier to visualise concrete words and put them in a variety of memorable contexts. In addition, words which are phonologically closer to the first language are better recalled, as are shorter words (see Chapter 4).

Transfer effects

If you analyse your own use of a second language, how much is it influenced by the grammar and vocabulary of your first language(s)? Quite a lot, we suspect. Research suggests that the differences and similarities between the first and second language can affect the acquisition of a structure in both a positive way (if the structures are the same across the two languages) or negative way (if they are different). This phenomenon is referred to in research as **positive** or **negative transfer**. This is a type of interference effect, but not those we described in Chapters 8 and 11 where similar items are confused in memory. Transfer has to be kept in mind when weighing up learnability and how you go about teaching a structure.

If we go back to adjective agreement in French, the fact that English nouns and adjectives do not have masculine and feminine endings makes agreement harder for English learners to acquire. Similarly, object pronouns in French are slow to develop since they require not only knowledge of gender, but also different positioning in relationship to the verb. (They usually come before the verb, not after.) Not surprisingly, many students struggle with adjectival agreement and object pronoun use for many years and never get to fully internalise them at all.

When it comes to vocabulary, we have already noted that learnability varies. Table 13.1, based on work by Paul Nation, helps to evaluate how learnable a new word might be, bearing in mind its meaning, form and use (L1 = first language). Remember that vocabulary acquisition is not subject to the same age or developmental stage constraints as grammar acquisition. For more on vocabulary learning, see Chapter 11.

Meaning	Form and meaning	Is the word a loan word in the L1?
	Concept and referents	Is there an L1 word with roughly the same meaning?
		Does the word fit into the same sets as an L1 word of similar meaning?
	Associations	
Form	Spoken form	Can learners repeat the word accurately if they hear it?
	Written form	Can learners write the word correctly if they hear it?
	Word parts	Can learners identify known affixes in the word?
Use	Grammatical functions	Does the word fit into predictable grammar patterns?
		Does the word have the same collocations in the L1?
	Collocation	Does the word have the same restrictions on its use as its L1 equivalent(s)?
	Constraints on use	

Table 13.1 Learnability: how hard are words to learn? (adapted from Nation, 2008)

Pienemann's Processability Theory

The basic idea underlying second language acquisition researcher Manfred Pienemann's *Processability Theory* is that at any stage of development a learner can produce and comprehend only those second language linguistic forms which the current state of the 'language processor' in the brain can handle. A student may be ready to acquire a new structure, or not ready. This varies from language to language, and from one individual to another.

A real difficulty, however, is determining the developmental stage a student is at (Meisel et al., 1981). Even measuring a student's current ability is not easy. How many error-free examples are needed in spontaneous speech or writing to decide if a student has internalised a grammatical form? Knowing if a student is ready or not for a structure is therefore hard to gauge and, in the end, comes down to the teacher's knowledge of each class and each student. In reality, because the range of natural aptitude and achievement in any class is considerable, deciding when to move on is bound to be a compromise.

Textbooks can compound the difficulty. They typically work through grammatical structures in a set order which may correspond poorly with the needs of individual classes and students. The same structures may be reviewed every few weeks or from one year to the next, but this degree of distribution is inadequate for many students when it comes to building long-term memory. Curriculum design and teacher pedagogy needs to take into account any possible mismatch between the grammar being taught and students' developmental readiness to understand and use it. An important takeaway for language teachers is that, because a traditional grammatical syllabus fails to take account of a student's current state of second language development, you have to select the most important structures, supplement the text book and build in more practice.

To build memory it's better to limit the repertoire of language and practise it more intensively. Less is more.

Grammar, vocabulary and phonology

It's generally accepted that you need both grammar and vocabulary to make progress in a language, but are both equally learnable? The research strongly suggests that people of any age can learn new vocabulary successfully. Indeed, younger learners may have no great advantage in this regard. On the other hand, it seems that the *system* of the language (its grammar) is harder to acquire for older learners. It takes an awful lot of language input for students to acquire that ability to master grammatical patterns without having to think of them. Words can enter long-term memory far more easily than rules.

In addition, our procedural memory of the phonological system of the language (being able to pronounce well) is very age-sensitive. Older learners may know a lot of words, but they often pronounce them inaccurately. It seems that the phonology of our first language(s) is so ingrained that it's hard to dislodge. What's more, very young humans are particularly sensitive to sounds.

To get around the difficulty of internalising grammar, some researchers, writers and teachers (including ourselves) suggest that combining vocabulary and grammar through a chunking approach makes learning easier, particularly for students learning a language in school settings. As a reminder, this is termed a lexicogrammatical approach (combining lexis – vocabulary – with grammar) to provide learners with lots of ready-made language chunks which they can learn and manipulate communicatively. For more about the advantages of chunking see Chapter 8.

Frequency is not always enough

As we've seen before, when it comes to learning and remembering language, frequency of exposure helps a lot, but this is not always enough to get learners to remember. A well-known example mentioned by Slabakova et al. (2020) is the fact that many learners of English forget to use the 's' on the end of present tense verbs, for instance they might say *he learn* instead of he *learns*. Yet they hear and read it a huge number of times.

Why is this? We aren't sure, but it could just be that it isn't ***salient*** to people, that is they don't notice it because it doesn't seem important for conveying meaning. In Bill VanPatten's Input Processing hypothesis (VanPatten, 1996 – see Chapter 8), it's claimed that learners focus on lexical items, not functional morphemes such as verb endings or adjectival agreements. Pienemann says that relating nouns to verb endings is just hard for learners whose first language is English, for example.

This suggests that teachers need to really highlight those items which are harder or apparently less salient for students.

Did you know...?

Very young infants, and even babies in the womb, are able to differentiate between the phonemes of their mother's language and another language.

Research by Christine Moon and colleagues has shown that the vowel sounds a baby in utero locks on to are the loudest, namely their mother's.

In a study, 40 infants, about 30 hours old and an even mix of girls and boys, were studied in Tacoma and Stockholm (Moon et al., 2013). While still in the nursery, the babies listened to vowel sounds in their native tongue and in other languages.

Their interest in the sounds was captured by how long they sucked on a pacifier (dummy) that was wired into a computer measuring the babies' reaction to the sounds. Longer or shorter sucking for unfamiliar or familiar sounds is evidence for learning, because it indicates that infants can differentiate between the sounds heard in utero.

In both countries, the babies at birth sucked longer for the unfamiliar language than they did for their mothers' native tongue.

Summary

- ✓ At a given point in time students may not be developmentally ready to acquire a grammar structure you teach. They may be able to explain the rule, but not use it spontaneously in speech or writing. Processability Theory claims that, at any stage of second language development, a learner can produce and understand only those linguistic forms which the current state of the language processor in the brain is able to deal with.
- ✓ The inherent difficulty of some grammatical structures means they are less likely to find their way into long-term procedural memory.
- ✓ Interference effects from the first language can affect how well vocabulary and grammar is remembered.
- ✓ In general vocabulary is easier to recall than the rules of the language's system (its grammar). Adults find the latter harder than the former. Similarly, adults find accurate pronunciation harder than younger learners.
- ✓ A lexicogrammatical approach allows students to manipulate language chunks communicatively.

For reflection

- In the language(s) you teach, which areas of language seem to be the least *learnable*? What did you find difficult to learn yourself?
- Are certain age groups more likely to benefit from grammar teaching than others? What is your experience of this so far?
- To what extent do you anticipate difficulties for students by considering the differences between the first and second language? Can you think of specific examples?
- How important is it to teach students to pronounce well? How much should we tolerate inaccuracy?

Further reading and viewing

- Kwon, E-Y. (2005). The "Natural Order" of Morpheme Acquisition: A Historical Survey and Discussion of Three Putative Determinants.
- Pienemann, M. (1998). *Language processing and second language development: Processability theory.* Amsterdam/Philadelphia: John Benjamins.
- Ruby Sallah talks (in 2020) about Pienemann's Processability Theory. Available at: https://www.youtube.com/watch?v=s2duRA7Vzdg&t=610s

The emotional factors affecting memory

14

Key concepts

In this chapter we consider:

- ☒ **Motivation, including the importance of curiosity, self-efficacy and other theories of motivation**
- ☒ **The role of anxiety and stress**
- ☒ **Growth mindset**
- ☒ **Emotional intensity**

Motivation

You might think we've left it until late in the book to talk about something more important than brain architecture, working memory, cognitive load and so on. Researchers have suggested that, alongside language learning aptitude, motivation is the key to success. Teachers know only too well how emotional states, motivation and desire to learn affect students' learning. These are key to everything. Less learning happens and fewer memories are formed if students are just not motivated to learn in the first place, or if they are stressed, anxious or plain disruptive. Much research has been carried out over the years on how these factors influence learning and memory.

If students are to pay attention and remember language they clearly need to be motivated to do so. Neuroscience research tells us that pleasurable experiences are driven by a ***reward circuit*** situated in the midbrain which stimulates the release of dopamine, the neurochemical involved in experiencing positive feelings. In neuroimaging studies, the reward circuit is active when we experience pleasurable events, such as eating chocolate, listening to music, or looking at a face. This circuit is linked directly to the frontal cortex and hippocampus, two brain areas central for efficient learning and memory.

In particular, it seems that *curiosity* activates the reward circuit, so it should be no surprise that when students are feeling inquisitive and interested, they will remember information more easily. Brain scanning reveals that the dopamine circuits 'light up' just at the thought of wanting to know something, even before you learn it. What might interest students is, of course, infinitely variable! Research suggests that stories stick better than factual information. That's where the teacher's skill comes in, providing content and activity which holds students' attention, discouraging wandering minds.

Did you know...?

Studies have shown that meditation can improve performance in memory tests. Researchers at the University of California at Santa Barbara found that college students who participated in 45-minute meditation sessions four times a week scored 60 points higher, after just two weeks, on tests measuring working memory capacity and reading comprehension (Mrazek et al., 2013). They wrote: "Our results suggest that cultivating mindfulness is an effective and efficient technique for improving cognitive function, with wide-reaching consequences" (abstract).

Now, motivation is a complex matter, well beyond the general scope of this book, and can stem from all sorts of factors. From the second language literature it has been described as either *instrumental* (such as the desire to pass an exam or learn the language needed to meet a specific goal – this is also referred to in other theories as *controlled motivation*) or *integrative*, (the desire to learn about and somehow become part of the target language culture) (Gardner and Lambert, 1972). The latter may have been important to you as a teacher.

From the psychology literature, another way to look at it is through *self-determination theory* (Deci and Ryan, 2008). This theory argues that the three key components of motivation are autonomy, competence and relatedness (the social aspect of learning). Self-determination theory claims that they must all be met and, if one of them is not, motivation will be lower. If these needs are satisfied, then work is more likely to be a source of *intrinsic motivation* – you do it just because you like it. If the source of motivation is external, this is known as *extrinsic motivation*. A teacher's role should be to help develop intrinsic motivation by enabling the basic psychological needs of autonomy, competence and relatedness to be satisfied.

Another influential way of looking at motivation comes from psycholinguist Zoltan Dörnyei's *Motivational Self* model. This suggests that motivation is based on three main considerations: the *ideal self*, the *ought-to self* and the *second language learning experience.* The ideal self (or possible self) is how you imagine you might be as a speaker of another language. The ought-to self concerns the beliefs you have about what is expected when you learn and how you should avoid negative outcomes. The second language learning experience is about the impact of the teacher, the curriculum, peer group or experience of success, but also many areas beyond the classroom. A good deal of Dörnyei's research has been about how classroom pedagogy can influence motivation.

So for the majority of your students, motivation may well arise from a range of factors, such as the desire to please the teacher or peers (relatedness) or simply to enjoy the sense of being good at the subject. The latter feeling ('competence' in self-determination theory) is also described by psychologists as *self-efficacy*. We believe this is the motivational key to success in classroom settings and any activity which develops and maintains self-efficacy will result in more learning and better memory.

Curiosity

In a 2017 study Shana Carpenter and Alexander Toftness divided students into two groups to test whether ***pre-questioning*** about material the students were going to learn from a video clip would increase their memory of the information afterwards. They found that the group who did pre-questions performed 24% better than the group who just watched the video without any questioning beforehand (Carpenter and Toftness, 2017). Further research has shown that pre-questions can be effective whether they take the form of multi-choice, gap-fill or open-ended questions.

It seems that pre-questions arouse curiosity and engagement with a task (recall the pre-test effect we described in Chapter 10). They can also reduce a sense of over-confidence students may have, believing they know everything. A word of caution is needed, however, since pre-questions can have a negative effect if they encourage selective processing of information during reading or listening. Students may skip information not related to the pre-questions.

Self-efficacy

The notion of self-efficacy originally comes from the work of Albert Bandura. Self-efficacy is defined as the "beliefs in one's capabilities to organise and execute the courses of action required to produce given attainments" (Bandura, 1997 p.3). In other words, it's about students having an expectancy of success. Bandura claims that self-efficacy beliefs "affect almost everything [people] do; how they think, motivate themselves, feel, and behave" (Bandura, 1997 p.19). Research shows that people with high expectations of success remember more and do better at tasks. If language teachers can create in their students this positive feeling of self-worth or self-concept about the subject, then they will pay more attention, work harder and remember more.

In language lessons this implies we should provide resources and tasks which are enjoyable, achievable and just challenging enough (germane cognitive load). It means providing language which is always comprehensible along with plenty of opportunities to communicate, using whichever methodology you prefer.

All this has important implications for pedagogy across all the four main language skills: listening, speaking, reading and writing. As we explained in Conti and Smith (2019), one skill area which can easily reduce motivation and increase anxiety is listening. Classroom activities which focus on developing the micro-skills of listening (listening as modelling, rather than listening as testing), should lead to greater self-efficacy as well as improved learning. Speaking and writing activities which demand too much spontaneity and use of unknown language also lead to feelings of failure. Written texts containing less than about 95% comprehensible input for most students, and which require too much guesswork to decode, may also reduce motivation and self-efficacy.

Anxiety and stress

What about the effects of stress and anxiety on memory? Research provides somewhat conflicting findings about their role. On the one hand, stress impairs memory owing to an increase in the release of cortisol which blocks pathways near the hippocampus (the part of the brain largely responsible for memory), making it harder to recall things. So in general, let's be clear, stress and anxiety are bad for memory.

But as we mentioned in Chapter 10, the study by Smith et al. (2016) found that retrieval practice was able to reduce the effect of stress. Increased stress (having to do an exam) did not negatively affect the students who used retrieval practice at all. Other studies, for example Agarwal et al. (2014) have found that school students' anxiety is reduced thanks to programmes of retrieval practice built into their courses. Regular low-stakes testing/ quizzing should ultimately reduce stress and increase self-efficacy.

In terms of language learning, we need to be aware of just how scary the experience is for many students! This is one of the main reasons language teachers in particular try to make lessons 'fun'. It's not just about sweetening the pill or gamifying learning - we know that relaxed students are happier and more successful. For many years, researchers have specifically studied what is called *foreign language classroom anxiety* (such as Zheng and Cheng, 2018). Some research has suggested that this is a greater issue in some countries than others. For example, Chinese and Korean students, used to certain styles of learning, may find speaking in class particularly threatening.

Foreign language classroom anxiety has a variety of causes. Price (1991) wrote that levels of difficulty in some lessons, students' perceptions of their own language aptitude, certain personality variables (for example, perfectionism or fear of public speaking) and stressful classroom experiences were all possible causes of anxiety. Students' individual personality traits, such as introversion or extraversion, are associated with anxiety arousal (Brown et al., 2001).

Young (1991) identified six possible sources of language anxiety from three origins: the learner, the teacher and the instructional practice. He claimed that language anxiety is caused by (1) learners' personal and interpersonal anxiety, (2) learners' beliefs about language learning, (3) teachers' beliefs about language teaching, (4) teacher-student interactions, (5) classroom procedures and (6) testing.

The research suggests that anxiety not only accompanies speaking, as you might expect, but also listening. Graham (2017) refers to studies (for example, Horwitz, Horwitz and Cope, 1986) which found that listening comprehension was a source of much anxiety. Students worry that they need to understand every word they hear in order to be able to comprehend. In addition, they often perceive listening activities as a test rather than a learning opportunity (Conti and Smith, 2019).

Sentence Chaos

1. Display a set of 10 sentences on the board.

2. Put students in groups of three: two players and a reader/referee.

3. The referee decides on a set order (different from the arrangement on the board) and reads out the sentences twice, at the beginning of the game. The 10 sentences are visible at all times.

4. Players then repeat the sentences in the same order. Players have five lives. Every time a player makes a mistake the other player has a go until they run out of lives. The player who stays alive, or has managed to reproduce the longest accurate sequence of sentences, wins.

So, teachers need to reduce the threatening nature of speaking and listening by whatever means. This can mean accepting error, being sensitive about correction, avoiding setting tasks beyond the capability of students and creating a supportive classroom environment in which activities are enjoyable and feasible. As far as listening is concerned, it means reducing anxiety by providing highly comprehensible language and tasks which model the micro-skills of the listening process, to build in success rather than guesswork and failure. We explore this way of teaching listening (Listening-as-Modelling) in *Breaking the Sound Barrier* (Conti and Smith, 2019).

Other researchers have looked into the idea that stress is not always a bad thing and that too much or too little stress are both undesirable. Crum et al. (2013) found that those study participants who had high levels of cortisol were able to lower it if they believed that stress can actually be good for you. Having a positive mindset about stress can help us feel better, perform better and make us more likely to seek out feedback. In essence, psychologists claim that a little bit of stress can help people learn and perform more effectively.

On the other hand, as noted earlier, research is clear that anxiety inhibits the processing and retention of learned material, and the effect is particularly strong in language learning which poses particular challenges for sometimes reluctant students – speaking in another language can feel embarrassing and even threatening. Reducing anxiety by providing input and practice at a suitable level, building a nurturing classroom environment, using humour and engaging, game-like tasks can all contribute to reducing anxiety and increasing retention.

Did you know...?

Depression affects memory. People who are depressed are 40% more likely to develop memory problems. Low levels of serotonin, a neurotransmitter connected with brain arousal, may make depressed individuals less attentive to new information.

Dwelling on sad events of the past, a symptom of depression, makes it difficult to pay attention and store short-term memories.

Isolation is another memory thief. A study by the Karen Ertel and colleagues in 2008 found that older people with higher levels of social integration had a slower rate of memory decline over a six-year period (Ertel et al., 2008). Researchers hypothesise that social interaction keeps our brains active. As we've said before, with memory, we use it or lose it.

Stress and growth mindset

A study by Hae Yeon Lee and colleagues in 2019 found that when students experience an academic setback such as a bad grade, the amount of cortisol (a stress hormone) in their bodies spikes. For most students it drops to normal levels a day later, but for some it stays high. These students remain fixated on the setback and have difficulty moving forward (Lee et al., 2019).

The researchers analysed the stress levels of students at two high schools in Texas during a stressful time, the transition into high school. Students completed daily surveys asking about the stress they experienced, and provided daily saliva samples to indicate their cortisol levels.

A clear majority of these students experienced a drop in grades in the first semester and reported feeling stressed as a result. In terms of how they handled that stress, two distinct groups emerged. Students who believed that intelligence can be developed (those with a growth mindset) were more likely to see setbacks as temporary, and not only had lower overall cortisol levels but were able to return to lower levels shortly after a setback. Students who believed that intelligence is fixed, on the other hand, maintained high cortisol level for longer, a stress response that tends to depress problem solving and intellectual flexibility.

The psychologist Carol Dweck is most associated with mindset theory. General advice to emerge from the theory includes explaining the difference between fixed mindset and growth mindset; praising effort, not ability; encouraging students to ask questions like "What could I do differently?"; embracing failure; setting achievable goals; explaining that some things take time and effort; talking about your own learning journey and developing resilience through hard work.

In sum, emotional factors play a huge role in getting students ready for learning and many teachers take the view that establishing the right relationship with a class is the key to everything. We wouldn't disagree in general, but once good relationships and the right classroom feel are established, that's when all the other gains can be made in terms of making language stick. It is possible to have a good relationship while not much learning happens.

Emotional intensity makes things more memorable

The brain processes huge amounts of information every day, so it needs a triage system for determining what's important and what can be forgotten. One way of doing this is to prioritise information by its emotional intensity. Things we have a strong emotional reaction to are likely to be more important than ones we barely notice. While there is no precise definition of what constitutes an 'emotional event', one strong correlation is the release of dopamine.

Dopamine is like a kind of a post-it note for the brain saying 'remember this!'. If we are learning in a way that engages us, emotionally, then we are more likely to remember it. If we understand the importance of something, rather than simply trying to memorise a list of facts, then the information will be stored better and for longer.

Summary

✓ Motivation is a key prerequisite for learning and therefore memory development. It has been described from many angles, but a key one is the notion of self-efficacy, the feeling that you are good at what you do.

✓ Self-efficacy is key to successful language learning. Classroom activities need to build and maintain self-efficacy, learning and memory. One key requirement is to provide comprehensible language and successful opportunities to engage with it.

✓ Stress and anxiety are bad for learning and memory on the whole. There is evidence, paradoxically, that tests (retrieval practice) can reduce the effects of stress. Regular low-stakes testing/quizzing should ultimately reduce stress and increase self-efficacy.

✓ Second language learning anxiety affects many students, especially in speaking and listening. Steps can be taken to anticipate and reduce it.

✓ There is evidence that having a growth mindset rather than a fixed mindset about your abilities, can reduce anxiety and help build resilience.

✓ We are likely to remember things better when we have an emotional attachment to them. Curiosity is another major driver of learning and memory.

For reflection

☒ How can you create a classroom atmosphere which is both well-disciplined and supportive for students?

☒ Given that we remember learning better when we have an emotional engagement with it, how can you create this engagement with the language or topics you are teaching?

☒ What strategies and techniques could you use to reduce stress and anxiety for students who worry about using the language or doing tests?

☒ How can you help students have a growth mindset when it comes to language learning?

Further reading and viewing

☒ Agarwal, P.K., D'Antonio, L., Roediger, H.L., McDermott, K.B. & McDaniel, M.A. (2014). Classroom-based programs of retrieval practice reduce middle school and high school students' test anxiety.

☒ Bandura, A. (1977). Self-efficacy: Toward a unifying theory of behavioral change. *Psychological Review, 84* (2), 191–215.

☒ Zheng, Y. & Cheng, L. (2018). How does anxiety influence language performance? From the perspectives of foreign language classroom anxiety and cognitive test anxiety. *Language Testing in Asia, 8,* Article 13. Available at: languagetestingasia.springeropen.com/articles/10.1186/s40468-018-0065-4

☒ Carol Dweck (in 2014) gives a short lecture on the subject of growth mindset. Available at: youtube.com/watch?v=hiiEeMN7vbQ

☒ Lee, H.Y., Jamieson, J.P., Miu, A.S., Josephs, R.A. & Yeager, D.S. (2019). An entity theory of intelligence predicts higher cortisol levels when high school grades are declining. *Child Development, 90* (6), 849-867.

☒ Edward Deci gives a talk about self-determination theory. Available at: youtube.com/watch?time_continue=184&v=m6fm1gt5YAM&feature=emb_logo

Learning from mistakes 15

Key concepts

In this chapter we consider:

- ☒ The importance of feedback
- ☒ Surprise as a driver of learning
- ☒ Errorful and error-free learning
- ☒ The concept of adaptation
- ☒ The role of grades and comments
- ☒ The best types of corrective feedback for memory
- ☒ When is it best to give feedback during oral work?
- ☒ Correcting written work
- ☒ Why some errors are better than others

The importance of feedback

Are you the type of language teacher who believes students need to be accurate from the start or that it's fine to make mistakes and that, indeed, we learn and remember more by doing so? Do you like to correct students' speech and writing? Do you think it's useful to show examples of erroneous language in the name of building memory? To what extent can producing and being exposed to errors increase memory? These are the subjects of this chapter.

In general terms, psychologists believe that feedback is a vital part of the learning process. Educationalists John Hattie and Helen Timperley define feedback as "information provided by an agent... regarding aspects of one's performance or understanding" (Hattie and Timperley, 2007 p.81). Winne and Butler (1994) note that feedback is "information with which a learner can confirm, add to, overwrite, tune, or restructure information in memory, whether that information is domain knowledge, meta-cognitive knowledge, beliefs about self and tasks, or cognitive tactics and strategies" (p. 5740).

For language learners feedback and error correction come mainly from the teacher and to a lesser extent peers. In classroom work this is an ongoing process of confirmation, recasting of responses and occasional explicit correction. On paper, it's a range of corrective practices which we look at later. For the best practitioners we're talking about a finely-tuned, subtle process of formative assessment, or what has been called **responsive teaching** (Fletcher-Wood, 2018) – the bread and butter of effective teacher practice.

Instinctively language teachers think feedback is vital and they devote countless hours of time to correcting students' written work. But when it comes to error correction, the second language acquisition literature has provided mixed messages over the years (Shintani and Ellis, 2013). Our best bet is that correcting spoken and written errors is useful if done at the right time, with the right students in the right way. Cognitive science and second language acquisition research provide some other useful insights about whether receiving feedback, and making, hearing or seeing mistakes, can enhance memory.

Surprise as a driver of learning

Let's turn to cognitive science first. Neuroscientist Stanislas Dehaene has suggested what he calls four 'pillars of learning' based on research into cognitive psychology and neuroscience (Dehaene, 2020). He argues that each of these pillars is vital for building long-term memory. He calls them **attention**, **active engagement**, **feedback** and **consolidation**.

To put these four pillars in everyday terms, imagine you are learning to do a dance. (1) pay attention to the teacher; (2) try out the steps; (3) get some wrong and correct them; (4) practise over and over again. It's the third pillar, responding to feedback, which we are considering in this chapter.

Firstly, Dehaene explains that we learn not so much by making **associations** between information, but by noticing things which seem wrong. As he puts it, surprise is the driving force of learning. Researchers Robert Rescorla and Allan Wagner hypothesised that the brain learns only if it perceives a gap between what it predicts and what it receives. This goes back to Jean Piaget's idea that cognitive development happens when there is a mismatch between a child's existing schemas and feedback from the environment. For learning, **cognitive conflict** (an error signal) is needed or, as Rescorla and Wagner (1972 p.75) put it, "organisms only learn when events violate their expectations". As a second language speaker you will be aware of those moments when you hear something unexpected or which does not match with what you thought. It's often at those times that you notice something interesting and remember it for later.

Put another way, you can see the brain as a type of machine that generates predictions, receives information, then compares the two. An error signal creates a better prediction for the future. The following sequence is continually repeated: prediction – feedback – corrections – new prediction. You can see this as a sort of statistical process when learning is only triggered if there is an error signal.

According to Dehaene, this doesn't mean we have to *make* mistakes to learn, but it's about a perception of a discrepancy between what we expect and what we get. Interestingly, however, in some theories of second language acquisition, it's argued that perception of errors we make ourselves is important for developing proficiency. The so-called **Interaction Hypothesis** (Long, 1996) claims that we need to test out our utterances with other speakers to get feedback and *notice* (Schmidt, 1990) when we make mistakes in order that we can improve. Interactions with teachers and other students can result in negative feedback and a re-modelling of the correct language form. Think of it like this: when a student makes a mistake they are trying out a hypothesis about the language; corrective feedback tells them if it was right.

You may have noticed that this theory ties in rather neatly with what we said about curiosity and the testing effect in previous chapters. The simple act of being curious about an answer and trying to retrieve it, even if you make a mistake, leads to learning and better memory.

Errorful and error-free learning

For some time cognitive psychologists have been exploring the extent to which making mistakes is good for memory. Just as Robert Bjork has argued that deliberately creating difficult tasks can enhance memory (we referred to the idea of desirable difficulty in Chapter 6), other researchers have produced counter-intuitive evidence that making mistakes is actually a good thing. In Chapter 10 we pointed out that the testing effect shows that the very act of retrieval, even if students get answers wrong, improves recall.

In the literature this is termed **errorful learning**. The general finding from research is that, except for people with specific neural issues such as amnesia, allowing learners to make errors is more productive than creating the conditions where errors are avoided at all costs (so-called **error-free learning**). In contrast, in behaviourist accounts of learning it was always felt best to avoid errors in case they persist.

In a nutshell, the process of finding an answer through making hypotheses then seeing them disproven creates deeper processing and better memory. You can see the parallel here with Dehaene's theory.

So, from a language teacher's point of view, should errors actually be encouraged? We would argue this is a step too far in language classrooms, but that students should be encouraged to generate educated guesses about language in certain circumstances and as part of their learning about metacognitive strategies. We can also say that recognising errors can help students notice how the language works, think about it more and process more deeply.

It would be a mistake in general to deliberately supply language input which provokes guesswork and error, since that goes against a fundamental principle of acquisition, namely the need for comprehensible input which can be processed. We should not forget that repeatedly hearing, reading and using correct language builds memory. Students like to be correct and derive confidence and motivation from knowing they're accurate.

On the other hand, as we'll see below, *once students have internalised language*, supplying incorrect forms can enhance memory.

Spot the error

This error-spotting task raises students' awareness of commonly made decoding errors in listening.

1. Display a list of words or short phrases.

2. Read one of them aloud, making a pronunciation mistake with one phoneme.

3. Students identify the error and explain it to the teacher or a partner.

(Conti and Smith, 2019)

Learning from failure

Following research by Potts and Shanks (2014), Tina Seabrooke and colleagues (Seabrooke et al., 2018) carried out a study in which participants had to learn the meanings of rare nouns in English and Euskara (the Basque language). During learning, participants either guessed the definition of the new word (usually getting it wrong), or just studied the words and their definitions for the same amount of time.

The results suggested that, when learning unknown words and their definitions, generating errors through guesswork strengthened recall of the definitions and words in isolation, but, interestingly, did not strengthen the association between them.

The researchers speculate, citing other research, that errorful learning may work better when pairs of words already have some kind of semantic relationship (for example, *pond – frog*) and that improved memory is mainly to do with the fact that the guessing process raises interest in the task.

For language teachers, a reasonable takeaway might mean, prior to setting vocabulary to learn, asking students in class to guess meanings of new or half-known words before they take the work home. This could promote curiosity and allow students to gauge their progress before and after learning.

Adaptation

Brain scans clearly show what happens when errors are perceived. For example, If you hear a series of identical notes, each note elicits a response in the auditory areas of the brain. But as the notes repeat, responses decrease, since the brain becomes accustomed to the signal. Psychologists call this **adaptation**. If a new note is suddenly played the primary auditory cortex shows a strong surprise reaction – adaptation dies away and additional neurons start to fire. The same phenomenon occurs if you hear the same pattern of notes repeated, then replace them with a new pattern. Think of it like the change of key in a pop song which has started to get too repetitive.

In linguistic terms, if we see or hear a sentence with an unexpected or inappropriate item of vocabulary, the strange word causes neurons sensitive to word meaning in the left of the brain to fire and 400 milliseconds later we perceive the anomaly. On the other hand, if we encounter a sentence with unexpected syntax, such as a word in the wrong part of speech or a word order issue, it is in Broca's Area that neurons 'light up' (600 milliseconds this time). In both cases, we notice a problem and learn from it.

This suggests that deliberately using errors in input is a productive practice for language teachers. And indeed, most teachers believe it's useful to do activities involving error-spotting and correction, sentence unjumbling or transcription correcting, for example. A counter argument to this practice which you may come across is that if we expose students to incorrect language, this will find its way into long-term memory and become, to use the jargon, **fossilised**. The solution is to only expose students to error once they have already reached a point where they have internalised (automatised) the correct form. After all, it's only if they sense an unexpected, incorrect form that the brain is likely to show added interest in the form of the language. Spotting the discrepancy leads to further processing and enhanced memory.

Effective teachers are well aware that giving feedback is a complex business and that correcting students' speech and writing needs to be handled sensitively. Interestingly, adults are better able to deal with negative feedback than adolescents. Some research suggests that whereas adults learn as much from reward and punishment, adolescents learn more from their successes (Palminteri et al., 2016). Clearly, neutral, informative feedback and correction should not veer towards anything perceived as punitive in classrooms. Keep in mind that, in the end, it's students who correct their errors, not you.

Did you know...?

Have you ever had a 'eureka!' moment while doing housework or having a shower? Procrastination can be a useful tool for memory. When we are not actively focusing on something, our sub-conscious is working on things in the background while we're doing other tasks. Psychologists suggest that when you procrastinate your mind wanders and you can stumble on unexpected patterns. You can see how this relates to what we said earlier in the book about consolidation and restructuring of memory.

What's more, psychologist Bluma Zeigarnik (Zeigarnik, 1927) found that memory of incomplete tasks can be better than for completed tasks. This is called the **Zeigarnik Effect**.

The role of grades and comments

What about using grades to improve future performance and memory? Back in 1958 a study was carried out which showed that students did better on subsequent assessments if work was given a grade alongside an individualised or standardised comment compared to a grade alone (Page, 1958). This research also revealed that when comments sent a message that the teacher was on the student's side, then results improved. So "I'm with you on this. Let's improve!" is better than "You must improve this mark!" Much research in the field of formative assessment has confirmed that comments are more useful than grades if you want students to learn and remember, but as with all these matters, it's not simple!

If grades are used they should always be based on clearly articulated assessment criteria which students are aware of; *not* norm-based criteria. Grades should normally reward performance, not effort, even if you choose to acknowledge effort in other ways.

As for comments, Benjamin Bloom (famous for the Bloom's Taxonomy) suggested the guidelines below (Bloom, 1968).

1. *Always begin with the positive.* Comments should point out what students did well and recognise their accomplishments.

2. *Identify what specific aspects of performance need to improve.* Students need to know precisely where to focus their efforts.

3. *Offer specific guidance and direction for making improvements.* Students need to know what steps to take to improve.

4. *Express confidence in students' ability to achieve at the highest level.* Students need to know teachers believe in them, are on their side, see value in their work, and are confident they can achieve the learning goals set for them.

The best types of corrective feedback for memory

What types of corrective feedback are there? Are some more effective than others? The term **recast** describes how you respond to a student's spoken error by repeating the same thing, correctly, without explicitly pointing out the mistake. A recast is, therefore, an implicit form of error correction which a student may or may not notice. Some studies have suggested that recasts are more effective with learners who have longer working memory spans (for example, Mackey et al., 2002). Others have indicated that recasts may work better for more proficient and older learners who are developmentally ready to respond to them (including Ammar, 2008).

Prompts, on the other hand, are an explicit sort of corrective feedback and include a variety of signals that get students to correct themselves. These include the following.

- ☒ **Elicitation**, where the teacher directly elicits a reformulation from students by asking questions such as "How do we say that in English?", by pausing to allow them to complete what the teacher says, or by asking a student to reformulate what they've said.
- ☒ **Metalinguistic clues**, where comments or questions are provided about a student's utterance such as "We don't say it like that in English".
- ☒ **Clarification requests**, where phrases such as "Pardon?" and "I don't understand" are said to indicate to students that what they've said is wrong in some way.
- ☒ **Repetition**, in which the teacher repeats something the student has said incorrectly, adjusting intonation (stress and pitch) to highlight the error – "The boy entered the *bedroom*?"

So, which are more effective, according to research? In fact both approaches have been shown to lead to better performance. But, although teachers tend to use recasts more than prompts (for example, Lyster and Lanta, 1997), prompts have been shown to be more effective, particularly with less advanced learners. Ellis, Loewen and Erlam (2006) compared the effectiveness of implicit and explicit corrective feedback on low-intermediate learners' performance, with analysis indicating that explicit feedback was superior to implicit.

A key takeaway here is that corrective feedback can get students to correct themselves and recall correct forms in the future.

When is it best to give feedback during oral work?

If you want students to remember correct language is it better to correct in the heat of the moment, or to delay feedback so as not to discourage them or interrupt their flow? In the research literature the jury is still out on this question (Ellis and Shintani, 2013), so teachers need to exercise judgement based on the individual student and context. Butler et al. (2007) speculate that there's a benefit to delayed correction since it takes advantage of the spacing effect, which means if you leave a corrective intervention until the next lesson, students are exposed to that language issue twice over a period of time. Given what we have previously said about making interventions memorable, then the manner of correction is likely to make more of a difference than the timing. Providing striking or even amusing examples of errors could well leave a stronger trace in students' memories.

Some teachers prefer to correct little, but reteach commonly occurring mistakes on a subsequent occasion. If you choose to pick up on errors to start a lesson, then students are more likely to remember what you tell them if you limit yourself to just one or two points rather than several. A judgement also needs to be made about how important an error is. In general, it makes sense to focus on major errors which can alter meaning, such as verb tenses, rather than minor ones such as adjectival agreement or gender.

In any case, why not discuss the issue of corrective feedback with students? Find out what they find useful and involve them in your thinking about the issue. (This applies to all areas of pedagogy, by the way.)

Correcting written work

Can the way we correct written work enhance long-term memory of language? One distinction made in the second language learning literature is between two different types of correction. **Direct error correction** means pointing out where a mistake has been made and providing the correct version. **Indirect error correction** involves indicating where an error has occurred, but getting the student to work out what was wrong. The rationale for the second approach is based on the observation that a substantial proportion of student errors are self-correctable if some form of cueing (highlighting, coding, etc.) is used to signal their presence. Research is mixed on the best way to correct written work, but it suggests that direct correction may be more effective (Ellis and Shintani, 2013).

As mentioned earlier, correction is a subtle business which can have psychological effects which vary from person to person, so teachers need to exercise judgment and skill when correcting. One observation we would make is that, although feedback can lead to better memory, language teachers can easily overestimate the value of correcting errors and may spend too much time doing so.

Some errors are better than others

If you have children of your own, or have spent time with infants, you'll know it's natural for mistakes to be made. But many errors are easy to understand and reveal a deeper understanding of grammar. So, when a child says *I goed* instead of *I went*, we can easily recognise this as an example of what is called **overgeneralisation** of a rule, that is, they have applied the rule of 'adding -ed' to make a past tense. Their error has actually revealed a command of grammar up to a point. Therefore, if your students do something similar, for example saying *J'ai allé* ('I went') instead of *je suis allé* you can be reassured that they have internalised the most common use of the auxiliary verb in the perfect tense.

Summary

- ✓ Feedback is a vital part of learning which confirms, retunes or restructures memory.
- ✓ Dehaene's four pillars of learning are vital for building long-term memory. He calls them attention, active engagement, feedback and consolidation.
- ✓ Surprise drives learning. Rescorla and Wagner hypothesised that the brain learns only if it perceives a gap between what it predicts and what it receives (cognitive conflict).
- ✓ Long's Interaction Hypothesis claims we need to test our utterances with other speakers to get feedback and to notice when we make mistakes in order to improve. When a student makes a mistake they are trying out a hypothesis. Corrective feedback tells them if it was right.
- ✓ Allowing students to make errors is more productive than creating the conditions where errors are avoided at all costs (as in the behaviourist model).
- ✓ Deliberately using errors in input is a productive practice for language teachers, but needs careful timing and implementation.
- ✓ Recasts and prompts are two ways to provide feedback. The latter may be more effective, notably with beginners.
- ✓ Research is unclear about the timing of error feedback, but experience suggests it's best to focus on only a very few major errors at one time.

- ✓ Although feedback can improve memory, language teachers can easily overestimate the value of correcting errors and may spend too much time doing so.
- ✓ Some errors may be more welcome than others. It's a good sign if a student has grasped a rule but over-generalised it.

For reflection

- ☒ To what extent do you use student errors to guide your teaching?
- ☒ What strategies could you employ to take advantage of Dehaene's third pillar of learning (feedback)?
- ☒ How do you correct spoken errors in your teaching? Do you think it's best to do it on the spot or some time later?
- ☒ What are the possible pitfalls of showing incorrect language to students?

Further reading and viewing

- ☒ Dehaene, S. (2020). *How We Learn: The New Science of Education and the Brain*. Allen Lane.
- ☒ Lyster, R., & Ranta, L. (1997). Corrective feedback and learner uptake: Negotiation of form in communicative classrooms. *Studies in Second Language Acquisition, 20*, 37-66. Available at: http://hyxy.nankai.edu.cn/jingpinke/buchongyuedu/corrective%20feedback%20and%20uptake%20by%20Lyster.pdf
- ☒ Roy Lyster gives a lecture on corrective feedback (in 2018). Available at: youtube.com/watch?time_continue=523&v=9bpbCzY0d20&feature=emb_logo

A memory-friendly curriculum

16

Key concepts

Chapter 16 has a curriculum and practical pedagogy bias, drawing on aspects of research described in previous chapters. We consider:

- ☒ Planning a vocabulary curriculum
- ☒ The role of regular quizzing
- ☒ Planning a grammar curriculum
- ☒ A communicative curriculum
- ☒ A sequence of lessons to make language stick (the MARS-EARS sequence)
- ☒ Testing in the curriculum
- ☒ Deep processing
- ☒ The importance of recycling
- ☒ Exploiting the priming effect
- ☒ Exploiting the protégé effect
- ☒ The role of pushed output
- ☒ Lesson scheduling
- ☒ Evaluating and adapting resources
- ☒ Making language comprehensible
- ☒ Mnemonics (memory hooks to help students remember grammar)
- ☒ Corrective feedback
- ☒ Stretching the high attainers
- ☒ General principles for curriculum design: sum-up

Planning a vocabulary curriculum

Ensure your curriculum plan creates opportunities for regular review and recycling of vocabulary. Don't assume for a moment that an item taught and practised once will be remembered. Provide the frequency and spacing of input needed to make the language stick. Intersperse new language items with those previously encountered.

Curriculum planning is one thing, but from day to day it's up to the teacher who knows their class intimately to use their judgment about how often to recycle known language. Entry and exit routines, register routines, lesson starters and fillers can be a convenient way to space out encounters with vocabulary.

When planning your vocabulary curriculum, we suggest keeping in mind the guidelines below which can be a good basis for departmental discussion.

1. A framework for vocabulary teaching in the classroom.

2. Criteria for selecting words to focus on.

3. Techniques for introducing new words.

4. Ways to practise using words.

5. Activities to build word learning strategies.

6. A vocabulary-rich environment to support learning.

7. Activities to help students collect words.

8. Ways to build motivation for word learning.

9. Activities that recycle texts and vocabulary.

10. A target number of word families to acquire.

Encourage students to employ a range of vocabulary learning techniques: keywords, paired associations and noting words in texts. Keep in mind that some words will be harder to recall than others, so during lessons give more attention to these. To repeat, favour distributed over massed practice of vocabulary. Regularly using vocabulary in meaningful communicative contexts yields better memory than learning from lists.

Consider all the dimensions of vocabulary knowledge and try to incorporate them as far as possible:

⊠ *form* (sound, spelling and morphology);

- ☒ *meaning*;
- ☒ *use* (collocations and stylistic appropriateness);
- ☒ *breadth* (vocabulary size);
- ☒ *depth* (how well a lexical item is known);
- ☒ *fluency* (how spontaneous are retrieval and use of lexis).

Remember the importance of a core vocabulary which consists of (a) high-frequency words and chunks (including sight words) and (b) high surrender-value words and chunks – those which provide the most potential for usage. A reduced curriculum featuring the most high-surrender value items allows more opportunities for recycling and deep and durable learning.

Encourage students to see the relationship between different members of a word family: to give an English example the links between words such as *care, carer, caring, to care* and *cared*. When students can see morphological relationships between parts of speech, they can more easily recognise unfamiliar words and generate more words applying the same patterns.

You might like to consider your vocabulary curriculum growing like a snowball, as in Figure 16.1. The first year of teaching could focus on 500 word families, the second on 500 more and the third on another 500.

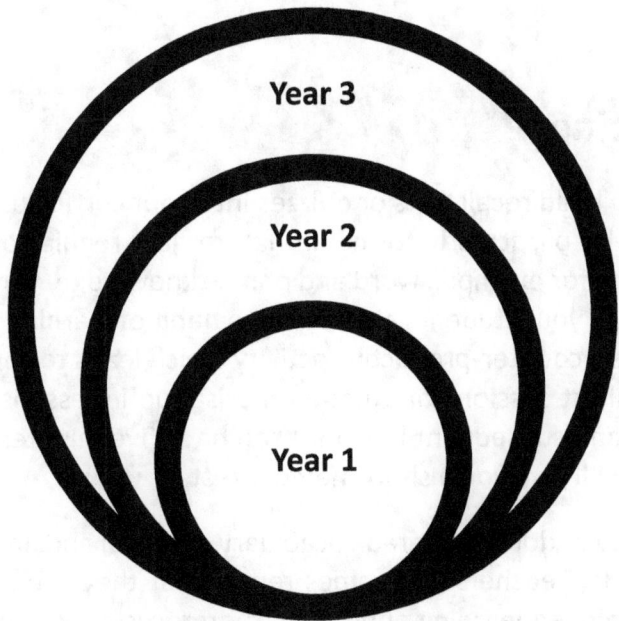

Figure 16.1   Planning the first three years of a vocabulary curriculum

Ten tips to help students memorise vocabulary from lists

1. Use the read, cover and write method.
2. Get someone to test you.
3. Concentrate on the difficult words and link them to something you know for example clay keys (the word for key is *clé* in French – pronounced *clay* in English).
4. Space out your learning in short five minute bursts.
5. Make up a rhythm – tap out the words as you say them.
6. Record the words onto a digital device and listen to them.
7. Write out the words with vowels missing, then do a gap-fill a little later.
8. Read the words out loud – fast, slow, loud, quiet. Take advantage of the production effect.
9. Break up the words into syllables – *mu/sique pro/fe/sseur*.
10. Group the words alphabetically.

Regular quizzing

Don't be reluctant to build recall tests or quizzes into your curriculum on a regular basis. They don't need to be particularly formal in nature, just regular opportunities to test specific knowledge of, for example, word and phrase knowledge, verb forms or pieces of cultural information. If your students are not in the habit of learning vocabulary at home for tests, this may be a counter-productive activity which leads to conflict and sanctions. Consider including short sessions of quiet memorisation in lessons, followed by recall quizzes in the same and subsequent lessons. "You have five minutes to memorise these words/phrases, then I'll give you a short memory test."

Apps provide one way of doing targeted vocabulary retrieval and are popular with many teachers and students. Teachers sometimes report that they use apps such as Quizlet before lessons (the flipped learning approach), then recycle the same language as part of their lesson plan.

Keeping in mind the TAP effect (Chapter 11), if students have been asked to learn isolated words or phrases from a bilingual list, they will recall them better if these words are tested in the same way, that is, by a traditional vocabulary test. If you choose to test the words through a different format, such as through definitions or a gap-fill exercise, then it is likely students will perform less well. Higher-achieving classes may benefit the most from a more challenging format, which could provide better germane cognitive load and encourage deeper processing, both of which build memory.

Five tips for running vocab tests

Many teachers do regular vocabulary tests so here are some tips on how to get the most out of them.

1. Set a target score. Research suggests that when students know what they have to achieve, this can affect the way they revise. They may see it as a challenge to beat the target.
2. With mixed attainment classes consider varying how you run the test. Use first to second language and vice versa. The latter is easier since recognition is easier than retrieval.
3. Use rewards for success, but let the class know this in advance. Research supports the use of rewards to aid learning.
4. Use sanctions, for example retests, if learning was inadequate. If you are going to run a series of tests, it's best to set the standard early on. Good habits breed good habits. In the end this leads to happier learners.
5. Allow a few moments of last minute learning before you conduct the test. This reinforces memory and allows students to mentally prepare for the coming task.

A grammar curriculum

A selection of grammatical structures has to be made, sequenced in some coherent way, but this doesn't necessarily mean organising your whole curriculum around an ordered sequence. Research offers little support for a curriculum based on 'the grammar point of the day' (a so-called *synthetic syllabus*). As we previously explained, students become developmentally ready to acquire grammar at different points. In addition, although teachers may find grammar fascinating, this is not necessarily the case for our students.

One way around this, as we have mentioned before, is to incorporate grammar and vocabulary through a lexicogrammatical approach. This means presenting and practising language in communicative chunks in a way which is more appealing to students and corresponds better with how memory works. We describe one such approach in Conti and Smith (2019), and have given further examples of how to generate chunked input in this book.

In a lexicogrammatical approach the grammar emerges from the language chunks used in communication. Grammatical points are explained and practised once students have had repeated receptive exposure through flooded input. Students may even seek explanations for themselves, but it's much more likely that you will have planned when and how you want the grammar point in question to be practised.

So, in sum, provide context for work on grammatical forms, using them in different communicative settings. When the focus is on comprehensible input and communicative practice, take every opportunity to refer to the form of the language being used, particularly items which are less salient, meaning they stand out less to students. For example, in French students may find the distinction between the relative pronouns *qui* and *que* not very obvious since they look and sound similar. Unless the difference in their usage is explained and practised students are less likely to use them correctly, particularly if the amount of input they receive is limited. In immersion contexts or with more able learners it is more likely that correct forms will develop naturally over time.

Be prepared to drill specific structures if the class is ready for it. Make grammatical exercises as meaningful as possible. Dull mechanical drills using random vocabulary are not likely to be engaging or promote the most effective retention. More communicative question-answer drills based on stories or personal experience work well.

It's worth repeating the fundamental issue derived from research that students may not be ready to acquire a structure when you choose to teach it. You have to judge how much time to devote to a particular grammar point. Keep in mind the factors below.

☒ How useful is the grammar point in question – what is its surrender value? For example, present and simple past tenses will have more surrender value than future tense, imperfect or conditionals.

☒ High frequency verbs should be a priority, as advised by the TSC Review (Bauckham, 2016).

☒ How complex is the grammar point? Is it simple enough to explain and for students to use? To go back to the chapter on cognitive load, how many interacting elements does it have?

☒ Is it the type of structure which is more likely to be acquired slowly over time through implicit learning? Examples of this might include relative pronouns, gender, adjectival agreement and the subjunctive.

☒ Is knowledge of the structure particularly useful for the syllabus being studied? For example, the GCSE examination in England, Wales and Northern Ireland requires the ability to express past, present and future time.

Sentence puzzle activities

These promote syntactic priming through both listening and reading. They help students remember word order and how it can affect meaning. Below is a listening example from Conti and Smith (2019).

1. Write the short-hand / symbols of a sentence pattern you have modelled and your students are familiar with. For instance (in French):

    a. Time marker + subject + verb + adverbial of place.

    b. Ask students to copy out the above on paper or on mini-whiteboards.

2. Then read out a jumbled-up version of a sentence which follows that pattern. Ensure students are very familiar with every word in the sentence.

3. Students now rearrange the sentence under each heading. The correct answer is:

Time marker	Subject	Verb	Adverbial of place
Hier	*je*	*suis allé*	*au cinéma*
Yesterday	*I*	*went*	*to the cinema*

A communicative curriculum

One way to avoid a purely grammatical or topic-based curriculum is to organise learning around a set of **communicative functions**. The list in the box on the next page you can see that curriculum planning doesn't have to be based on either topic or grammar. Although the communicative functions and their associated language constructions may be set within topic areas, topics are chosen for their suitability for the teaching of the communicative function. For instance, in the case of *Reporting events in the past*, you could choose the topics of *Talking about last weekend, Last year's holiday* or *What I did in school yesterday*.

The grammatical content of the curriculum also stems from the choice of communicative functions; you teach the grammar needed to enable students to manipulate the content of sentence builders or texts creatively. What does this mean in practice? Having practised the construction 'Time marker + *I went to* + place + *by* + means of transport' (*Last weekend I went to London by train*) you may want students to be able to use the same construction with other persons of the verb, or in a different tense, or with a prepositional phrase other than '*by* + noun' (for example, '*with* + noun'). In other words, the teaching of grammar serves a communicative goal and is driven by vocabulary.

In this approach vocabulary and grammar are selected, but are not the prime drivers of the curriculum. The fact that students see a communicative value for the language they hear, see and use should enhance both motivation and memory building. Remember that students tend to be much more interested in meanings than grammar.

A possible alternative to this would be to design the curriculum around communicative tasks – meaning-focused, 'real life' activities where the language to be learned is an inherent part of the task. It is often argued this approach presents challenges for beginners who have little or no existing language to work with and who haven't automatised the language needed to carry out a task. One way around this is to design tasks based primarily on input in the early stages. In this case, students are not required to produce much language before they are ready to do so.

A set of communicative functions

1. **Describing and identifying people, including yourself** (providing personal data, describing appearance, describing personality, etc.)

2. **Describing places, objects and natural phenomena** (describing location, size, appearance, weather, etc.)

3. **Creating questions** (requesting factual information - including directions, making invitations, asking for an opinion, etc.)

4. **Expressing feelings** (expressing positive and negative emotions, reacting to events, providing reasons for your emotions/reactions, etc.)

5. **Making arrangements** (making suggestions, inviting, accepting, refusing, etc.)

6. **Comparing and contrasting** (expressing likes and dislikes, supporting an opinion, explaining preferences, talking about the best and the worst of someone or something, etc.)

7. **Describing routine behaviour in the present** (talking about what you usually do, indicating time, expressing a purpose, etc.

8. **Describing routine behaviour in the past** (talking about what you used to do, indicating time, expressing a purpose, etc.

9. **Describing past events** (setting the scene, sequencing events, evaluating the consequences of actions and events, etc.)

10. **Making plans for the future** (indicating time, making predictions, hypothesising, discussing probabilities, etc.)

11. **Indicating agreement and disagreement** (expressing opinions on events and phenomena, explaining why, supporting an argument, providing examples, etc.)

12. **Solving problems** (describing the problem, providing solutions, discussing possible consequences, arguing for and against, etc.)

To give an idea of the type of progression you could achieve, Table 16.1 shows how recycling and interleaving are woven into the curriculum. Over a 14-week cycle the communicative function 'Describing and identifying people' is carefully developed. Only by week 12 does more spontaneous work on automatising the language begin. Keep in mind that this would not be the only communicative function developed over this period.

It's very likely that memory of the language used for these communicative functions will be better by the end of the cycle than if the language were covered over a much shorter time scale, without being interleaved with other functions. It is also likely that this knowledge will be retained for longer in the future.

Weeks 1 to 2	Weeks 3-4	Weeks 5-8	Weeks 9-11	Weeks 12-14
Describing people's physical appearance				
	Describing people's personality Describing people's physical appearance (R)			
		Comparing people Describing physical appearance (R) Describing people's personality (R)		Practice in automatising all the areas on the table
			Describing people's clothes Comparing people (R) Describing physical appearance (R) Describing personality (R)	

Table 16.1 Planning the delivery of a communicative function 'Describing and identifying people'. R = revision.

A sequence of lessons to make language stick

The sequence of lesson activities in Table 16.2 below is adapted from Conti and Smith (2019) and is based on the sequence devised by Gianfranco called MARS-EARS. We've highlighted selected words from cognitive science which you have come across in the book so far. We believe a sequence along these lines aligns with what we know about long-term memory building and language acquisition.

Modelling	Constructions, chunks and words are presented and modelled aurally using sentence builders including translations, displayed on the board. The translations ease **cognitive load** and ensure comprehensibility. Read out sentences drawn from the sentence builder which students translate into English on mini-whiteboards.
Awareness-raising	Raise students' awareness of any phonological, grammatical or syntactic issues you want them to **notice explicitly** ('pop-up grammar').
Receptive processing	Students do listening and reading tasks containing 95-98% comprehensible input and input-flooding. The aim is for students to hear and read **many repetitions** of the patterns in order to strengthen their receptive learning. Do these until you are satisfied that students have developed a solid receptive knowledge.
Structured production	The receptive knowledge acquired through listening and reading is now converted into productive knowledge through **pushed output,** taking advantage of the **production effect.** This means using highly structured tasks which force students to produce orally and in writing every lexical item lots of times. Such tasks can be (1) gamified pair work translation tasks; (2) picture tasks and any other tasks which elicit **retrieval practice.**
Expansion	Two things happen in this phase: (1) the target patterns/chunks are explained to help students make sense of them. This resembles a typical grammar lesson, except that it occurs after students have already memorised the chunks and have become aware of the underlying grammar through exposure and use; (2) the chunks are practised with old and new vocabulary and structures over time through systematic recycling (**interleaving**).
Autonomy	The language is practised productively without scaffolding, but still in familiar contexts. This phase continues throughout the remainder of the year and through extensive recycling and interleaving.
Routinisation	The focus here is on **automaticity**, i.e. working on developing fast retrieval (both in the receptive and productive skills). This requires task repetition and performing tasks more and more quickly.
Spontaneity	Spontaneity development is about practice in unfamiliar contexts, i.e. requiring students to perform tasks with little or no preparation.

Table 16.2 The MARS-EARS pedagogical cycle

Testing in the curriculum

If we wish students to perform at their best in tests of retrieval, it's wise to design tests which resemble the way the language was presented and practised in lessons (remember the TAP effect). Assessments should not suddenly present students with language and questions in an unfamiliar format. For example, if students have not practised translation or essay writing in lessons, it would be inadvisable (and unfair) to present them with a test containing translation or essay writing.

Of course, one corollary of this is that an unfamiliar format will expose how well students are able to apply their knowledge and skills to a new context. If this is the aim of the test, then it should be designed accordingly. It is possible to design tests which incorporate tasks identical to those done in class alongside similar, but slightly less familiar ones, in order to diagnose how well students can apply their knowledge in a different context. Remember that research suggests that having to apply knowledge to unfamiliar contexts also has its benefits for memory.

Deep processing

One way to encourage deep processing of language structures is to use a range of question types and other interactions (for example, true/false, giving false statements to correct) to recycle a limited number of items, rather than to teach more items through one activity type. By doing this you can intensively focus as much as possible on the key items to be practised. In other words, work repeatedly on a limited repertoire of language rather than superficially on a wider range. You could call this **thorough and extensive processing** (Conti and Smith, 2019), or **intensive input-output work** (Swan, no date). Favour mastery over coverage. A lesson may be fun and memorable whilst failing to teach the key items. (Although a fun, memorable lesson may have other benefits in terms of overall motivation.)

The importance of recycling

When teaching words and phrases don't just rely on written lists of isolated words. Provide in your curriculum and day-to-day planning as many rich opportunities for students to hear, read and produce as many examples of the word (at higher levels in various forms and contexts). Make as many connections as possible to encourage deep processing. Use objects, pictures, video, texts, rhymes, music, definitions, synonyms, antonyms, associations, anecdotes – whatever it takes to provide multiple and memorable connections with the word or phrase.

Exploiting the priming effect

Providing as much comprehensible input as possible takes advantage of the priming effect. So, allow students to hear and see examples of comprehensible language, even if it is not being explicitly taught. This is the main argument for teaching in the target language. One way to do this in a lesson sequence is through Gianfranco's EPI (Extensive Processing Instruction) method, where the same target language chunks are recycled multiple times with the aid of sentence builders, reading aloud games and narrow reading and listening tasks. Narrow reading/listening means providing, say, four to six short paragraphs of text along with a range of exercises to exploit them, including matching, translation in both directions, questions and various types of gap-fill exercise.

Deep processing through questioning

At intermediate and advanced level, questioning, both oral and written, can be planned to elicit deep processing and retrieval. Look at this short paragraph and how the carefully chosen questions beneath get students to manipulate or recycle language and retrieve other language forms from memory. Target language questions also have the benefit of providing further comprehensible input.

10 November 2020: Bordeaux is one of the five areas in France where the anti-proximity bracelet has been tested since September before being spread across the whole country on December 31. The perpetrator will therefore not be able to approach within 3 km of his ex-wife. During a previous prison stay, he harassed his former wife by means of letters.

1. Is Bordeaux the only area where ths tag is being used? (Elicits: ***There are*** *four* ***other*** *areas.*)
2. When did they start to test the electronic tag? (Elicits: ***They started to test*** *the tag* ***in*** *September.*)
3. What will happen on the 31st December? (Elicits: *The tags* ***will be spread*** *across the country.*)
4. What might happen if the perpetrator didn't have a tag? (Elicits: ***He might approach*** *his ex-wife.*)
5. How did he harass his wife from prison? (Elicits: ***By writing*** *letters* ***to her.***)

Questions which invite direct lifting from the text are less desirable, but can have their place if you want to encourage weaker students to respond.

In the TPRS approach (Teaching Proficiency through Reading and Storytelling) the co-creation of stories (known as 'story asking'), often based on the students' or teacher's personal experience, is one means by which a small range of target structures are recycled multiple times. Frequent question-answer sequences (circling) help provide the repetition conducive to memory building.

Many teachers have a repertoire of go-to activities based on one short text, on paper, displayed on a screen or a combination of both. A sequence involving a combination of those below, suitably scaffolded for the class, ensures plenty of repetitions. Teachers new to a department may welcome a check-list of evidence-informed activities.

- ☒ The teacher reads aloud.

- ☒ Choral reading aloud.

- ☒ Teacher reads the text and stops at chosen points, requiring students to say the next word (with a particular focus, for example on verbs or adjectives).

- ☒ Students do the previous activity in pairs.

- ☒ Teacher makes false statements which the class must correct.

- ☒ In pairs, students do the above exercise.

- ☒ Teacher asks questions (yes/no, either/or, multiple choice or question word questions with *who, when, what, how, why*, etc.)

- ☒ Students write down answers to questions read out by the teacher.

- ☒ Students complete sentences begun by the teacher orally.

- ☒ Students read aloud to each other.

- ☒ Students recall the original text from a gapped version ('Disappearing text').

- ☒ Students do delayed dictation or delayed copying.

- ☒ Students do paired gapped dictation, where each partner has the source text with different gaps.

- ☒ Students translate sentences from the text into English, then translate back with the text hidden.

Storytelling from a picture

An easy, low preparation way to build in comprehensible input is to use a picture as the basis for co-creating a story with a class. Teachers who use the TPRS (Teaching Proficiency through Reading and Storytelling) approach refer to this as Picture Talk. Pictures which can suggest a back-story work best. But those which communicate cultural information are also useful. Through repeated questioning (yes/no, either/or and so on) and eliciting ideas, writing up suggestions on the board, students hear, read and use multiple repetitions of target structures and vocabulary.

We know that stories and repetition play an important role in memory building. The emotional engagement with the story, to which the students have contributed, makes the lesson both more enjoyable and memorable.

Exploiting the protégé effect

It's easy to set up learning situations where one student has to teach others. Students can be told in advance that they will have to explain to a partner, or to you, how an area of grammar works, or to explain an aspect of the target language culture. Even when setting up pair or group work tasks, warn students that at the end of the task they will have to perform it or explain how they reached an outcome.

In the flipped learning model, where students learn something at home before applying that knowledge in class, tell students that they will have to explain what they learned to a partner. Examples include grammatical explanations on YouTube or listening comprehension tasks done at home based on online videos or audio (such as *audio-lingua.eu*).

Memorising conjugations with tunes

Don't expect students to be able to transfer rote learned verbs straight to spontaneous use, but singing a whole verb to a tune is fun, memorable and provides a sense of achievement. Many teachers and students enjoy using singalong videos on YouTube. It's a great lesson starter or filler. Here are a few examples.

French

Auld Lang Syne for *être* in the present tense.

The Pink Panther theme for *avoir* in the present tense.

Mission Impossible for *aller* or *être* in the present tense.

Spanish

Don't Stop Me Now (Queen) for *ser* in the present tense.

German

When the Saints Go Marching In for *sein* the present tense

The role of pushed output

Keep the production effect in mind. Don't assume language will stick if it is just heard or read. Comprehensible input is key, but provide opportunities for output, either voluntary or pushed, such as requiring a response to a prompt or question from students. But ensure that students have had the necessary receptive input before you expect them to produce language. If you get them to produce unstructured language too early, their memory will be overloaded, retrieval will be hesitant and a feeling of failure may be the result. The production effect and retrieval practice effect support exercises which force students to recycle, write or say language from memory, and limit the use of multi-choice and true/false style tasks which just require a tick or a number. But keep in mind that this kind of task is also a source of comprehensible input.

Vocabulary storage and retrieval

Find the near synonym

1. Write a numbered list of five words or short sentences on the board.

2. Say in random order, six words or sentences (with one item a distractor) which are near-synonyms of the items on the board.

3. Students match each item on the board to the number of its near-synonym and write it down.

Gapped sentences

1. Write a few gapped sentences on the board and tell students you are going to say in random order a number of words or phrases needed to complete the sentences.

2. Say the words or phrases and ask students to match them to the correct sentence.

(Conti and Smith, 2019)

Lesson scheduling

Although there's little research on this issue, school timetables which promote spaced repetition with three, four or five lessons a week, are likely to be better than those where, for example, students have only one or two contact sessions a week. Little and often!

Where lessons can't be arranged in this way, teachers can only do their best to plan individual lessons and give homework to ensure the best possible distribution of learning, favouring multiple encounters with language over time, rather than massed practice.

Memorising presentations

It's common for students to have to set oral presentations to memory when they have a classroom task or exam to prepare for. Research with actors shows that memorising a text is much more than just learning words. Deep processing, physical movement and emotional associations all play a role. For budding linguists, useful techniques include:

- ☒ repeatedly reciting the text out loud to take advantage of the production effect;
- ☒ where possible, using bodily actions or gesture to embody language used;
- ☒ where relevant, associating content with feelings;
- ☒ visualising the subject matter of the talk to engage visual memory;
- ☒ practising with a listener to take advantage of the protégé effect;
- ☒ recording and listening back to the talk;
- ☒ focusing on the starts of sentences – once a sentence is underway it may keep going;
- ☒ focusing on intonation to reinforce meaning.

Evaluating and adapting resources

Your knowledge of how students acquire and remember language enables you to evaluate critically any textbooks or other resources you are presented with. We believe that textbooks are usually overloaded with vocabulary and grammar and that a selection needs to be made. Many languages departments choose to do without textbooks.

Nation and Macalister (2009) suggest the following ways you can adapt a textbook, to which we have added our own gloss:

1. **Add or omit content.** (This is a common approach whereby you skip over the bits you don't like or add your own materials, for example more grammar practice examples, sentence builders or texts.)

2. **Change the sequencing of the content**. (You may choose to do this for all sorts of reasons. For example, if you use a text of your own containing new grammatical structures, you may use material from further ahead in the book. Or

you may just feel unsatisfied with the way grammar is selected and ordered and introduce more complex structures sooner.)

3. **Change the format**. You might resequence a particular unit, starting with an activity presented later. (Keep in mind that good books often sequence their content in a predictable fashion, so one reason for resequencing would be to simply provide some variation. This might even depend on the mood of the class that day (and yours!).

4. **Change the presentation**. Use different techniques for teaching the content to those suggested in the book or Teacher's Book. Usually, lack of space in textbooks means that texts are exploited superficially, so you need to develop a range of tasks to enable a text to be understood and processed, and for language to be recycled sufficiently (for example, the MARS-EARS sequence described earlier).

5. **Add or omit monitoring**. For example, you can get students to test each other to check progress, as opposed to doing so yourself.

6. **Add or omit assessment**. You can add extra quizzes or tests as you go along, to supplement the published end of unit test. Or you may feel that you don't need to use the published test at all.

Nation and Macalister go on to suggest that one significant way to adapt a book is by adding a programme of reading, or supplying extra listening material. This would be to respect three core principles they describe earlier in the book. These are:

☒ **Comprehensible input**. There needs to be substantial amounts of interesting written and spoken input.

☒ **Fluency**. The course should provide opportunities to increase fluency by repeatedly using language students already know.

☒ **Time on task**. As much time as possible needs to be spent focusing on language use (as opposed to descriptions of the language – 'talking about the language').

You may already successfully adapt your course book in an instinctive fashion, without necessarily thinking through your rationale. You just have a gut feeling that an exercise will work, a text is dull or a task too hard. Some teachers, often less experienced or trainees, may need more help refining the skill of evaluating and adapting course books. The key thing is this: does the book apply sensible, research-informed principles of language teaching, such as the primacy of interesting comprehensible input, repetition, spacing, retrieval, interaction and practice? Does it create the conditions for memories to stick?

Making language comprehensible

We have explained that for students to be able to process, learn from and remember language, the input they receive needs to be very highly comprehensible (ideally at least 95% known words). But comprehensibility can't be measured by knowledge of vocabulary alone. Other factors come into play, for example speed of delivery, accent, intonation and a student's pre-existing knowledge.

A key language teacher skill concerns how to make language comprehensible (Pica, Doughty and Young, 1987). When planning a curriculum as a department, it is useful to have shared strategies for doing this. Alongside the skilled use of question and answer, a number of specific techniques can be used to make language comprehensible and learnable when talking to students. These techniques include Long's (1981) *modified input* and *modified interaction*, where we simplify input and check for understanding (as a caregiver would with a young infant). They are part of your repertoire of formative assessment techniques.

- In general, pitch your language at or fractionally above the current level of the students' comprehension. Avoid using too many new words or phrases.

- Modify the input to make it accessible by simplifying the syntax, for example by using simple sentences and avoiding subordinate clauses.

- Select vocabulary that students are more likely to recognise, for example cognates or vocabulary encountered previously.

- Do not speak at native speaker speed; use repetition, rephrasing and pausing.

- Allow students to ask questions or seek clarification, including by gesture. Teach them simple phrases such as, *Can you repeat, please?*

- Maintain eye contact with as many students as possible, using facial expression to enhance meaning.

- Use generic teacher skills to hold attention, such as varying your physical position in the class, scanning left to right and front to back.

- Use humour to reduce anxiety and produce more engagement. Research suggests that students echo their teacher's behaviour (emotional priming) and are more likely to use language spontaneously when relaxed (Hawkes, 2012).

- Make use of translation into the first language when there is no efficient alternative. Do not feel obliged to use 100% target language.

- Use gesture, pictures and classroom objects. You can spot a language teacher by the number of gestures they use in everyday conversation!

- Be predictable in your routines, including questioning style, use of choral and individual repetition; students become familiar with what is expected of them.

- Reinforce listening by using the written word, for example, writing words and chunks on the board or providing transcripts of dialogues.

- Use formative assessment techniques such as mini-whiteboard responses to check for meaning, for example students write *true* on one side of their board and *false* on the other. Or check for understanding by asking individual students to translate back what you've said.

- Avoid talking for too long; observe when a class may be losing enthusiasm for an activity. Make use of your emotional and cognitive empathy skills.

Below is an example of a typical classroom dialogue which shows how you can model language repeatedly in an organic, communicative fashion. We used this example in Conti and Smith (2019). It was adapted from a lesson observed in Nava and Pedrazzini (2018). Suppose you want to explain the new word *sporty*.

Teacher:	*Are you sporty? I love sport. I'm very sporty. I play football, tennis and love to go walking (gestures). Do you like sport? Hands up (gesture) if you like sport.*
	(Students raise hands)
Teacher:	*Lionel Messi is sporty, isn't he? Harry Kane is sporty. Who else is sporty?*
Student:	*Rafael Nadal.*
Teacher:	*Yes! He's sporty. Is Homer Simpson sporty?*
Students:	*No!*
Teacher:	*Homer loves sport!*
Students:	*No! He loves donuts!*
Teacher:	*Is an elephant sporty?*
Students:	*No!*
Teacher:	*Is a hippopotamus sporty?*
Students:	*No!*
Teacher:	*All together: "sporty".*

And so on. Note how students receive plenty of modelled and chunked target language input, including multiple repetitions of the words *sport* and *sporty*, before they are expected to produce much language themselves.

One clear advantage for the style of sentence builder frame or knowledge organiser we have previously referred to, is that all the language is comprehensible since translations are provided.

Memory hooks (mnemonics)

When you learned a language you were probably taught memory hooks to help you remember various points of language. We collated responses from language teachers on social media for mnemonics of this type. They are laid out in Tables 16.3, 16.4 and 16.5. They can help students monitor the accuracy of their speech and writing, remember rules of phonics or remind them of elements to include in written assignments. A list of these could be kept as part of a curriculum plan.

Spanish mnemonics	What they refer to
DOCTOR PLACE	When the verbs *ser* an *estar* are used *Ser*: Date, Occupation, Characteristic, Time, Origin, Relation *Estar*: Position, Location, Action, Condition, Emotion
CAROLINA	Letters in Spanish which can be doubled, for example, the 'r' in *carro* or 'l' in *llave*
UWEIRDO	Use of the subjunctive: Uncertainty, Wishes, Emotions, Impersonal expressions, Recommendations and requests, Doubt and denial, *Ojalá*
Vin Diesel has ten weapons	Irregular imperatives: *sé, ven, di, sal, haz, ten, ve, pon*
My Big Dog Poops Under Trees	Qualifiers : *muy, bastante, demasiado, poco, un poco, tan*
DISHES	Irregular subjunctives : *dar, ir, ser, haber, estar, saber*

Table 16.3 Spanish mnemonics

French mnemonics	What they refer to
EN for engine	Using *en* in repositional phrases for motorised means of transport, for example, *en voiture* versus *à pied*
A TV AND MRS PERM MR DRAPERS MT VAN MR VAM RRED PANTS DR PV MASTERMAN DR VEMS MANTRAP MR DREAMPANTS	The verbs which take the auxiliary *être* in the perfect tense (allowing for slight variations of verbs included)
WEDDINGS	Uses of the subjunctive: Will, Emotions, Doubt, Desire, Interrogation, Negation, General characteristics, Superlative
BANGS BRAGS (R = rank)	Adjectives which precede the noun: Beauty, Age, Number (ordinal), Greatness, Size
CRFL (careful)	Consonants which are most commonly pronounced at the end of words
CROISSANT	Elements to include in a piece of intermediate writing; Connectives, Reasons, Opinions, Infinitive expressions, Subject pronouns (a range thereof), Star phrases, Adjectives and adverbs, Negatives, Tenses (a range thereof)
AVOCADO	Similar to above, but: Adjectives, Verbs, Opinions, Connectives, Adverbs, Description, Originality
STuPiD DPSTXZ (dipsticks)	Consonants which are usually not pronounced at the end of words
'A' and 'le' will never do, what do you do, you put A-U!	To remind students not write 'à le' instead of 'au'
♫ *me te nous vous, me te nous vous le la les, le la les lui leur, lui, leur y en, y en* (to the tune of Frère Jacques)	Order of pronouns
A donkey says *y en*	Order of pronouns

Table 16.4 French mnemonics

German mnemonics	What they refer to
FUDGEBOW BE DOG WUF	Prepositions which take the accusative case
BRATWURST	Elements to include in a piece of intermediate writing: Belief (opinion), Reason, Adjectives and adverbs, Tenses, Word order, Umlauts, Range, Structures, Time phrases
RAINCOAT	Similar to above, but Reasons, Adjectives, Intensifiers, Nouns (need capitals), Connective, Opinions, Adverbs (of time, manner, place) and Tenses
Elephants STir Tetley ENglish Tea ENergetically	Present tense regular verb endings
VBZGASMAN (Very Busy Gasman)	Prepositions which take the dative case
WEIL is so vile, the verb runs a mile!	Verbs goes to the end of the clause or sentence
WOW DAD	Subordinating conjunctions: *weil*, *obwohl*, *wenn*, *da*, *als*, *dass*
Tickle Me Pink	Order of adverbs: Time, Manner, Place
I AM a DR	Prepositions which take the accusative involve movement (Accusative Movement), while those which take the dative indicate rest (Dative Rest)

Table 16.5 German mnemonics

Corrective feedback

Given the very mixed research on corrective feedback, but bearing in mind the general view that it helps build memory for correct language, below are some general pointers, based on Ellis and Shintani (2013). There is a useful departmental discussion to be had on how corrective feedback should be used as part of the curriculum. Ellis and Shintani acknowledge that these points remain up for debate!

- It's a good way to get students to focus on the form of the language.
- Its effectiveness depends on students' developmental readiness to acquire the language feature being corrected. For example, there may be little point in correcting errors on relatively complex areas of grammar with near-beginners. Most students won't get much out of it.
- It's worth doing, whether your focus during any task is on accuracy or fluency. With fluency tasks such as loosely structured information gap tasks or role plays error correction can be very light-touch.
- It may be useful whether it is immediate or delayed. Written feedback is usually delayed (for example, when homework is being corrected) and has been shown to be effective. But be realistic about just how effective it is and whether you should be spending a lot of time correcting when there are other things to be done, such as preparing good lessons. A case can be made for selective correction of written work. It may be that higher-attaining students benefit from more detailed correction.
- There is no best way to carry out oral feedback. Explicit prompts and recasts (and combinations of both) can be effective, but lower-aptitude learners pick up and respond to recasts less readily.
- Direct correction of written work is probably better than indirect correction (getting students to work out the correction themselves).

Keep in mind that error correction is a subtle business which can affect students' self-efficacy and to which they will respond differently. Think of any ways you can to make correction memorable. A simple facial expression or gesture can encourage a student to think about the accuracy of what they have just said, prompting them to correct themselves and remember the correct form in the future. Whole class feedback based on just one or two learnable points may pay dividends, especially if the correction is repeated over time.

LIFT (Learner Initiated Feedback Technique)

Tell students to write in the margin of their work any questions they have regarding the grammatical accuracy of what they've written. For example, to take English as an example, "Should I use *with* or *by* here?"; "should this be *whose* or *which*?" Think of examples for the language(s) you teach. You can respond to these questions at the end of the piece of work or orally.

This is a good example of a metacognitive strategy, namely getting students to think about and monitor accuracy as they write. It also informs you about the kind of difficulties students are experiencing. A brief exchange on an area of accuracy encourages dialogue and should make the correction more memorable.

Stretching the high attainers

Part of curriculum planning is to take into account the needs of students with various levels of language learning aptitude. In Chapter 3 we gave a list of suggestions for identifying students with lower working memory capacity. But it's just as important to be able to recognise those students who need to be stretched more than average. Research over the years shows that the two main factors influencing progress are language aptitude and motivation. These are said to operate independently, so motivation can help mitigate any lack of aptitude, while high aptitude counts for a lot when motivation is lacking or work ethic poor. As we have previously pointed out, some researchers (for example, Wen, 2016) argue that working memory is fundamental to aptitude.

There's no doubt that aptitude for language learning exists and back in 1959 John Carroll and Stanley Sapon attempted to identify the factors which make up aptitude and predict a person's ability to learn another language (Carroll and Sapon, 1959). The audio and pen and paper tests they designed (called the MLAT – Modern Language Aptitude Test) are still used today, as well as later variations. Of course, proficiency is also a product of acquired knowledge, not just aptitude. The aptitude test shows potential, not achievement.

Carroll is considered by many to be one of the premier psychologists in terms of contributions to educational linguistics. Below are the factors he identified and which you can use to identify higher aptitude learners.

1. **Phonetic coding ability** — the ability to identify distinct sounds, to form associations between those sounds and the symbols representing them, and to retain these associations.

2. **Grammatical sensitivity** — the ability to recognise the grammatical functions of words (or other linguistic entities) in sentence structures.

3. **Rote learning ability for second language materials** — the ability to learn associations between sounds and meanings rapidly and efficiently, and to retain these associations.

4. **Inductive language learning ability** — the ability to infer or induce the rules governing a set of language materials, given samples of language materials that permit such inferences.

Although working memory was not on the agenda in 1959, you can see how it is involved in the above factors. Students have these characteristics to varying degrees. You have encountered the good mimic who is not so good at grammar, and the accurate, grammatically aware writer who has more difficulty pronouncing accurately or speaking fluently.

Guess how often

1. Display a series of time-frequency words on the board: *never, occasionally, sometimes, often, every day.*

2. Read to the class a series of statements about your personal life, sticking to easy, comprehensible language that students are familiar with, e.g. *I go to the cinema; I eat pizza; I visit Spain; I play tennis,* etc. Students must guess how often you do these things by choosing one of the words or phrases displayed. Answers may be written on mini-whiteboards.

3. Give the answers. Students could get points for correct guesses.

Peter Skehan's 2002 model of language aptitude and four stages in the acquisition process is summarised in Table 16.6 (adapted from Ellis and Shintani, 2013). He combines the notion of aptitude with cognitive processes involved in the type of information processing model we have been describing in the book.

Stage	Processes involved	Aptitude components
Noticing	The student directs attention to a feature in the input	Auditory segmentation; attention management; working memory; phonemic coding
Patterning	The student forms a hypothesis (explicitly or implicitly) about the feature, then extends the range of the hypothesis before recognising its limitations, restructuring it and integrating the new representation into the developing language system	Working memory; grammatical sensitivity; inductive language learning ability; restructuring capacity
Controlling	The student can use the integrated feature with increasing ease and accuracy	Automatisation; proceduralisation; retrieval processes
Lexicalising	The student can now produce the feature as a remembered whole rather than by applying a rule	Long-term memory; chunking; retrieval processes

Table 16.6 Peter Skehan's classification of aptitude and acquisition processes

Once we know something about aptitude and the acquisition process, how can this information be used to benefit the highest attainers – often those who will go on to study languages to a more advanced level? Below are some factors to bear in mind when curriculum planning.

☒ The provision of open-ended oral and written tasks. Does the curriculum specifically include such tasks with the aim of stretching the most able?

☒ Classroom techniques designed to match questions to students (as opposed to random 'cold-call' questioning). Are all teachers versed in skilled questioning techniques?

☒ Opportunities for extra listening and reading input. Does the department have the necessary sources available?

- ☒ A consideration of class grouping by aptitude or prior achievement. If the school culture supports ability groups, what would be the best format and how would you assign teachers to each group for the benefit of all students?
- ☒ Differentiated tasks, for example, varying the length of oral presentations or the titles of written essays. How could this be incorporated without sacrificing a 'mastery for all' approach?
- ☒ Provision for high-aptitude linguists who may have conditions such as ADHD or dyslexia. Can you identify them (e.g. the good mimic who may produce inaccurate written work)? Can you adjust teaching and resources to cater for their needs?

Principles of Instructed Language Learning

Second language acquisition researcher Rod Ellis produced a research-informed list of *Principles of Instructed Language Learning*, which was reproduced in Ellis and Shintani (2013 pp.22-27). These have exerted a powerful influence on curriculum design in some countries and are listed for you below.

1. Instruction needs to ensure that learners develop both a rich repertoire of formulaic expressions and a rule-based competence.

2. Instruction needs to ensure that learners focus on meaning.

3. Instruction needs to ensure that learners also focus on form.

4. Instruction needs to be predominantly directed at developing implicit knowledge of the second language while not neglecting explicit knowledge.

5. Instruction needs to take into account the order and sequence of acquisition.

6. Successful instructed language learning requires extensive second language input.

7. Successful instructed language learning also requires opportunities for output.

8. The opportunity to interact in the second language is central to developing second language proficiency.

9. Instruction needs to take into account individual differences in learners.

10. Instruction needs to take account of the fact that there is a subjective aspect to learning a new language.

11. In assessing learners' second language proficiency it is important to examine free as well as controlled production.

Summary

- ✓ Have clear, evidence-informed guidelines for the teaching of vocabulary and grammar.
- ✓ Remember the importance of a core vocabulary which consists of high-frequency words and chunks and high surrender value words and chunks.
- ✓ Remember the fundamental issue that students may not be ready to acquire a structure when you choose to teach it. You have to judge how much time to devote to a particular grammar point.
- ✓ Build into your curriculum recall tests or quizzes on a regular basis.
- ✓ Consider the value of a curriculum based on lexicogrammar and communicative functions.
- ✓ Plan sequences of lessons to integrate the four skills, recycling language chunks and consolidating memory. Begin with receptive activities, work through controlled tasks before gradually allowing students to produce language more spontaneously. Keep in mind the importance of thorough and extensive processing.
- ✓ Make skilled use of oral and written questioning to encourage thorough processing of language.
- ✓ Keep in mind the importance of the repetition priming effect and use ways to generate repetition across all the skills.
- ✓ Evaluate and adapt text book materials keeping in mind the science of learning. Consider not using text books at all.
- ✓ Use every technique possible to manage cognitive load and keep input comprehensible.
- ✓ Use memory hooks to help students develop their explicit knowledge of grammar and metacognitive strategies, for example how to write effective essays.
- ✓ Bear in mind the general view from research that corrective feedback helps build memory for accurate language, but be aware of its limitations. Time may be better spent doing other things than writing corrections on students' work. Consider the value of the LIFT technique.
- ✓ Be aware of the characteristics of high aptitude language students and have departmental strategies for dealing with their needs. These students may be the linguists of the future.
- ✓ Be aware of the general advice from research about second language learning when designing a curriculum.

For reflection

- ☒ To what extent does your languages department have a principled approach to curriculum planning?
- ☒ What adaptations would need to be made to your existing curriculum to make it as memory-friendly as possible?
- ☒ What are the pros and cons to a curriculum based on a sequence of grammatical structures: a 'structure of the day' curriculum?

Further reading and viewing

- ☒ Conti, G. (2018) How I Teach Lexicogrammar (parts 1 and 2). Available at: gianfrancoconti.com
- ☒ Conti, G. & Smith, S.P. (2019). *Breaking the Sound Barrier: Teaching language Learners How to Listen.* Independently published, available through Amazon.
- ☒ The TSC Review of MFL Pedagogy (Bauckham, 2016). Available at: ncelp.org
- ☒ Ellis, R. & Shintani, N. (2013). *Exploring Language Pedagogy through Second Language Acquisition Research.* London: Routledge.
- ☒ Macalister, J. & Nation, I.S.P. (2019). *Language Curriculum Design*. London: Routledge.
- ☒ Arifah Mardiningrum gives a short illustrated lecture based on the 2010 edition of the languages curriculum book by Paul Nation and John Macalister. Available at: youtube.com/watch?v=f5Hg_jTI734

Conclusion – applying cognitive science to language teaching

In the introduction to this book we pointed out that learning a language is not necessarily the same as learning other things in life. It's also the case that learning a new language is not the same as learning our first language(s). How could it be, when we already know so much from the first?

One of the big debates in the field of second language acquisition surrounds the nature of any innate ability humans have for language acquisition. It seems so remarkable that young children master the rules of a language in such a short time that many believe there must be special, language acquisition cognitive mechanisms involved. Are these mechanisms still in play when we learn a second language?

Some scholars believe that our ability to learn first and additional languages can only be explained by the existence of an innate, so-called **Universal Grammar** which dictates, across all languages, the way in which we generate rules from the input we receive, allowing us to produce novel utterances. By contrast, a growing number of researchers have come to believe that we use the same general learning mechanisms for language learning as we do for other types of learning (for example, Ellis and Larsen-Freeman, 2006). Some view it as a sort of statistical learning – we remember and adapt language based on the number of times we hear or see it used (Ellis, 2006). Some argue that, to a degree, we have the ability to learn language rules consciously, then to practise them until they become automatised (DeKeyser, 2007).

We don't know which of these perspectives is the most accurate or if some sort of combination of them is at work.

In terms of memory retention, these debates may not seem particularly relevant to language teachers, but in fundamental ways they are. If learning a new language is largely a natural, unconscious, implicit process then it's clear that our main role is to provide language input, allow learners to interact with it, nature will take its course and long-term memory will grow.

On the other hand, if learning is a conscious process involving working memory, one where declarative knowledge becomes procedural, then teaching has to take this into account. Our own belief is that, in school settings, both learning routes are necessary to maximise both implicit and explicit learning. Earl Stevick put it this way: "Learning and acquisition.. are separate strands which you as a teacher wind together so that they supplement each other" (cited in Swarbrick, 1994 p.106). This is how long-term memory is most likely to develop and how school learners are most likely to become proficient.

In our handbook *The Language Teacher Toolkit* (Smith and Conti, 2016) we proposed a list of 12 methodological principles to help teachers think about what they do and why. These principles very much align with findings from cognitive science and second language acquisition research.

Returning to these principles it's possible to show how knowledge of memory can help you refine or even transform your teaching, and could play a role in your departmental discussions on curriculum more broadly. Each principle is highlighted here, supplemented by reflections based on the various chapters in this book.

1. **Make sure students receive as much meaningful, stimulating input as possible. Place a high value on listening and reading. To quote Lightbown and Spada (2013): "Comprehension of meaningful language is the foundation of language acquisition".**

   Comprehensible input allows the processes of implicit learning and priming to take place. Meaningful input means lower cognitive load and less language learning anxiety. Texts which are at least 95% comprehensible, sentence builders, knowledge organisers, parallel texts, pictures, gesture, skilled questioning, classroom realia – all of these help keep language meaningful. In addition, we have seen that the more distinctive the input is, the more likely it is to be encoded and recalled.

2. **Make sure students have lots of opportunities to practise orally, both in a tightly structured fashion led by the teacher and through communication with other students. Have them repeat and recycle language as much as possible.**

   Oral practice is supported by the production effect, builds phonological memory and encourages noticing, including the noticing of errors. We have argued that automatisation develops best when there is a careful progression from receptive tasks, through controlled activities, leading to more spontaneous production. Controlled oral games and drills generate repetition and encourage retrieval. Remember that when we speak we activate the same areas in the brain (the Phonological Loop) as when we listen.

When the teacher is in charge the quality of input is higher, but pair and group work allows more students to practise in ways they find enjoyable and less anxiety-inducing.

3. **Use a balanced mixture of the four skills of listening, speaking, reading and writing.**

Lessons and sequences of lessons which integrate all the skills permit repetition through recycling of language structures. They promote dual coding, schema building and long-term memory development. In lesson planning, changing the mode (skill) creates variety for students and encourages deeper processing, for example when students encounter vocabulary in different settings.

It's particularly important to make sure listening is not neglected, since it is at the heart of language acquisition.

4. **Promote independent learning outside the classroom.**

Extra tasks beyond the classroom create more opportunities for implicit learning and recycling. They can also be motivational. Immersion experiences are the best of all for developing motivation and implicit learning.

5. **Select and sequence the vocabulary and grammar you expose students to. Do not overload them with too much new language at once. Focus on high frequency language.**

This helps manage cognitive load, while taking into account readiness and learnability issues. By limiting the input to higher frequency language you enable this language to be recycled multiple times, giving it a greater chance to find its way to long-term memory. Think of the snowball effect, as new knowledge schemas attach to existing ones. Limiting the number of words and chunks allows these to be repeated more often and processed more deeply, for example in collocations.

Selecting and sequencing vocabulary and grammar does not necessarily mean designing the whole curriculum around this selection. Communicative functions and tasks, often tied in with topics, are a valid way to plan a curriculum. In this way the vocabulary and grammar serve the communicative functions.

Make sure students focus on less salient vocabulary and grammar.

6. **Be prepared to explain how the language works, but don't spend too much time on this. Students need to use the language, not talk about it. Research provides some support for the explicit teaching and practice of rules.**

Explanations develop declarative knowledge which has the potential, through practice and automatisation, to form schemas in long-term memory and procedural knowledge. Take advantage of the worked example effect and Rosenshine principles when presenting and practising new language.

Declarative knowledge of grammar has value in its own right. It's all too easy, however, to believe that declarative knowledge instantly becomes procedural. In other words, it is tempting to believe that when students know the rules they will be able to apply them. A key takeaway from our book is that long-term memory only develops with repeated exposures and practice over time.

7. **Aim to enhance proficiency – the ability to independently use the language promptly in real situations.**

Spontaneous speech and writing are the ultimate goal (though not necessarily for all students), but these develop slowly, often in a non-linear fashion. Taking into account your knowledge of memory you can encourage the process of acquisition at the right pace. For too many students, proficiency never develops at all because knowledge is never thoroughly processed, embedded and retained. The motto 'less is more' is worth keeping in mind.

A realistic goal for many students is to be able to understand and produce a narrow repertoire of language for communicative purposes.

Keep in mind the TAP effect when designing classroom tasks (do they resemble real life communicative tasks?) and tests (is the format and language of the test the same or similar to those previously experienced in lessons?).

8. **Use listening and reading activities to model good language use rather than test; focus on the process, not the product.**

Activities which enable thorough processing to occur promote more secure memory. Listening and reading for modelling tasks develop phonological awareness and memory, along with phonics skill. When listening and reading exercises are purely focused on testing comprehension they encourage superficial processing of language and guesswork. Reading aloud tasks take account of dual coding and the generation effect.

Listening comprehension tasks which are too hard and encourage guesswork, not only stop language from being processed, but also cause anxiety.

9. **Be prepared to judiciously and sensitively correct students and get them to respond to feedback. Research suggests negative feedback can improve acquisition.**

The research from cognitive science on errorful learning and the research from second language acquisition support the use of corrective feedback. Activities which involve students spotting and correcting mistakes encourage schema building and deeper processing.

Making errors is a natural part of the process of acquisition and the research on readiness and natural orders reminds us that some errors take time to disappear. Over-generalisation errors can be a sign of effective learning.

10. **Translation (both ways) can play a useful role, but if you do too much you may neglect general language input.**

Translation is valuable in making language comprehensible, thus reducing cognitive load. We know from research that knowledge schemas in both languages are simultaneously activated when students translate.

11. **Make sensible and selective use of digital technology to enhance exposure and practice.**

Technology use can be valuable for motivation, promote spaced learning, recycling and dual coding. But we must not forget that it can create divided attention which may slow down the process of memory building. The best apps and programmes enable more thorough processing through a range of manipulation exercises based on whole chunks of language and exploiting the full range of language skills.

12. **Place a significant focus on the second language culture. This is one way of many to increase student motivation and to broaden outlooks.**

When motivation is increased, more learning happens and more memories are created. Embedding language in culturally interesting and valuable contexts not only broadens horizons, but also makes language memorable.

Every book about second language learning tells you at some point how complex a process it is, and how difficult it can be to say how a language should be taught. As one scholar, Wilga Rivers, has put it, when we try to describe second language learning, we are like the blind men of Indian legend, trying to describe an elephant (Rivers, 1983). What it's like to you depends on the part you happen to touch and having a clear vision of the whole is hard. Memory building is slow and incremental. But knowing more about how memory works can help us devise lessons and a whole curriculum with greater clarity and skill.

If students are hearing, reading and interacting with comprehensible language regularly, in ways they find meaningful and enjoyable, they are more likely to remember it.

Bibliography

We have indicated where sources were freely available online at the time of writing.

Abbott, E.E. (1909). On the analysis of the factor of recall in the learning process. *The Psychological Review: Monograph Supplements, 11*(1), 159–177. Available at: teachertoolkit.co.uk/wp-content/uploads/2020/09/abott1909.pdf

Adams, A.-M. & Gathercole, S.E. (1996). Phonological working memory and spoken language development in young children. *Quarterly Journal of Experimental Psychology, 49*, 216-233.

Agarwal, P.K., D'Antonio, L., Roediger, H.L., McDermott, K.B. & McDaniel, M.A. (2014). Classroom-based programs of retrieval practice reduce middle school and high school students' test anxiety. *Journal of Applied Research in Memory and Cognition, 3* (3), 131-139.

Alain, C., Khatamian, Y., He, Y., Lee, Y., Moreno, S., Leing, A.W.S., & Bialystok, E. (2018). Different neural activities support auditory working memory in musicians and bilinguals. *Annals of the New York Academy of Sciences, 1423*(1), 435-446.

Alderson, J. (2007). The CEFR and the Need for More Research. *The Modern Language Journal, 91*, 659-663.

Ammar, A. (2008). Prompts and recasts: Differential effects on second language morphosyntax. *Language Teaching Research, 12* (2), 183-210.

Anderson, F.T., & McDaniel, M.A. (2019). Retrieval in prospective memory: Multiple processes or just delay? *Quarterly Journal of Experimental Psychology, 72* (9), 2197–2207.

Anderson, J.R. (1982). Acquisition of cognitive skill. *Psychological Review, 89* (4), 369–406.

Anderson, R.C. (1984). Role of the Reader's Schema in Comprehension, Learning, and Memory. In R.C. Anderson, J. Osborn & R.J. Tierney (Eds.) *Learning to Read in American Schools: Basal Readers and Content Texts, 243-257.* Hillsdale, New Jersey: Erlbaum.

Andrade, J. (2010). What does doodling do? *Applied Cognitive Psychology, 24*, 100-106.

Arndt, H.L. & Woore, R. (2018). Vocabulary learning from watching YouTube videos and reading blog posts. *Language, Learning and Technology. 22*, 124-142. Available at: researchgate.net/publication/328138374

Askvik, E.O., van der Weel, F.R. & van der Meer, A.L.H. (2020). The Importance of Cursive Handwriting Over Typewriting for Learning in the Classroom: A High-Density EEG Study of 12-Year-Old Children and Young Adults. *Frontiers in Psychology*. Available at: frontiersin.org/articles/10.3389/fpsyg.2020.01810/full

Atkinson, R.C., & Shiffrin, R.M. (1968). Human memory: A proposed system and its control processes. In K.W. Spence & J.T. Spence (Eds.) *The psychology of learning and motivation* (Volume 2), 89–195. New York: Academic Press.

Baddeley, A.D. (1997). *Human memory: Theory and Practice (Revised)*. Hove: Psychology Press.

Baddeley, A. D. (2000). The episodic buffer: A new component of working memory? *Trends in Cognitive Sciences, 4* (11): 417-423.

Baddeley, A.D., Eysenck, M.W. & Anderson, M.C. (2020). *Memory*. London: Routledge.

Baddeley, A.D., Gathercole, S. & Papagno, C. (1998). The phonological loop as a language learning device. *Psychological Review, 105* (1), 158-173.

Baddeley, A.D. & Hitch, G. (1974). Working memory. In G.H. Bower (Ed.), *The psychology of learning and motivation: Advances in research and theory* (Vol. 8), 47–89. NY: Academic Press.

Baddeley, A.D. & Logie, R.H. (1999). Working memory: The multiple-component model. In A. Miyake & P. Shah (Eds.), *Models of working memory*, 28-61. Cambridge: Cambridge University Press.

Bahrick, H.P. (1984). Semantic memory content in permastore: Fifty years of memory for Spanish learned in school. *Journal of Experimental Psychology: General, 113* (1), 1–29.

Bahrick H.P., Bahrick L.E., Bahrick A.S. & Bahrick P.E. (1993). Maintenance of foreign language vocabulary and the spacing effect. *Psychological Science, 4*, 316–321.

Bandura, A. (1997). *Self-efficacy: The exercise of control.* WH Freeman/Times Books/Henry Holt & Co.

Barg, J.A. & Schul, Y. (1980). On the Cognitive Benefits of Teaching. *Journal of Educational Psychology, 73*, 593-604.

Bartlett, F.C. (1932). *Remembering.* Cambridge: Cambridge University Press.

Bartol, T.M., Bromer, C., Kinney, J., Chirillo, M.A., Bourne, J.N., Harris, K.M., & Sejnowski, T.J. (2015). Nanoconnectomic upper bound on the variability of synaptic plasticity. eLife Nov 30. Available at: ncbi.nlm.nih.gov/pmc/articles/PMC4737657/

Bauckham, I. (2016). Modern Foreign Languages Pedagogy Review. Available at: ncelp.org/wp-content/uploads/2020/02/MFL_Pedagogy_Review_Report_TSC_PUBLISHED_VERSION_Nov_2016_1_.pdf

Benati, A. (2017). The role of input and output tasks in grammar instruction: Theoretical, empirical and pedagogical considerations. *Studies in Second Language Learning and Teaching, 7* (3), 377-396. Available at: eric.ed.gov/fulltext/EJ1155604.pdf

Bilbrough, N. (2011). *Memory Activities for Language Learning*. Cambridge: CUP.

Bjork, R.A. (2011). On the symbiosis of learning, remembering, and forgetting. In A.S. Benjamin (Ed.), *Successful remembering and successful forgetting: a Festschrift in honor of Robert A. Bjork*, 1-22. London, UK: Psychology Press. Available at: bjorklab.psych.ucla.edu/wp-content/uploads/sites/13/2016/07/RBjork_2011.pdf

Bloom, B.S. (1968). Learning for mastery. *Evaluation Comment (UCLA-CSEIP), 1* (2), 1–12.

Bock, J.K. (1986). Syntactic persistence in language production. *Cognitive Psychology, 18*, 355–87.

Bock, K., & Griffin, Z.M. (2000). The persistence of structural priming: Transient activation or implicit learning? *Journal of Experimental Psychology: General, 129* (2), 177–192.

Bransford, J.D., Brown, A.L., & Cocking, R.R. (2000). *How People Learn: Brain, Mind, Experience, and School.* Washington DC: National Academy Press.

Brown, J. (1958). Some Tests of the Decay Theory of Immediate Memory. *Quarterly Journal of Experimental Psychology, 10*, 12-21.

Brown, J.D., Robson, G. & Rosenkjar, P.R. (2001). Personality, motivation, anxiety, strategies, and language proficiency of Japanese students. In Z. Dörnyei, R.W. Schmidt (Eds.), *Motivation and second language acquisition*, 361–398. Honolulu: University of Hawaii.

Brown, R. (1973). *A First Language*. Cambridge, MA: Harvard University Press.

Busch, B. & Watson, E. (2019). *The Science of Learning: 77 Studies That Every Teacher Needs to Know.* London: Routledge.

Butler, A.C. (2010). Repeated testing produces superior transfer of learning relative to repeated studying. *Journal of Experimental Psychology: Learning, Memory, and Cognition, 36* (5), 1118-1133.

Butler, A.C., Karpicke, J.D. & Roediger, H.L. III (2007). The Effect of Type and Timing of Feedback on Learning from Multiple-Choice Tests. *Journal of Experimental Psychology: Applied, 13* (4), 273-281. Available at: memory.psych.purdue.edu/downloads/2007_Butler_Karpicke_Roediger_JEPA.pdf

Bygate, M., Norris, J. & van den Branden, K. (2015). Task-Based Language Teaching. In C.A. Chapelle (Ed.) *The Encyclopedia of Applied Linguistics*.

Carpenter, S.K. (2017). Spacing effects on learning and memory. In J.T. Wixted (Ed.) *Cognitive psychology of memory: Volume 2: Learning and Memory: A comprehensive reference*, 465–485. 2nd edition. Oxford: Academic Press.

Carpenter, S.K., & Toftness, A.R. (2017). The effect of prequestions on learning from video presentations. *Journal of Applied Research in Memory and Cognition, 6,* 104-109.

Carroll, J.B., & Sapon, S.M. (1959). *Modern language aptitude test.* Psychological Corporation.

Cepeda, N.J., Vul, E., Rohrer, D., Wixted, J.T. & Pashler, H. (2008). Spacing effects in learning: a temporal ridgeline of optimal retention. *Psychological Science, 19* (11), 1095-1102.

Chandler, P. & Sweller, J. (1992). The split-attention effect as a factor in the design of instruction. *British Journal of Educational Psychology, 62* (2), 233–246.

Chomsky, N. (1965). *Aspects of the theory of syntax*. Cambridge, MA: M.I.T. Press.

Collins, L., Halter, R.H., Lightbown, P.M. & Spada, N. (1999). Time and the Distribution of Time in L2 Instruction. *TESOL Quarterly, 33*, 655-680.

Conti, G. (2004). *Metacognitive enhancement and error correction: An investigation of the impact of self-monitoring strategies on L2 Italian student writing*. PhD thesis, University of Reading, UK.

Conti, G. & Smith, S.P. (2019). *Breaking the Sound Barrier: Teaching Language Learners How to Listen*. Independently Published. Available at Amazon.

Cowan, N. (2010). The Magical Mystery Four: How is Working Memory Capacity Limited, and Why? *PMC US national Library of Medicine*. Available at: ncbi.nlm.nih.gov/pmc/articles/PMC2864034/

Cowan, E., Liu, A., Henin, S., Kothare, S., Devinsky, O. & Davachi, L. (2020). Sleep spindles promote the restructuring of memory representations in ventromedial prefrontal cortex through enhanced hippocampal–cortical functional connectivity. *Journal of Neuroscience, 40* (9), 1909-1919.

Craik, F.I.M. & Lockhart, R.S. (1972). Levels of processing: A framework for memory research. *Journal of Verbal Learning and Verbal Behavior, 11*, 671-684.

Craik, F.I.M., & Tulving, E. (1975). Depth of processing and the retention of words in episodic memory. *Journal of Experimental Psychology: General, 104* (3), 268–294.

Craik, F.I.M. & Watkins, M.J. (1973). The role of rehearsal in short-term memory. *Journal of Verbal Learning and Verbal Behavior, 12* (6), 599-607.

Crum, A.J., Salovey, P. & Achor, S. (2013). Rethinking Stress: The Role of Mindsets in Determining the Stress Response. *Journal of Personality and Social Psychology, 104* (4) 716-33.

Cuevas, J. & Dawson, B.L. (2018). A test of two alternative cognitive processing models: Learning styles and dual coding. *Theory and Research in Education, 16* (1), 40-64.

Daneman, M. & Carpenter, P.A. (1980). Individual differences in working memory and reading. *Journal of Verbal Learning and Verbal Behavior, 19* (4), 450-466.

Daneman, M. & Merikle, P.M. (1996). Working memory and language comprehension: A meta-analysis. *Psychonomic Bulletin and Review, 3* (4), 422-433. Available at: link.springer.com/content/pdf/10.3758%2FBF03214546.pdf

Deci, E.L. & Ryan, R.M. (2008). Self-determination theory: A macrotheory of human motivation, development, and health. *Canadian Psychology/Psychologie Canadienne, 49*(3), 182–185.

De Jong, N. (2005). Can second language grammar be learned through listening? An experimental study. *Studies in Second Language Acquisition, 27* (2), 205-234.

De Jong, N. (2010). Cognitive load theory, educational research, and instructional design: some food for thought. *Instructional Science, 38*, 105–134. Available at: link.springer.com/article/10.1007/s11251-009-9110-0

Dédéyan, A., Largy, P. & Negro, I. (2006). Working memory and detection of verbal agreement errors: A study in novice and skilled writers. *Langages, 164*, 57-70.

Dédéyan, A., Olive, T., Largy, P. (2006,). *Involvement of working memory in detecting subject-verb agreement errors: Developmental approach.* Paper presented at the International Symposium on Cognitive Approaches to Learning Written Language, Rennes, France.

Dehaene, S. (2009). *Reading in the Brain: The Science and Evolution of a Human Invention*. Viking Adult.

Dehaene, S. (2020). *How We Learn: The New Science of Education and the Brain*. Allen Lane.

DeKeyser, R.M. (1995). Learning Second Language Grammar Rules: An Experiment with a Miniature Linguistic System. *Studies in Second Language Acquisition*. *17* (3), 379–410.

DeKeyser, R.M. (2007). Skill acquisition theory. In B. VanPatten and J. Williams (Eds.), *Theories in Second Language Acquisition: an Introduction*. Mahwah, NJ: Lawrence Erlbaum.

Dell, G.S. & Sullivan, J.M. (2004). Speech errors and language production: neuropsychological and connectionist perspectives. In B.H. Ross (Ed.) *The psychology of learning and motivation: advances in research and theory, 63-108*. Vol 44. New York: Elsevier Science.

Dickerson, K.C. & Adcock, R.A. (2020). Motivation and Memory. In Stevens' *Handbook of Experimental Psychology and Cognitive Neuroscience*, J.T. Wixted (Ed.). First published 2018.

Diekelmann, S., Buchel, C., Born, J., & Rasch, B. (2011). Labile or stable: opposing consequences for memory when reactivated during waking and sleep. *Nature Neuroscience, 14*, 381–386.

Drondric, V. (2019). How (not) to teach English vocabulary. *The CATESOL Journal, 31* (1), 29-54. Available at: eric.ed.gov/fulltext/EJ1238807.pdf

Dulay, H.C., & Burt, M.K. (1974). Natural sequences in child second language acquisition. *Language Learning, 24*, 37-53.

Dunlosky, J. & Thiede, K.W. (2013). Metamemory. *The Oxford Handbook of Cognitive Psychology,* 283-298.

Dunlosky, J., Rawson, K.A, Marsh, E.J., Nathan, M.J. & Willingham, D.T. (2013). Improving Students' Learning With Effective Learning Techniques: Promising Directions From Cognitive and Educational Psychology. *Association for Psychological Science. Psychological Science in the Public Interest*, *14* (1), 4-58. Available at: pcl.sitehost.iu.edu/rgoldsto/courses/dunloskyimprovinglearning.pdf

Ebbinghaus, H. (1885). Memory: A Contribution to Experimental Psychology. New York: Dover. Translated and available at: psychclassics.yorku.ca/Ebbinghaus/index.htm

Ellis, N. C. (2005). At the interface: Dynamic interactions of explicit and implicit language knowledge. *Studies in Second Language Acquisition, 27*, 305–352.

Ellis, N.C. (2006). Language acquisition as rational contingency learning. *Applied Linguistics, 27*, 1-24.

Ellis, N.C. & Larsen-Freeman, D. (2006). Language emergence: implications for applied linguistics – introduction to the special issue. *Applied Linguistics, 27*, 558-589.

Ellis N.C. (2017). Implicit and Explicit Knowledge About Language. In: J. Cenoz, D. Gorter, S. May (Eds.) *Language Awareness and Multilingualism. Encyclopedia of Language and Education* (3rd ed.). Springer, Cham.

Ellis, R. (2008). *The Study of Second Language Acquisition*. Oxford: Oxford University Press.

Ellis, R. (2015). Researching Acquisition Sequences: Idealization and De-idealization in SLA. *Language Learning, 65*, 181-209.

Ellis, R., Loewen, S., & Erlam, R. (2006). Implicit and explicit corrective feedback and the acquisition of L2 grammar. *Studies in Second Language Acquisition, 28*, 339-368.

Ellis, R. & Shintani, N. (2013). *Exploring Language Pedagogy through Second Language Acquisition Research.* London: Routledge.

Ertel, K.A., Glymour, M.M., & Berkman, L.F. (2008). Effects of social integration on preserving memory function in a nationally representative US elderly population. *American Journal of Public Health, 98* (7), 1215–1220. Available at: ncbi.nlm.nih.gov/pmc/articles/PMC2424091/

Feld, G.B. and Diekelmann, S. (2015). Sleep smart—optimizing sleep for declarative learning and memory. *Frontiers in Psychology*. Available at: frontiersin.org/articles/10.3389/fpsyg.2015.00622/full#h3

Ferreira, V., Bock, K., Wilson, M.P. & Cohen, N.J. (2008). Memory for syntax despite amnesia. *Psychological Science, 19* (9), 940–946.

Fisher, R.P. & Craik, F.I.M. (1980). The effects of elaboration on recognition memory. *Memory and Cognition, 8*, 400–404.

Flavell, J.H. (1970). Developmental studies of mediated memory. In H.W. Reese & L.P. Lipsitt (Eds.) *Advances in child development and behavior* (Vol. 5). New York: Academic Press.

Flavell, J.H. (1979). Metacognition and cognitive monitoring: a new area of cognitive-developmental inquiry. *American Psychology, 34*, 906–911.

Flavell, J. H. (1985). *Cognitive development.* Englewood Cliffs, NJ: Prentice Hall.

Fletcher-Wood, H. (2018). *Responsive Teaching: Cognitive Science and Formative Assessment in Practice.* London: Routledge.

Forrin, N.D. & MacLeod, C.M. (2018). This time it's personal: the memory benefit of hearing oneself. *Memory, 26 (4)*, 574-579.

Gardner, R.C., & Lambert, W.E. (1972). *Attitudes and motivation in second language learning.* Rowley, MA: Newbury House.

Gathercole, S.E. & Pickering, S.J. (2000) Working memory deficits in children with low achievements in the national curriculum at 7 years of age. *British Journal of Educational Psychology, 70* (2), 177-94.

Gathercole, S.E. & Alloway, T.P. (2007). *Understanding Working Memory: A Classroom Guide.* Available at: www.mrc-cbu.cam.ac.uk/wp-content/uploads/2013/01/WM-classroom-guide.pdf

Geary, D.C. (2008). An Evolutionarily Informed Education Science. *Educational Psychologist, 43*(4), 179-195.

Germine, L.T., Duchaine, B. & Nkayama, K. (2010). Where cognitive development and aging meet: Face learning ability peaks after age 30. *Cognition, 11*, 201-210. Available at: lab.faceblind.org/papers/Germine11Cognition.pdf

Geva, E. & Ryan, E. (1993). Linguistic and cognitive correlates of academic skills in first and second languages. *Language Learning, 43*, 5-42.

Goo, J. (2012). Corrective feedback and working memory capacity in interaction-driven L2 learning. *Studies in Second Language Acquisition, 34*, 445-474.

Grabe, W. & Stoller, F.L. (2019). *Teaching and Researching Reading* (3rd ed.) London: Routledge.

Gradisar, M., Wolfson, A.R., Harvey, A.G., Hale, L., Rosenberg, R. & Czeisler, C.A. (2013). The Sleep and Technology Use of Americans: Findings from the National Sleep Foundation's 2011 Sleep in America Poll. *Journal of Clinical Sleep Medicine: 9* (12), 1291-1299.

Graham, S. (2017). Research into practice: Listening strategies in an instructed classroom setting. *Language Teaching, 50*, 107-119.

Habók, A. & Magyar, A. (2018). The Effect of Language Learning Strategies on Proficiency, Attitudes and School Achievement. *Frontiers in Psychology, 8.* Available at: researchgate.net/publication/322397091

Hakuta, K. (1974). Prefabricated patterns and the emergence of structure in second language acquisition. *Language Learning, 24* (2), 287-297.

Hall, C. (2020). *Gesture as a bridge between non-declarative and declarative knowledge.* PhD thesis, University of Chicago. Available at: knowledge.uchicago.edu/record/2759

Hallam, S., Price, J. & Katsarou, G. (2002). The effects of background music on primary school pupils' task performance. *Educational Studies, 28* (2), 111-122.

Han, Z. & Finneran, R. (2014). Re-engaging the interface debate. *International Journal of Applied Linguistics, 24,* 370-389.

Hattie, J. & Timperley, H. (2007). The Power of Feedback. *Review of Educational Research, 77*(1), 81-112.

Hawkes, R. (2012). Learning to talk and talking to learn: how spontaneous teacher-learner interaction in the secondary foreign languages classroom provides greater opportunities for L2 learning. Unpublished doctoral thesis. Available at: www.rachelhawkes.com/RHawkes_FinalThesis.pdf

Heath, C. & Heath, D. (2008). *Made to Stick: Why Some Ideas Take Hold and Others Come Unstuck.* London: Arrow Books.

Hendrickson, J.M. (1978). Error correction in foreign language teaching: recent theory, research and practice. *The Modern Language Journal, 62,* 387-398.

Hicks, J.L., Marsh, R.L. & Cook, G.I. (2005). Task interference in time-based, event-based, and dual intention prospective memory conditions. *Journal of Memory and Language, 53* (3), 430-444.

Hoey, M. (2005). *Lexical Priming: A New Theory of Words and Language.* Psychology Press.

Horwitz, E.K., Horwitz, M.N. & Cope, J. (1986). Foreign language classroom anxiety. *The Modern Language Journal, 70* (2), 125–132.

Hu, M. & Nation, I.S.P. (2000). Unknown vocabulary density and reading comprehension. *Reading in a Foreign Language 13* (1), 403-430. Available at: researchgate.net/publication/234651421

Hudson, T. (2007). *Teaching Second Language Reading.* Oxford: Oxford University Press.

Hunt, R.R. & Smith, R.E. (1996). Accessing the particular from the general: The power of distinctiveness in the context of organization. *Memory and Cognition, 24,* 217–225.

James, W. (1890). *The Principles of Psychology.* Dover Publications.

Jäncke, L., & Sandmann, P. (2010). Music listening while you learn: No influence of background music on verbal learning. *Behavioral and Brain Functions, 6,* 1-14.

Juffs, M. & Harrington, M. (2011). Aspects of working memory in second language learning and teaching. *Language Teaching, 44,* 137-166.

Karpicke, J.D. & Roediger, H.L. (2008). The critical importance of retrieval for learning. *Science, 319,* 966-8.

Kirschner, P.A., Sweller, J. & Clark, R.E (2006). Why Minimal Guidance During Instruction Does Not Work: An Analysis of the Failure of Constructivist, Discovery, Problem-Based, Experiential, and Inquiry-Based Teaching. *Educational Psychologist, 41*(2), 75-86.

Kobayashi, K. (2018). Learning by Preparing-to-Teach and Teaching: A Meta-Analysis. *Japanese Psychological Research, 61* (3), 192-203.

Kornell, N. (2011). Failing to predict future chances in memory: a stability bias yields long-term overconfidence. In A.S. Benjamin (Ed.), *Successful Remembering and Successful Forgetting: A Festschrift in Honor of Robert A. Bjork*, 365–386. New York, NY: Psychology Press.

Krashen, S.D. (1982). *Principles and Practice in Second Language Acquisition*. Oxford: Pergamon Press. Available at: sdkrashen.com/content/books/principles_and_practice.pdf

Kuhl, P.K., Tsao, F-M. & Liu, H.M. (2003). Foreign-language experience in infancy: Effects of short-term exposure and social interaction on phonetic learning. *Proceedings of the National Academy of Sciences, 100* (15), 9096-9101. Available at: pnas.org/content/100/15/9096

Kuhn, M.R. & Stahl, S.A. (2003). Fluency: A review of developmental and remedial practices. *Journal of Educational Psychology, 95* (1), 3–21.

Kvavilashvili, L., Messer, D.J. & Ebdon, P. (2001). Prospective memory in children: the effects of age and task interruption. *Developmental* Psychology, *37* (3), 418-430.

Kwon, E-Y. (2005). The "Natural Order" of Morpheme Acquisition: A Historical Survey and Discussion of Three Putative Determinants. Teachers College, *Columbia University Working Papers in TESOL & Applied Linguistics, 5* (1). Available at: journals.cdrs.columbia.edu/wp-content/uploads/sites/12/2015/06/3.-Kwon-2005.pdf

Laufer B. & Rozovski-Roitblat, B. (2011). Incidental vocabulary acquisition: The effects of task type, word occurrence and their combination. *Language Teaching Research, 15* (4), 391-411.

Lee, H.Y., Jamieson, J.P., Miu, A.S., Josephs, R.A. & Yeager, D.S. (2019). An Entity Theory of Intelligence Predicts Higher Cortisol Levels When High School Grades Are Declining. *Child Development, 90* (6), 849-867.

Leow, R.P. (2015). *Explicit Learning in the L2 Classroom: A Student-Centered Approach*. New York: Routledge.

Lessard-Clouston, M. (2013). Word Lists for Vocabulary Learning and Teaching. *The CATESOL Journal, 24,* 287-304.

Lewis, M. (1993). *The Lexical Approach.* Hove: Language Teaching Publications.

Lightbown, P.M. (2008). Transfer appropriate processing as a model for classroom second language acquisition. In Z. Han (Ed.), *Understanding second language process,* 27-44. Clevedon, UK: Multilingual Matters.

Lightbown, P.M. & Spada, N. (2013). *How Languages are Learned*. Oxford: OUP.

Likourezos, V., Kalyuga, S., & Sweller, J. (2019). The variability effect: when instructional variability is advantageous. *Educational Psychology Review, 31*.

Loewen, S. & Sato, M. (2017). *The Routledge Handbook of Instructed Second Language Acquisition*. London: Routledge.

Loewen, S., Isbell, D.R. & Sporn, Z. (2020). The effectiveness of app-based language instruction for developing receptive linguistic knowledge and oral communicative ability. *Foreign Language Annals, 53*, 209-233.

Logie, R.H. (1995). *Visuo-spatial working memory.* Hove: Erlbaum.

Long, M.H. (1981). Input, interaction, and second- language acquisition. *Annals of the New York Academy of Sciences, 379*(1), 259-278.

Long, M.H. (1996). The role of the linguistic environment in second language acquisition. In W. Ritchie & T. Bhatia (Eds.), *Handbook of Second Language Acquisition,* 413–468. San Diego: Academic Press.

Loprinzi, P.D. & Frith, E. (2018). The Role of Sex in Memory Function: Considerations and Recommendations in the Context of Exercise. *Journal of Clinical Medicine, 7* (6), 132.

Lyster, R. & Ranta, E. (1997). Corrective feedback and learner uptake: negotiation of form in communicative classrooms. *Studies in Second Language Acquisition, 19* (1), 37-61.

Macalister, J. & Nation, I.S.P. (2019). *Language Curriculum Design.* London: Routledge.

Macedonia, M. (2014). Bringing back the body into the mind: gestures enhance word learning in foreign language. *Frontiers in Psychology, 5.* Available at: ncbi.nlm.nih.gov/pmc/articles/PMC4260465/

Mackey, A., Philp, J., Egi, T., Fujii, A., & Tatsumi, T. (2002). Individual differences in working memory, noticing of interactional feedback and L2 development. In P. Robinson (Ed.), *Individual Differences and Instructed Language Learning,* 181–208. Philadelphia: John Benjamins.

Marian V. & Neisser, U.G. (2000). Language-dependent recall of autobiographical memories. *Journal of Experimental Psychology, 129* (3), 361-368.

Mattys, S.L., Baddeley, A. & Trenkic, D. (2018). Is the superior verbal memory span of Mandarin speakers due to faster rehearsal? *Memory and Cognition, 46*(3). Available at: ncbi.nlm.nih.gov/pmc/articles/PMC5880866

Mayer, K.M., Yildiz I.B., Macedonia M. & von Kriegstein, K. (2015). Visual and Motor Cortices Differentially Support the Translation of Foreign Language Words. *Current Biology, 25* (4), 530-535.

Mayer, R.E., & Gallini, J.K. (1990). When is an illustration worth ten thousand words? *Journal of Educational Psychology, 82*, 715-726.

Mayer, R.E. & Moreno, R. (2003). Nine ways to reduce cognitive load in multimedia learning. *Educational Psychologist 38* (1), 43-52. Available at: researchgate.net/publication/253772914

McLeod, S.A. (2007). Levels of processing. *Simply Psychology.* Available at: simplypsychology.org/levelsofprocessing.html

McLeod, S.A. (2012). *Working memory.* Simply Psychology. Available at : simplypsychology.org/working%20memory.html

McLaughlin, B. (1987). *Theories of Second-Language Learning.* London: Arnold.

Meacham, J.A. & Singer, J. (1977). Incentive effects in prospective remembering. *Journal of Psychology, 97*, 191–197.

Meisel, J.M., Clahsen, H. & Pienemann, M. (1981). On determining developmental stages in natural second language acquisition. *Studies in Second Language Acquisition, 3* (2), 109-135. Available at: cambridge.org/core/services/aop-cambridge-core/content/view/S0272263100004137

Melton, A.W. (1970). The situation with respect to the spacing of repetitions and memory. *Journal of Verbal Learning and Verbal Behavior, 9,* 596-606.

Miller, G.A. (1956). The magical number seven, plus or minus two: some limits on our capacity for processing information. *Psychological Review, 63* (2), 81–97.

Miller, G.A. & Taylor, W.J. (1948). The perception of repeated bursts of noise. *Journal of the Acoustical Society of America, 20,* 171-182.

Milton, J. (2006). Language lite? Learning French vocabulary in school. *Journal of French Language Studies, 16*, 187-205.

Mitchell, R., Myles, F. & Marsden, E. (2013). *Second Language Learning Theories* (3rd edition). London; Routledge

Miyake, A., & Shah, P. (Eds.) (1999). *Models of working memory: Mechanisms of active maintenance and executive control.* Cambridge: Cambridge University Press.

Moon, C., Lagercrantz, H. & Kuhl, P.K. (2013). Language experienced *in utero* affects vowel perception after birth: a two-country study. *Acta Paediatrica, 102*, 156-160.

Moreira, B.F.T., Pinto, T.S.S., Starling, D.S.V & Jaeger, A. (2019). Retrieval Practice in Classroom Settings: A Review of Applied Research. *Frontiers in Education, 4*. Available at: frontiersin.org/article/10.3389/feduc.2019.00005

Morris, C.D., Bransford, J.D. & Franks, J.J. (1977). Levels of Processing Versus Transfer Appropriate Processing. *Journal of Verbal Learning and Verbal Behavior, 16*, 519-533.

Mrazek, M., Franklin, M., Phillips, D., Baird, B. & Schooler, J. (2013). Mindfulness Training Improves Working Memory Capacity and GRE Performance While Reducing Mind Wandering. *Psychological Science, 24* (5), 776-781.

Murre, J. & Dross, J. (2015). Replication and Analysis of Ebbinghaus' Forgetting Curve. *PLOS One*. Peer-reviewed open access journal. Available at: journals.plos.org/plosone/article?id=10.1371/journal.pone.0120644

Nation, I.S.P. (2001) *Learning vocabulary in another language.* Cambridge: Cambridge University Press. (1st edition).

Nation, I.S.P. (2008). The four strands. *Innovation in Language Learning and Teaching, 1*, 1–12.

Nation, I.S.P. (2013). *Learning vocabulary in another language.* Cambridge: Cambridge University Press. (2nd edition).

Nation, I.S.P. (2014). Developing fluency. In T. Muller, J. Adamson, P.S. Brown, & S. Herder (Eds.), *Exploring EFL Fluency in Asia,* 11–25. Basingstoke: Palgrave.

Nation, I.S.P. (2015). Principles guiding vocabulary learning through extensive reading. *Reading in a Foreign Language, 27* (1), 136-145. Available at: nflrc.hawaii.edu/rfl/item/320

Nation, I.S.P. & Macalister, J. (2010). *Language Curriculum Design.* New York & London: Routledge.

Nation, I.S.P. & Yamamoto, A. (2012) Applying the four strands to language learning. *International Journal of Innovation in English Language Teaching, 1* (2). Available at: victoria.ac.nz/__data/assets/pdf_file/0003/1626123/2012-Yamamoto-Four-strands.pdf

Nava, A. & Pedrazzini, L. (2018). *Second Language Acquisition in Action: Principles from Practice.* Bloomsbury Academic.

North, A.C. (2012). The effect of background music on the taste of wine. *British Journal of Psychology, 103* (3), 293-301.

North, A., Hargreaves, D. & McKendrick, J. (1999). The Influence of In-Store Music on Wine Selections. *Journal of Applied Psychology, 84.* 271-276.

O'Brien, I., Segalowitz, N., Collentine, J. & Freed, B. (2006). Phonological memory and lexical, narrative and grammatical skills in second language oral production by adult learners. *Applied Psycholinguistics, 27,* 377-402.

Olive, T. & Passerault, J-M. (2012). The Visuospatial Dimension of Writing. *Written Communication, 29,* 326-344.

Ophir, E., Nass, C. & Wagner, A.D. (2009). Cognitive control in media multitaskers. PNAS, 106 (37). Available at: pnas.org/content/106/37/15583

Ortega, L. (2013). *Understanding Second Language Acquisition.* London: Routledge.

Oxford, R.L. (1990). *Language Learning Strategies: What Every Teacher Should Know.* Boston: Heinle and Heinle.

Ozeri-Rotstain, A., Shachaf, I., Farah, R. & Horowitz-Kraus, T. (2020). Relationship Between Eye-Movement Patterns, Cognitive Load, and Reading Ability in Children with Reading Difficulties. *Journal of Psycholinguistic Research, 49,* 491–507.

Page, E.B. (1958). Teacher Comments and Student Performance: A Seventy-Four Classroom Experiment in School Motivation. *Journal of Educational Psychology, 49,* 173–181.

Paivio, A. (1969). Mental imagery in associative learning and memory. *Psychological Review, 76* (3), 241–263.

Paivio, A. (1971). *Imagery and verbal processes.* New York: Holt, Rinehart and Winston.

Paller, K.A. & Voss, J.L. (2004). Memory reactivation and consolidation during sleep. *Learning Memory, 11* (6), 664-70. Available at: ncbi.nlm.nih.gov/pmc/articles/PMC534694/

Palminteri, S., Kilford, E. J., Coricelli, G., & Blakemore, S.J. (2016). The computational development of reinforcement learning during adolescence. *PLOS Computational Biology, 12* (6).

Pan, S.C., Tajran, J., Lovelett, J., Osuna, J. & Rickard, T.C. (2019). Does interleaved practice enhance foreign language learning? The effects of training schedule on Spanish verb conjugation skills. *Journal of Educational Psychology, 111* (7), 1172–1188.

Park, Y., Brownwell, M.T., Reed, D.K., Tibi, S., & Lombardino, L.J. (2020). Exploring how initial response to instruction predicts morphology outcomes among students with decoding difficulties. *Language, Speech, and Hearing Services in Schools, 51* (3), 655–670.

Perham, N. & Currie, H. (2014). Does listening to preferred music improve reading comprehension performance? *Applied Cognitive Psychology*, *28*, 279-284.

Peterson, L.R. & Peterson, M.J. (1959). Short-term retention of individual verbal items. *Journal of Experimental Psychology*, *58*, 193-198.

Pham, A.V. & Hasson, R.M. (2014). Verbal and Visuospatial Working Memory as Predictors of Children's Reading Ability. *Archives of Clinical Neuropsychology, 29*(5), 467-477.

Piaget, J. (1952). *The origins of intelligence in children*. New York, NY: International University Press. Translated by M.T. Cook.

Pica, T., Doughty, C. & Young, R.F. (1987). The Impact of Interaction on Comprehension. *Tesol Quarterly, 21*.

Pienemann, M. (1998). *Language processing and second language development: Processability theory.* Amsterdam/Philadelphia: John Benjamins.

Potter, M.C., Wyble, B., Hagmann, C.E. & McCourt, E.S. (2014). Detecting meaning in RSVP at 13 ms per picture. *Attention, Perception & Psychophysics, 76* (2), 270–279.

Potts, R. & Shanks, D. (2014). The Benefit of Generating Errors During Learning. *Journal of Experimental Psychology. 143* (2), 644-667.

Pressley, M., Levin, J.R., Kulper, N.A., Bryant, S.L. & Michener, S. (1982). Mnemonic versus non-mnemonic vocabulary learning strategies: Additional comparisons. *Journal of Educational Psychology*, *74*, 693-707.

Price, M.L. (1991). The subjective experience of foreign language anxiety: interviews with highly anxious students. In E.K. Horwitz, D.J. Young (Eds.), *Language anxiety: From theory and research to classroom implications*, 101–108. Englewood Cliff: Prentice Hall.

Rasch, B. & Born, J. (2013). About sleep's role in memory. *Physiological reviews, 93* (2), 681–766.

Rescorla, R.A. & Wagner, A.R. (1972). A theory of Pavlovian conditioning: Variations in the effectiveness of reinforcement and nonreinforcement. In A.H. Black & W.F. Prokasy, (Eds.), *Classical Conditioning II*, 64–99. Appleton-Century Crofts.

Riggs, N.R., Jahromi, L.B., Razza, R.P., Dillworth-Bart, J.E. & Mueller, U. (2006). Executive function and the promotion of social-emotional competence. *Journal of Applied Developmental Psychology*, *27*(4), 300-309. Available at: sciencedirect.com/science/article/pii/S0193397306000426

Rivers, W.M. (1983). *Communicating Naturally in a Second Language: Theory and Practice in Language Teaching.* New York: Cambridge University Press.

Roediger, H.L. & Karpicke, J.D. (2006). Test-enhanced learning: taking memory tests improves long-term retention. *Psychological Science, 17*, 249-255.

Rogers, J. & Cheung, A. (2018). Input spacing and the learning of L2 vocabulary in a classroom context. *Language Teaching Research*, *24*(5), 616-641.

Rogowsky, B.A., Calhoun, B.M. & Tallal, P. (2015). Matching Learning Style to Instructional Method: Effects on Comprehension. *Journal of Educational Psychology*, *107* (1), 64-78. Available at: apa.org/pubs/journals/features/edu-a0037478.pdf

Rosell-Aguilar, Fernando (2018). Autonomous language learning through a mobile application: a user evaluation of the busuu app. *Computer Assisted Language Learning*, *31* (8), 854–881.

Rosenshine, B. (2012). Principles of Instruction. Research-Based Strategies that All Teachers Should Know. *American Educator*. Available at: teachertoolkit.co.uk/wp-content/uploads/2018/10/Principles-of-Insruction-Rosenshine.pdf

Rosner, Z.A., Elman, J., & Shimamura, A. (2013). The generation effect: Activating broad neural circuits during memory encoding. *Cortex*, *49*, 1901-1909.

Rubinstein, J.S., Meyer, D.E. & Evans, J.E. (2001). Executive control of cognitive processes in task switching. *Journal of Experimental Psychology: Human Perception and Performance*, *27* (4), 763-797.

Rumelhart, D. & Norman, D. (1978). Accretion, tuning and restructuring: Three modes of learning. In. J.W. Cotton & R. Klatzky (Eds.), *Semantic Factors in Cognition.* Hillsdale, NJ: Erlbaum. Available at: pdfs.semanticscholar.org/4d8d/303fd622cf3bd0899bfe532fbee41202e718.pdf

Sahu, A., Christman, S.D. & Propper, R.E. (2016). The contributions of handedness and working memory to episodic memory. *Memory Cognition*, *44* (8), 1149-1156.

Samuels, S.J. (2006). Toward a Model of Reading Fluency. In S.J. Samuels & A.E. Farstrup (Eds.), *What research has to say about fluency instruction,* 24–46. International Reading Association.

Schmidt, R. (1990). The Role of Consciousness in Second Language Learning. *Applied Linguistics*, *11*, 129-158.

Schmidt, R. (2001). Attention. In P. Robinson (Ed.), *Cognition and second language instruction,* 3-32. Cambridge: Cambridge University Press.

Schmidt, R. (2010). Attention, awareness, and individual differences in language learning. In W.M. Chan, S. Chi, K.N. Cin, J. Istanto, M. Nagami, J.W. Sew, T. Suthiwan & I. Walker, *Proceedings of CLaSIC 2010*, Singapore, December 2-4, 721-737. Singapore: National University of Singapore, Centre for Language Studies. Available at: nflrc.hawaii.edu/PDFs/SCHMIDT%20Attention,%20awareness,%20and%20individual%20differences.pdf

Schmitt, N. (2008). Review article: Instructed second language vocabulary learning. *Language Teaching Research*, *12* (3), 329-363.

Schneider, W. (2017). Memory. In *Reference Module in Neuroscience and Biobehavioral Psychology*. Elsevier.

Schneider, W. & Pressley, M. (1997). *Memory Development between Two and Twenty.* Mahwah, NJ: Erlbaum.

Schreiber, P.A. (1991) Understanding prosody's role in reading acquisition. *Theory Into Practice, 30* (3), 158-164.

Schwartz, B.L. & Metcalfe, J. (2017). Metamemory: An update of critical findings. Available at: columbia.edu/cu/psychology/metcalfe/PDFs/SwartzMetcalfe2017.pdf

Seabrooke, T., Hollins, T.J., Kent, C., Wills, A.J. & Mitchell, C.J. (2018). Learning from failure: Errorful generation improves memory for items, not associations. *Journal of Memory and Language, 104*, 70-82.

Segalowitz, N. (2003). Automaticity and second languages. In C.J. Doughty and M.H. Long. (eds.), *Handbook of Second Language Acquisition*, 382-408. Malden: Blackwell.

Segalowitz, N. (2016). Second language fluency and its underlying cognitive and social determinants. *International Review of Applied Linguistics*, *54* (2), 79-95. Available at: core.ac.uk/download/pdf/78101209.pdf

Service, E. (1992). Phonology, Working Memory and Foreign-language Learning. *The Quarterly Journal of Experimental Psychology A, 45* (1), 21-50. Available at: researchgate.net/publication/21519743

Shepard, R.N. & Metzler, J. (1971). Mental Rotation of Three-Dimensional Objects. *Science, 171* (3972), 701–703.

Shipstead, Z., Harrison, T.L. & Engle, R.W. (2016). Working memory capacity and fluid intelligence: Maintenance and disengagement. *Perspectives on Psychological Science, 11*, 771–799.

Shimamura, A. (2018). *MARGE: A Whole-Brain Learning Approach for Students and Teachers*. (E-book). Available at: shimamurapubs.files.wordpress.com/2018/09/marge_shimamura.pdf

Sievertsen, H.H., Gino, F. & Piovesan, M. (2016). Cognitive fatigue influences students' performance on standardized tests. *Proceedings of the National Academy of Sciences, 113*(10), 2621-2624.

Siok, W.T., Perfetti, C.A., Jin, Z. & Tan, L.H. (2004). Biological abnormality of impaired reading is constrained by culture. *Nature, 431*, 71-76.

Slabakova, R., Leal, T., Dudley, A. & Stack, M. (2020). *Generative Second Language Acquisition.* Cambridge: Cambridge University Press.

Smith, A., Floerke, V. & Thomas, A. (2016). Retrieval practice protects memory against acute stress. *Science. 354*, 1046-1048.

Smith, S.P. (2017). *Becoming an Outstanding Languages Teacher*. London: David Fulton, Routledge.

Smith, S.P. & Conti, G. (2016). *The Language Teacher Toolkit*. Independently published. Available at Amazon.

Smoker, T., Murphy, C. & Rockwell, A. (2009). Comparing Memory for Handwriting versus Typing. *Human Factors and Ergonomics Society Annual Meeting Proceedings. 53* (22), 1744-1747.

Soderstrom, N.C., & Bjork, R.A. (2015). Learning Versus Performance: An Integrative Review. *Perspectives on Psychological Science, 10* (2), 176–199.

Sommer, S. & Gruneberg, M. (2002). The use of Linkword Language computer courses in a Classroom situation; A case study at Rugby school. *Language Learning Journal, 26*, 48-53.

Sommerville, S.C., Wellman, H.M., & Cultice, J.C. (1983). Young children's deliberate reminding. *Journal of Genetic Psychology, 143*, 87-96.

Sosic-Vasic, Z., Hille, K., Kröner, J., Spitzer, M. & Kornmeier, J. (2018). When Learning Disturbs Memory - Temporal Profile of Retroactive Interference of Learning on Memory Formation. *Frontiers in Psychology, 9*. Available at: frontiersin.org/articles/10.3389/fpsyg.2018.00082/full

Sozler, S. (2012). The Effect of Memory Strategy Training on Vocabulary Development of Austrian Secondary School Students. *Procedia - Social and Behavioral Sciences, 46*, 1348-1352. Available at: researchgate.net/publication/271583859

Speciale, G., Ellis, N. & Bywater, T. (2004). Phonological sequence learning and short-term store capacity determine second language vocabulary acquisition. *Applied Psycholinguistics, 25* (2), 293-321.

Squire, L.R. (1992). Memory and the hippocampus: a synthesis from findings with rats, monkeys and humans. *Psychological Review, 99* (2), 195-231.

Stahl, A.E. & Feigenson, L. (2015). Observing the unexpected enhances infants' learning and exploration. *Science, 348* (6230), 91-94.

Standing, L.G., Conezio, J. & Haber, R.N. (1970). Perception and memory for pictures: Single-trial learning of 2500 visual stimuli. *Psychonomic science, 19* (2), 73-74.

Swan, M. (no date). Using texts constructively 2: intensive input-output work. British Council. Teaching English. Available at: https://www.teachingenglish.org.uk/article/using-texts-constructively-2-intensive-input-output-work

Swarbrick, A. (Ed.) (1994). *Teaching Modern Languages*. London: Routledge.

Sweller, J. (1988). Cognitive load during problem solving: Effects on learning. *Cognitive Science 12* (2), 257-285.

Sweller, J. (2017). Cognitive Load Theory and Teaching English as a Second language to Adult Learners. *TESL Ontario. Contact Magazine.* Available at: contact.teslontario.org/wp-content/uploads/2017/05/Sweller-CognitiveLoad.pdf

Sweller, J., Ayres, P. & Kalyuga, S. (2011). *Cognitive Load Theory*. New York: Springer.

Tam H., Jarrold C., Baddeley A.D. & Sabatos-DeVito M. (2010). The development of memory maintenance: children's use of phonological rehearsal and attentional refreshment in working memory tasks. *Journal of Experimental Child Psychology*, *107*, 306–324.

Thakur, M. & Saxena, V. (2019). The effects of chewing gum on memory and concentration. *International Journal of Scientific Research and Engineering Development, 2,* 77-82. Available at: researchgate.net/publication/335974196

Thorndike, E.L. (1914). *The Psychology of Learning*. New York: Teachers College.

Tinkham, T. (1997). The effects of semantic and thematic clustering on the learning of second language vocabulary. *Second Language Research*, *13*, 138-163.

Tong, X. & McBride-Chang, C. (2010). Chinese-English biscriptal reading: Cognitive component skills across orthographies. *Reading and Writing*, *23*, 293–310.

Tulving, E. (1972). Episodic and semantic memory. In E. Tulving and W. Donaldson (Eds.), *Organization of Memory*, 381–403. New York, NY: Academic Press. Available at: alumni.media.mit.edu/~jorkin/generals/papers/Tulving_memory.pdf

Tulving, E., & Madigan, S.A. (1970). Memory and verbal learning. *Annual Review of Psychology*, *21*, 437–484.

Ullman, M. (2006). The declarative/procedural model and the shallow structure hypothesis. *Applied Psycholinguistics*, *27*, 97-105.

Uttl, B., White, C.A., Cnudde, K. & Grant, L.M. (2018). Prospective memory, retrospective memory, and individual differences in cognitive abilities, personality, and psychopathology. *PLoS One, 13* (3). Available at: ncbi.nlm.nih.gov/pmc/articles/PMC5870974/

VanPatten, B. (1996). *Input Processing and Grammar Instruction in Second Language Acquisition.* Norwood: Ablex.

Vredeveldt, A., Baddeley, A.D. & Hitch, G.J. (2013). The effectiveness of eye-closure in repeated interviews. *Legal and Criminal Psychology*, *19*, 282-295.

Wadsworth, B. J. (2004). *Piaget's theory of cognitive and affective development: Foundations of constructivism*. New York: Longman.

Walker, I., & Hulme, C. (1999). Concrete words are easier to recall than abstract words: Evidence for a semantic contribution to short-term serial recall. *Journal of Experimental Psychology: Learning, Memory, and Cognition*, 25 (5), 1256–1271.

Walter, S. & Meier, B. (2014). How important is importance for prospective memory? A review. *Frontiers in Psychology*. Available at: frontiersin.org/articles/10.3389/fpsyg.2014.00657/full

Warrington, E.K., & Weiskrantz, L. (1968). A study of learning and retention in amnesic patients. *Neuropsychologia, 6* (3), 283-291.

Webb, S. (2007). The Effects of Repetition on Vocabulary Knowledge. *Applied Linguistics*, *28*, (1), 46-65.

Wen, Z. (2016). *Working Memory and Second Language Learning.* Bristol: Multilingual Matters.

Wen, Z. & Li, S. (2019). Working memory in L2 learning and processing. In J. Schwieter & A. Benati (Eds.), *The Cambridge Handbook of Language Learning,* 365-389. Cambridge University Press.

Wilkins, D.A. (1972). *Linguistics in Language Teaching*. Edward Arnold.

Winne, P. H. & Butler, D. L. (1994). Student Cognition in learning from teaching. In T. Husen & T. Postlewaite (Eds.), *International Encyclopedia of Education* (2nd ed), 5738-5745. Oxford: Pergamon.

Wooldridge, C.L., Bugg, J.M., McDaniel, M.A. & Liu, Y. (2014). The testing effect with authentic educational materials: a cautionary note. *Journal of Applied Research in Memory and Cognition, 3*, (3), 214-221.

Xu, K. M., Koorn, P., de Koning, B., Skuballa, I.T., Lin, L., Henderikx, M., Marsh, H.W., Sweller, J. & Paas, F. (2020). A growth mindset lowers perceived cognitive load and improves learning: Integrating motivation to cognitive load. *Journal of Educational Psychology* (advance online publication).

Young, D.J. (1991). Creating a low-anxiety classroom environment: what does language anxiety research suggest? *The Modern Language Journal, 75*, 426–439.

Zechmeister, E.B., & McKillip, J. (1972). Recall of place on the page. *Journal of Educational Psychology, 63* (5) 446-453.

Zeigarnik, B. (1938). On finished and unfinished tasks. In W.D. Ellis (Ed.), *A source book of Gestalt psychology,* 300–314. London: Kegan Paul, Trench, Trubner & Co..

Zheng, Y. & Cheng, L. (2018). How does anxiety influence language performance? From the perspectives of foreign language classroom anxiety and cognitive test anxiety. *Language Testing in Asia, 8*, Article 13. Available at: languagetestingasia.springeropen.com/articles/10.1186/s40468-018-0065-4

Zhou, H., Chen, B. & Rossi, S. (2017). Effects of Working Memory Capacity and Tasks in Processing L2 Complex Sentence: Evidence from Chinese-English Bilinguals. *Frontiers in Psychology, 8*. Available at: frontiersin.org/articles/10.3389/fpsyg.2017.00595/full

Index